PAUL AND THE POWER OF GRACE

PAUL AND THE POWER OF GRACE

John M. G. Barclay

WILLIAM B. EERDMANS PUBLISHING COMPANY

GRAND RAPIDS, MICHIGAN

Wm. B. Eerdmans Publishing Co.
4035 Park East Court SE, Grand Rapids, Michigan 49546
www.eerdmans.com

26 25 24 23 22 21 20   1 2 3 4 5 6 7

ISBN 978-0-8028-7461-0

Library of Congress Cataloging-in-Publication Data

Names: Barclay, John M. G., author.
Title: Paul and the power of grace / John M. G. Barclay.
Description: Grand Rapids, Michigan : William B. Eerdmans Publishing
    Company, 2020. | Includes bibliographical references and index. | Summary:
    "A condensed and developed version of Barclay's previous book, Paul and
    the Gift, with extended applications to the other letters of Paul and to select
    contemporary issues"—Provided by publisher.
Identifiers: LCCN 2020020627 | ISBN 9780802874610
Subjects: LCSH: Bible. Epistles of Paul—Theology. | Grace (Theology)—Biblical
    teaching.
Classification: LCC BS2655.G65 B375 2020 | DDC 227/.06—dc23
LC record available at https://lccn.loc.gov/2020020627

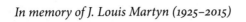

In memory of J. Louis Martyn (1925–2015)

Contents

Preface

A few years ago, I wrote a heavy-weight book called *Paul and the Gift* (Grand Rapids: Eerdmans, 2015), which explored Paul's theology of grace in Galatians and Romans; for that task I used resources from the study of gifts in the discipline of anthropology, and I explored crucial episodes in the history of interpretation of Paul. That book has been widely discussed by both New Testament scholars and theologians, and many have urged me to write a shorter version for a broader audience. As I reflected on this suggestion, I found I also wanted to explore more features of the terrain of gift. At the same time reviews, debates, and discussions of *Paul and the Gift* pressed me to develop my arguments, to extend their scope, and to relate the gift-theme more explicitly to the contemporary world. This new book is entitled *Paul and the Power of Grace* as a reflection of its goal to bring out more fully the dynamic in Paul's theology of grace and of the resources it offers for practice today.

This book thus performs two tasks. First, in chapters 1–9, it offers a shortened and sharpened version of the main ingredients of *Paul and the Gift*, omitting most of its technicalities (including the Greek and Hebrew) and drastically reducing its first two parts. As in *Paul and the Gift*, the primary focus of these chapters is on Paul's letters to the Galatians and to the Romans, and I have offered here, in outline, a reading of those letters that brings out the radical social implications of Paul's theology of the gift of Christ. Secondly, in chapters 10–13, I have extended the discussion of grace and gift into other letters, added comment on how this reading of Paul relates to other interpretations of Paul, and suggested (in chapter 13) how the ideas in this book might offer a resource for handling some contemporary issues.

Thus, this new book as a whole offers both an accessible summary of *Paul and the Gift* and an extension and development of that work. (It is not, however, the major follow-up volume promised in *Paul and the Gift*, regarding gift-exchange and the formation of community: that is an ongoing work-in-progress.)

It has been a challenge to strike the right balance between repeating myself, saying some things differently, and adding some things new. Those who have already read *Paul and the Gift* will find the first nine chapters of this book very familiar, but I have written this new book primarily for those who have *not* read *Paul and the Gift*, or who found it intimidatingly long. (Conversely, those who find this book frustratingly brief can go to the longer and fuller version in *Paul and the Gift*!)

I am very grateful to the publishers, Eerdmans, for their patience in waiting for this book, and especially to my editors (in succession) Michael Thomson and Trevor Thompson, and to the expert project editor, Linda Bieze, and copy editor, Cody Hinkle. I am indebted to friends who kept urging me to write it, of whom Paul Trebilco, Todd Brewer, and Jonathan Linebaugh should get special mention. The latter two also generously read through the whole manuscript and offered many valuable suggestions for improvement, while Logan Williams, who did likewise, also picked up many an error in content or prose. I am immensely grateful to them all.

I dedicate this book to the memory of J. Louis Martyn, an outstanding New Testament scholar and profound theologian of grace, from whom I learned much that undergirds this book.

Prologue: What Do We Mean by Grace?

In June 2019, a remarkable event took place on the Pyramid Stage of Glastonbury Festival in the UK. The British rapper Stormzy took to the stage and led a huge crowd in a rendition of his hit song "Blinded by Your Grace." The lyrics speak of the grace of God given to the unworthy and were sung with real emotion.

Moreover, they were taken up with enthusiasm by the rapturous festival crowd. What was striking was how much resonance they seemed to have with this audience, even in the secularized youth culture of modern Britain.

Those with ears to hear will pick up the echoes of John Newton's famous hymn, which is still deeply embedded in the Western collective consciousness:

> Amazing grace—how sweet the sound—
> That saved a wretch like me.
> I once was lost, but now am found,
> Was blind, but now I see.

The imagery in the lyrics of Stormzy and Newton echo Jesus's parable of the prodigal son, lost and broken (Luke 15:11–32), and accounts in the New Testament gospels of Jesus's healing of the blind (e.g., John 9:1–34). But the term "grace," rarely used in the Gospels, is an echo of Paul, whose letters are full of references to grace. More accurately, they are full of references to God's favor, gift, or benefaction, using a variety of Greek terms including the word *charis*, which we normally translate "grace." Paul sums up the effect of the life, death, and resurrection of Jesus as "the grace (*charis*) of our Lord Jesus Christ" (2 Cor 8:9); "where sin abounded, grace (*charis*) super-abounded"

(Rom 5:20).[1] Sinful human beings have been "justified as a gift, by his [God's] grace (*charis*), through the redemption that is in Christ Jesus" (Rom 3:24). Paul says his converts were called "in *charis*" (Gal 1:6), and the same is true of Paul (Gal 1:15). "By the *charis* of God I am what I am, and his *charis* toward me was not in vain; rather, I worked harder than them all—not I, but the *charis* of God with me" (1 Cor 15:10). By contrast, to be disjoined from Christ is to "fall from *charis*" (Gal 5:4).

What did Paul mean by this word *charis*, and how is it related to other terms for gift (and the verb, "to give"), which are common throughout his letters? *Charis* is an ordinary term in the Greek of Paul's day, not loaded with any special theological meaning. It means an act (or attitude) of favor or benevolence—not a special kind of gift, just any favor or benefit (see further, chapter 1). As we shall see, most gifts and benefits in the ancient world were distributed discriminately to fitting or worthy recipients. In Christian theology, however, *charis* (and its Latin translation, *gratia*) acquired a distinctive tenor: they came to mean a favor or gift *given to the undeserving*. That is how we normally hear the term "grace" now: it depicts a benefit or gift given to an unfitting or helpless recipient—in Newton's terms, a "wretch." Is that what is meant by Paul? Did he endue ordinary words for gift with this special meaning? If so, how did *charis* and other gift-terms acquire the sense of an undeserved gift? And what difference did that make?

"Grace" has often been supplemented with adjectives or qualifiers, designed to clarify its meaning or to maximize its force. The Protestant Reformers of the sixteenth century insisted that salvation is "by grace alone." What did they mean to exclude by that phrase, and why did it matter to them? In fact, both before and after their time, Christians have often spoken of "pure grace," "sheer grace," or "free grace." But pure from what? Or free of what? What is the point of this kind of emphasis?

One might understand "pure grace" to mean that God's relation to the world consists *only of* love, benevolence, and kindness, excluding any notions of wrath or judgment, any sense that God might punish evil or condemn evildoers. On this reading, "pure grace" signifies unmixed, unqualified love, on the understanding that God has adopted this singular stance toward the world in Christ, without reservation and without limit. To speak of "grace" and then also to speak of judgment or condemnation is, on this reading of "grace," a complete self-contradiction.

"Sheer grace" or "free grace" could have other connotations. These might mean that grace is free of any notion of reward, any *quid pro quo*. Grace, on

---

1. All translations from the New Testament are my own.

this understanding, escapes all notions of reciprocity or return; in fact, it is not just different from them but directly contrary to them. "Free grace" is "free," on this interpretation, when it is noncircular, that is, rid of any hint of return or exchange: it just gives (and gives again). A "grace" that is given in return for some prior act, or a "grace" that demands or expects some return, seems to some people like the very opposite of grace. If grace is "free," should it not be unilateral, unconditional, outside the normal cycles of reciprocity and return that inhibit or burden human gifts?

Grace may, in fact, be said to be free in two senses. It might be free of prior conditions, without regard to worth or desert, "free" in the sense of undeserved. Or (and this is not the same) it might be considered "free" of subsequent obligation, debt, or demand, given, as we might say, "with no strings attached." In the second sense, "grace" might seem incompatible with any system of condition, law, rule, or demand. In fact, one might consider it a contradiction to speak of "grace" and then to instruct people to repent, work, sacrifice, serve, or obey, especially if these are viewed as somehow *necessary* for salvation. On this reading, grace is not only *unconditioned*—given without regard to prior desert—but also *unconditional*—given without expectation of a necessary response.

"Grace," it seems, is not a simple concept but is capable of many possible meanings. Grace without obligation, sacrifice, or demand was the object of Dietrich Bonhoeffer's famous critique of "cheap grace"—a form of comfortable, undemanding Christianity that he considered the besetting sin of German Lutherans in the 1930s.[2] No one preached grace more passionately than Bonhoeffer, but Bonhoeffer's understanding of grace did not carry the sense "with no strings attached." In contemporary churches, the meaning of grace is still a matter of sharp controversy. Does grace liberate us from "legalistic" moralism and the judgmentalism that crushes believers and nonbelievers alike?[3] Or is "grace" then a mask for an irresponsible and "antinomian" message that falsely affirms people as they are, without looking for Spirit-given transformation? Some contemporary versions of "pure grace" have been dubbed by their critics "hyper-grace," judging the grace that they preach to be, in some sense, excessive. But from its advocates' point of view, anything less than "pure grace" is a "mixed-grace" gospel (mixed, that is, with law or works).[4]

Do these differences represent different degrees of grace, such that some

2. Dietrich Bonhoeffer, *The Cost of Discipleship* (London: SCM, 1948, with many subsequent reprints); originally published as *Nachfolge* (1937).

3. See Paul Zahl, *Gift in Practice: A Theology of Everyday Life* (Grand Rapids: Eerdmans, 2007).

4. For criticism, see Michael L. Brown, *Hyper-Grace* (Lake Mary, FL: Charisma House,

believe in grace *more than* others? Or are they, rather, different ways of understanding grace? As we shall see, it is possible that those on opposite sides of these disputes may all believe in grace to the same degree; they just believe in it *differently*.

Such controversies are nothing new: disputes about the meaning of "grace" go back to the beginning of Christianity. It would be hard to find a Christian theology that does not affirm the importance of grace. But Christians have differed greatly in what they mean by that term, what they associate with it, and what they consider its antithesis. This topic provides, in fact, a good example of how people may talk past one other: they appear to disagree violently on the same issue, but in fact they mean different things, even when they use the same vocabulary.

This is a book about Paul and grace, and it starts by wondering what we mean by that term, and by trying to clarify how and why it has been differently understood. Our focus will be on the letters of Paul, the source of most Christian discourse on this topic.[5] We need to read these first-century documents with a clear sense of what *Paul* was talking about in his own social, linguistic, and cultural context, and we need to trace the connection between this topic and his life's work as "apostle to the nations." (When Paul spoke about "the nations" [*ta ethnē*], he meant "the non-Jewish nations," the peoples we often call "gentiles" [from the Latin *gentiles*, "nations"].) His mission to the gentiles was highly controversial since he did not require his gentile converts to observe the Jewish law in the way that other Jewish believers thought essential. The letters where he speaks most fully about his mission—his letters to the Galatians and to the Romans—are the texts where the language of "gift" and "grace" is used most intensively. Is there some connection between his understanding of the good news as grace and his conduct of the gentile mission? Did his association of the Christ-event with grace shape the way he built boundary-crossing communities? Is grace relevant not only for the comfort of the individual (Newton's "wretch like me") but also, socially, for the formation of new communities that challenged taken-for-granted norms?

The first step in this book will be to examine the language of grace and

---

2014); for response, Paul Ellis, *The Hyper-Grace Gospel* (Birkenhead, New Zealand: KingsPress, 2014).

5. We will focus primarily on the seven "undisputed" letters of Paul, i.e., those generally acknowledged in critical, historical scholarship to be written by the apostle Paul: Romans, 1 Corinthians, 2 Corinthians, Galatians, Philippians, 1 Thessalonians, and Philemon. The grace language is, however, continued and developed in subsequent letters in the Pauline tradition (Ephesians, Colossians, 2 Thessalonians, 1 Timothy, 2 Timothy, and Titus).

gift with the aid of anthropology, which has long studied gifts, both what they mean and how they work, in various societies over time (chapter 1). On that basis, we will be able to clarify the different ways in which divine gift (or grace) has been defined—often by drawing it out to some end-of-the-line extreme. We will thus get a sense for why "grace" has been, and continues to be, understood differently in Christian theology (chapter 2). In fact, we can also see why the grace or mercy of God could be variously understood by Jews contemporary with Paul (chapter 3). Those itching to get to the "Paul" part of the book are urged to be patient! The first few chapters of this book are an essential foundation, and they will help us see whether or how Paul's theology was radical.[6]

At the heart of this book is an extended reading of Galatians (chapters 4 to 6) and of Romans (chapters 7 to 9). These are the letters of Paul with the greatest and most significant concentration of gift-language. Since there are some differences between these two letters, besides their many points in common, it is important to read them separately and in sequence. Paul is a contextual theologian, and we should first attend to each letter in its own right. (The full exegetical arguments for my readings of those letters, with reference to the Greek text, can be found in *Paul and the Gift*; here I offer the essential features.)

Thereafter, our perspective will broaden to trace the contours of grace and its practices across other Pauline letters (chapters 10 and 11), noting both the peculiar "grammar" of Paul's theology, and the practical expressions of grace in Pauline communities. Since this book offers a reading of Paul that goes beyond the recent clash between classic Protestant readings of Paul and "the new perspective" on Paul, in chapter 12 I will outline where it stands in these and other contemporary debates about Paul. Moreover, Paul remains not just a figure of the past but a significant (if underrecognized) voice in contemporary culture, and we should be alert to the potential of Paul's theology to speak to current issues. Accordingly, I will conclude with some observations on how the reading of Paul that is advanced in this book can contribute to issues of gift, community, and worth that press on us today (chapter 13).

Paul, we shall see, had an unusual, creative, and socially radical understanding of the grace of God, arising from *the Gift*: Christ. Whereas good gifts were (and still are) normally thought to be distributed best to fitting or worthy

---

6. Those wanting *more* may consult my *Paul and the Gift* (Grand Rapids: Eerdmans, 2015), where the material outlined in the first three chapters of the present book is discussed at much greater length.

recipients, Paul took the Christ-gift, the ultimate gift of God to the world, to be given without regard to worth, and in the absence of worth—an unconditioned or incongruous gift that did not match the worth of its recipients but created it. This is the root of his mission to gentiles and his formation of communities that crossed social boundaries and ignored old hierarchies of worth. In fact, it was in the formation and the practices of these communities that the grace of God was evidenced. Moral and social transformation was not an optional extra in Paul's understanding of grace but its necessary expression, because the gift of God in Christ brought into question the whole value system of the ancient world and took place in relationships, not just in the heart. Grace, it turns out, is not an idea or a thing but a radical, divine dynamic. Our aim is to trace the *power* of grace in Paul's letters, its capacity to reorient the self and to recalibrate community. But to get to that goal we need first to think more deeply about "gift" and "grace," and to place Paul's ideas in their ancient cultural context.

CHAPTER 1

Grace as Gift

Our first step is to place the topic of "grace" within the field of social relations that come under the heading of "gift." There is a simple linguistic reason for this strategy. As we have already noted, the Greek term we normally translate as "grace" (*charis*) is a normal, nonspecialized word for benefit, favor, or gift, which Paul mixes with other ordinary gift-terms. He celebrates the *charis* of the Lord Jesus Christ (2 Cor 8:9) and then gives thanks to God for his inexpressible "gift" (*dōrea*, 2 Cor 9:15). At one point, he uses four roughly synonymous gift-terms to describe the event of Christ (*charis, dōrea, dōrēma, charisma*, Rom 5:15–17). When he speaks of "the Son of God who loved me and gave himself for me" (Gal 2:20), he refers again to this gift when he says, in the next sentence, that he will not reject the *charis* of God (Gal 2:21). The gift that he wants the Corinthians to give to Jerusalem is called a *charis* (2 Cor 8:7), and the gifts of the Spirit that they enjoy are labelled *charismata* (1 Cor 12:4). Although we distinguish in English between "gift" and "grace," it is often the case that either could serve as a translation for *charis*, which is part of a pool of regular Greek terms for gift, favor, or benefit.[1]

The word *charis* has, in fact, three main classes of meaning that reflect the circular structure of gift-giving in antiquity.[2] It can mean, firstly, what is charming or attractive, an object of favor (as of Jesus in Luke 2:52). Secondly, it may mean a gift, favor, or benefit, or the attitude of benevolence that accompanies a gift. Sometimes there is a distinction between the gift and the

---

1. A translation, of course, has to bring out the nuance of each word in context, and there is no one-to-one relationship between *charis* and any single English term: it is best translated sometimes as gift, sometimes as grace, sometimes as favor, and sometimes as thanks. The claim that it falls within the domain of gift-relations does not imply that it is always best *translated* as "gift."

2. For details, see the appendix in my *Paul and the Gift* (Grand Rapids: Eerdmans, 2015), 575–82. Relevant Hebrew terms, and their Greek translations, are also discussed there.

attitude of benevolence. But often the two overlap, because what is given is not only a thing, but also a service or favorable treatment that represents the giver's attitude. Thus, in Paul's letters, *charis* can describe gifts (e.g., 1 Cor 16:3: "your *charis* to Jerusalem") or the favor or generosity of God ("*charis* and peace be with you from God our Father and the Lord Jesus Christ," Rom 1:7). Thirdly, *charis* (like the related term, *eucharistia*) can mean the return of gratitude or thanksgiving (e.g., 2 Cor 9:15: "*charis* [thanks] be to God for his inexpressible gift"). These three meanings of *charis* represent the circular movement of gifts: a gift given to a favored person creates gratitude in return. The Greeks played on these interrelated meanings, as did Paul throughout 2 Corinthians 8–9.

However, our focus in this book is *not* limited to the word *charis* or to texts that happen to use this term. To study Paul's theology of grace is not the same as doing a word-study on *charis*. This word is mixed with a set of other gift-terms in Pauline theology, and we would confine ourselves wrongly if we fixated on one term alone. Every language has many words for gifts, depending on their context and their social meaning. In English, a monetary gift could be styled simply a gift, but it might be what we call a tip, a donation, an honorarium, a present, a benefit, or a bribe. Each of these terms has a slightly different nuance, reflecting the purposes, contexts, and effects of the gift. Indeed, what one person considers a donation, another might denounce as a bribe. This alerts us to the fact that gifts are complex and multifaceted phenomena. The same word can mean subtly different things, and different words can overlap in meaning, depending on the social relationships they describe or the different ways they are figured rhetorically. We need to clarify the meaning of words, but we also need to observe the social meaning of "gifts" and the social expectations they convey. Rather than fixating on one term, we need to explore a cluster of words and their associated *ideas*, grouped under the heading of "gift."

But what do we mean by "gift"? It is time for a definition. By "gift" I mean the sphere of voluntary, personal relations characterized by goodwill in the giving of a benefit or favor, which generally elicits some form of reciprocal return that is necessary for the continuation of the relationship. "Voluntary" is crucial: we do not regard the taxes we pay as a gift; by law, we have to pay them, and we do not expect a thank-you letter from the tax inspector! Even if, as we shall see, gifts can be both obliged and voluntary, some element of voluntariness in their giving is crucial to their status as gifts (as Paul notes in 2 Cor 9:7). "Personal" is also important: gifts in all cultures express a personal connection between giver and recipient, and are generally viewed as qualitatively different, in that sense, from commercial exchange.[3] "Goodwill" is significant: all gifts express something of a beneficent attitude (the same thing given with malicious intentions is not a gift but a form of harm). And, as we shall see in a moment, in most cultures and at most times, gifts are part of a circular exchange, an ongoing cycle where the gift is intended to create or maintain a social relationship. Payment for goods and services is generally the end of a transaction, but a gift is not the end of a relationship, and neither is the return. One gives or gives back (typically at a later time and in some nonidentical form) in order to *continue* a relationship that is in principle open-ended.

Working from this broad definition, our question is this: if Paul configures God's relationship to the world in Christ as gift (voluntary, personal, and with goodwill), what sort of gift is it, and how does it work?

THE ANTHROPOLOGY OF GIFT

Differing cultural patterns of favor or benefit, all under the heading of "gift," have been the subject of a long and fascinating discussion among anthropologists. If you have travelled to another continent, or have come to know people from another culture, you will know that gifts operate under different rules in different cultures. Who is expected to give gifts, and when? What sort of gift is appropriate for what occasion? What is expected in response to a gift? Like me, you may have been embarrassed by misreading a gift-situation—failing to provide a gift when one was expected, or failing to reciprocate in the proper way. Anthropologists have long studied the functions and social meanings of gifts, stimulated by a famous essay by Marcel Mauss, now translated and published as a book, called simply *The Gift*.[4] Starting from ethnographical studies around the Pacific Rim, Mauss explored how gifts (broadly defined) knit societies together and how they have altered over time in changing cultural and economic conditions. Mauss identified three key obligations in societies structured by gifts: the obligation to give, the obligation to receive, and the obligation to return the gift (often in a different form). Because they are personal, gifts may be closely attached to the person of the giver (think of heirlooms,

---

3. The distinction is not absolute and the two spheres may overlap: a shopkeeper may give me a personal discount for being a loyal customer.

4. Marcel Mauss, *The Gift*, trans. W. D. Halls (London: Routledge, 1990). The original was a long essay in French ("Essai sur le don"), published in 1925.

or hand-crafted gifts), and in some cases gifts are "inalienable"—given, but in an important sense still the property of the person or group that gave it.

Mauss was particularly interested in what creates the obligation to return a gift, an obligation that still leaves the return, however, voluntary and free. His own explanation (concerning the "spirit" of the gift) has not persuaded everyone, but the question is valid. The best answer may lie in the fact that gifts are a means of creating or sustaining relationships. Failure to return a gift weakens the invited relationship and may bring it to an end.[5] Even in modern Western culture, where the sphere of gifts has been limited and their power reduced (see below), we are conscious that family relations and friendships are maintained by a continuous circle of favors and benefits. To receive many favors but never to return them usually means that the relationship does not last. For instance, if I gave a gift to a friend each year for his birthday, but he never thanked me for it, let alone reciprocated in some form, I would probably conclude that the friendship did not count for much.

Mauss and his successors showed that in most cultures standard Western polarities simply do not apply. We contrast "free" gifts with notions of obligation, but at many times in history and in many (perhaps most) cultures today, gifts can be both obligatory and free. We contrast a "disinterested" gift with one that furthers the interest of the giver, but that polarity may be a modern construct, falsely imposed on others. We might consider a gift that has an element of obligation or interest as less than "pure," but that might represent the imposition of a cultural standard that is uniquely our own. We might judge that others are deceiving themselves by claiming to be givers, when they "really" want something in return.[6] In fact, we should learn from anthropology to be wary of imposing *our* assumptions about gifts on other people or other periods of time, and we should operate with an open mind, since modern, Western construals of gift are by no means inherently "right." In general, cultural awareness teaches us that:

A. "Gifts" may take many forms, including all kinds of favors, benefactions, and services. Material gifts are often returned not in kind, but by according honor or prestige to the giver, especially in unequal relationships.

5. For influential anthropological discussions, see Marshall Sahlins, *Stone Age Economics*, 2nd ed. (London: Routledge, 2004) and Maurice Godelier, *The Enigma of the Gift*, trans. Nora Scott (Chicago: University of Chicago Press, 1999).

6. For a classic analysis of gifts that expect a return as collective self-deception, see Pierre Bourdieu, *Outline of a Theory of Practice*, trans. Richard Nice (Cambridge: Cambridge University Press, 1977), 171–97. Excerpts from his and others' views on gifts are collected in Alan D. Schrift, ed., *The Logic of the Gift* (London: Routledge, 1997).

B. What constitutes a gift is culturally defined, and how gifts relate to other forms of transaction (e.g., commerce or pay) has to be observed in each context.

C. Unless there is strong evidence to the contrary, we should expect that gifts carry some expectation of return. Reciprocity is the norm. Exchange and return are characteristic not only of trade-relations but also of gift-giving, even if the return takes place in indirect forms.

D. We should beware of labels such as "free" and "pure," lest they carry the connotations of modern ideologies of gift. Even dictionary definitions are culturally determined. We should be open to the possibility that gifts can be both "voluntary" and "obliged," both "disinterested" and "interested," both "generous" and "constrained." At the very least, we should let sources from past times and different cultures speak of gifts in their own terms. And that includes the letters of Paul.

GIFTS IN PAUL'S GRECO-ROMAN CONTEXT

How did gifts operate in Paul's cultural environment, that is, in his Greco-Roman context and in his Jewish culture that operated within it?[7] A fundamental principle of Greek social life was the norm of reciprocity in giving, receiving, and returning gifts.[8] This norm operated at all social levels, from the extravagant hospitality and political favors exchanged among the rich to the ordinary, beneath-the-radar swapping and sharing that helped the poor survive (if they did). It was good advice to "be cordial to your neighbor, for if trouble comes at home, a neighbor's there, at hand."[9] Generosity to others was the best form of insurance, and those known for being stingy or uncooperative were liable to find themselves without help when illness, accident, or bereavement brought financial disaster. "Give something and get something," said the popular maxim, or "One hand washes another" (the Greek equivalent of "You

---

7. For a fuller description, see *Paul and the Gift*, 24–51. For a broad collection of sources, see James R. Harrison, *Paul's Language of Grace in its Graeco-Roman Context* (Tübingen: Mohr Siebeck, 2003). There are good summaries also by David A. deSilva, *Honor, Patronage, Kinship, and Purity: Unlocking New Testament Culture* (Downers Grove, IL: InterVarsity Press, 2000); Gerald W. Peterman, *Paul's Gift from Philippi: Conventions of Gift Exchange and Christian Giving* (Cambridge: Cambridge University Press, 1997).

8. See Sitta von Reden, *Exchange in Ancient Greece* (London: Routledge, 1995); Christopher Gill, Norman Postlethwaite, and Richard Seaford, eds., *Reciprocity in Ancient Greece* (Oxford: Oxford University Press, 1998).

9. Hesiod, *Works and Days*, trans. Dorothea Wender (London: Penguin, 1973), 343–44.

scratch my back and I'll scratch yours").[10] Recipients of favors would commonly describe themselves as being "in debt" since it was taken for granted that gifts carry obligations. Nonetheless, since gifts were personal, informal, and resistant to exact calculation, they were in a different category from loans, wages, or trade-exchange. A contractual loan was a matter of law, and a defaulter could be taken to court, but the social obligations arising from gifts, although morally powerful, were not actionable in law. Gifts, however, did create circular exchange: something was expected to come back to the giver, even if only gratitude or honor. The structure of gift-giving was commonly identified in the popular image of the Three Graces (*Charites*), who danced in a ring, bound together in gift-and-return.[11]

This system of reciprocal exchange also characterized the relationship between humans and the gods, despite the difference in status.[12] In Greek and Roman religion, the gods were recognized as benefactors of humanity: they gave gifts of nature, health, safety, and success, and it was incumbent on humans to reciprocate in sacrifice and worship. As in the normal cycle of reciprocity among friends, one did not need to calculate who started the exchange. Sacrifices could be figured as return gifts for benefits already given, or as gifts inducing future benefits. Greek and Roman religion has often been represented as a system of *do ut des* ("I give in order that you give"). That rightly recognizes the reciprocity of religious practice, but it is misleading if it suggests that the human giver is always the initiator of the cycle. Ancient philosophers, at least, would insist that the world, human life, and the benefits of nature were prior gifts, initiated by the gods/God.

If gifts, both human and divine, were given within a cycle of reciprocal exchange, it was important to give wisely and discriminately. This is partly a matter of practical prudence: one would be wary of giving to someone unlikely or unwilling to reciprocate. But it also concerns the donor's social reputation. Gifts tied persons and groups together: the giving and receiving of a gift constituted a social bond. For that reason, one might refuse a gift, wary of association with a disreputable giver, and, as a donor, one would be careful to give gifts only to those recognized to be in some sense "worthy" of them.[13]

10. For these and other maxims on this topic, see Teresa Morgan, *Popular Morality in the Early Roman Empire* (Cambridge: Cambridge University Press, 2007).

11. E.g., Aristotle, *Nicomachean Ethics* 1133a2–4.

12. See Robert T. Parker, "Pleasing Thighs: Reciprocity in Greek Religion," in Gill, Postlethwaite, and Seaford, *Reciprocity in Ancient Greece*, 105–25.

13. Among Cicero's three principles of generosity is the rule that benefits should be given "on the basis of worth" (*pro dignitate*; Cicero, *On Duties*, 1.42–45, my translation).

"Worth" could be measured in many different ways, according to social status, gender, age, ethnicity, ancestry, education, or morality. Worshippers presented themselves to the gods as "worthy" of their benefits, and donors noted the worth of the people they had benefitted. As we shall see (chapter 3), the Jewish philosopher Philo of Alexandria thought it obvious that God would act on the principle of worth in the discriminate distribution of gifts; otherwise, the just ordering of the cosmos could be questioned. An indiscriminate gift might be considered both foolish and dangerous. Who would wish to degrade their reputation by tying themselves to people without worth?

The Greco-Roman system of gift-giving is particularly evident in inscriptions, which record gifts and services performed by the elite for the benefit of their cities or of subgroups within them. This system of "euergetism" (the giving of public benefits) was the means by which the rich attempted to legitimate vast inequalities in wealth.[14] By paying for public buildings, feasts, competitions, and civic amenities, the wealthy benefitted their cities, which reciprocated with public honors, proclamations, privileges, statues, and inscriptions. In these and other unequal relations, what the inferior party gives back is what the wealthy most want: not material goods but honor. On a smaller scale, benefactors supported clubs and associations, subsidizing their buildings, sacrifices, or meals; they were honored in exchange with titles, votes of thanks, and extra-large portions at banquets.

As the Greek world passed under Roman rule, the emperor became the supreme benefactor who gave financial relief to "Caesar-loving" cities, and who was honored with obsequious praise, sometimes with honors like those of the gods. Under his rule, elite Roman families and members of his household became patrons of cities and other interest groups, providing access to power in exchange for honor or financial reward.[15] For their subordinates, it was a matter of "who you knew" and what power they had to exercise influence in your favor. This complex network of reciprocity was, from a modern Western perspective, one vast system of "corruption" and "graft."

We are fortunate to possess a treatise on gifts from the first-century Roman world, namely, *On Benefits* by the Stoic philosopher Seneca. This treatise is partly a restatement of common assumptions about gift-reciprocity, partly an analysis of the problems in gift exchange, and partly a set of Stoic solutions

14. The classic on this topic is Paul Veyne, *Bread and Circuses* (abbreviated and translated by Brian Pearce; London: Penguin Books, 1990; French original in 1976).

15. On Roman patronage, see Richard P. Saller, *Personal Patronage under the Early Empire* (Cambridge: Cambridge University Press, 1982); Andrew Wallace-Hadrill, ed., *Patronage in Ancient Society* (London: Routledge, 1989).

to those problems, aimed at keeping the gift system flowing for the benefit of all.[16] One common assumption is that gifts go around in circles: for Seneca, gift-giving is like a continuous ball game where one person throws a ball to another in such a way that it can be easily caught and thrown back (*On Benefits* 2.17.3–5). Seneca knows that, in some cases, the only possible return-gift is gratitude, but since that is a virtue (and thus for a Stoic, the only true good), that is quite good enough. An anonymous gift is occasionally necessary but is not, for Seneca, ideal since the recipient can show no personal gratitude to the giver. Gifts are, for Seneca, what tie society together, and it is important that they be distributed well: generosity is excellent, but even lavish giving should be carefully directed. To give wisely, and to avoid disappointment or embarrassment, one should direct one's gifts to those worthy (*dignus*) of them.

Seneca shares the universal assumption that gifts oblige but is highly conscious of the unequal power-dynamics that may result: gifts can overwhelm their recipients or create patronizing relationships. His solution is to look always to the spirit (*animus*) of the gift, both in the giver and in the recipient. If donors give wisely in a generous spirit, it does not matter if they get no material return; it is enough for recipients to be grateful—although, where possible, they should give some counter-gift. This treatise is full of Stoic paradoxes and extremes, but it is notable that Seneca never idealizes the one-way, unreciprocated gift. He retains the universal ancient assumption that the proper expression of gift-giving is reciprocal exchange.

Were Jewish gifting practices in Paul's day any different in this regard? In brief: mostly no, but in one respect, yes. Jews gave to each other, and to God, with the normal expectation of a return. Their communities were knit together by mutual service, including the service of wealthier members, who were benefactors to the Temple or to local synagogues, expecting and receiving honor in return.[17] Jewish wisdom texts—such as Proverbs, Sirach, and Tobit—place gift-giving within the usual framework of reciprocity (e.g., Prov 11:25; Sir 12:1–2). But there is one important exception (echoed also in biblical laws, such as Exod 22:25–27): one should give to the poor, even though they cannot reciprocate (e.g., Prov 19:17). In most ancient societies, those on the margins of society were beyond the realm of gifts (not counting the occasional

16. For introduction and translation, see Miriam Griffin and Brad Inwood, *Seneca: On Benefits* (Chicago: University of Chicago Press, 2011).

17. A claim to Jewish exceptionalism has been made by Seth Schwartz, *Were the Jews a Mediterranean Society?* (Princeton: Princeton University Press, 2010). He associates Jews with solidarity rather than reciprocity (which he equates with inequality and dependency), but the antithesis is false, and the argument influenced by modern notions of the "pure gift."

coin tossed to a beggar) because they had nothing they could offer in return: that was the experience of the prodigal son, to whom "no one gave anything" (Luke 15:16).[18] The Jewish ethic is unusual in the emphasis it places on giving to the vulnerable and poor, even though they had nothing to give back.

In fact, however, when gifts to the poor are placed in a Jewish theological frame a form of reciprocity takes place even here. According to Deuteronomy, the poor recipients of gifts will "bless you" (that is, invoke God's blessing on the donor), such that the gift will be "to your credit before the LORD your God" (Deut 24:13, NRSV). Thus, even if the poor are unable to reciprocate themselves, there will be a return—in the form of blessing *from God*. In some wisdom literature, such divine blessing may be expected in this life (e.g., Sir 12:2), but in other Jewish material, the "reward" for humanly unreciprocated gifts is located in the afterlife.[19] We find this assumption in Jesus's teaching about giving in secret and without certainty of return: he bases this not (as we might expect) on the grounds that a unilateral, unreciprocated gift is morally better but on the promise that *God* will reward such gifts in the eschatological future (e.g., Matt 6:1-4; Luke 6:38; 14:14). The return-gift is delayed and, we might say, "outsourced," but since it comes from God it is guaranteed. Jews were perhaps more likely than non-Jews to give to the truly destitute, not because they did not care about a return but because they had stronger grounds for expecting one—not from the destitute but from God.

THE WESTERN "PURE" GIFT

Giving in hope of a return seems to many Westerners morally deficient, even a denial of the spirit of gift. But is there something peculiarly modern about this suspicion of reciprocity? Philosophers in antiquity (such as Aristotle, Cicero, and Seneca) certainly insisted that no gift should be given *only* for one's own benefit. But they assumed that gift-giving is a reciprocal business, in which friendships will be of benefit to both parties, and the best sort of giving will enable the sharing of goods in common. They did not assume a stark polarity between "disinterest" and "self-interest," and they displayed no concern to "purify" the gift from any element of return. Gifts, they knew, carried obli-

18. On ancient poverty, see Bruce W. Longenecker, *Remember the Poor: Paul, Poverty, and the Greco-Roman World* (Grand Rapids: Eerdmans, 2010); Margaret Atkins and Robin Osborne, eds., *Poverty in the Roman World* (Cambridge: Cambridge University Press, 2006).

19. See Gary A. Anderson, *Charity: The Place of the Poor in the Biblical Tradition* (New Haven: Yale University Press, 2013).

gations, and if they had known the phrase they would certainly have shared our acknowledgment that "there is no such thing as a free lunch." But, unlike them, we acknowledge that truth reluctantly, with a hint of cynicism, while we idealize the "gift-without-return" and prefer to mask or deny any elements of circular exchange. Why do we have such sensitivity on this matter?

Many social, economic, political, and ethical shifts have created the modern, distinctively Western ideal of the "pure gift," but we may note here in outline some of the key changes. Gifts and gift-exchange have not, of course, disappeared from the modern West. At Christmas we indulge in a profusion of gifts, and in personal relations we give gifts (e.g. hosting a meal) that follow an implied ethic of reciprocity. But in general gift-giving has been limited to the private sphere and restricted or banned in the public domain. At the same time, the ideology of gift has been separated out from the ideology of exchange. Already in antiquity, gifts were distinguished in certain respects from market exchange and contractual employment, but both were forms of exchange. Now we assume an ethical and structural contrast: the market is associated with profit, utilitarian transaction, and reciprocal exchange (*quid pro quo*), while gifts are associated with solidarity, sentiment, and disinterest. As Jonathan Parry has argued regarding the modern era, "the ideology of a disinterested gift emerges in parallel with an ideology of a purely interested exchange" and both are, in an important sense, "*our* invention."[20]

Our moral preference for a one-way, nonreciprocal, and wholly "disinterested" gift has many intellectual roots. When Martin Luther (1483–1546) challenged contemporary Catholic teaching about merit, and the concept of an instrumental cycle of gift-and-return between humans and God, his theology encouraged an ethic which limited or even banned notions of a return for human generosity. If a believer is to be a "Christ" to others, he should cheerfully "live only for others and not for himself."[21] Immanuel Kant (1724–1804), anxious that virtue be free of external constraint, and that no gift should put another under obligation, considered it a universal moral duty to promote the happiness of others without hoping for something in return. The more we prize individual autonomy, the more we disown the ties and social obligations traditionally created by gifts, and the more we idealize gifts given without thought or expectation of return. The French philosopher Auguste

20. Jonathan Parry, "*The Gift*, the Indian Gift, and the 'Indian Gift,'" *Man* 21 (1986): 453–73, at 458 (italics original).

21. Classically expressed in Luther's treatise, *The Freedom of the Christian*, translated in Jaroslav Pelikan and Helmut T. Lehmann, eds., *Luther's Works* (St. Louis: Concordia; Philadelphia: Fortress, 1955–1986), 31:343–77.

Comte (1798–1857) coined the term "altruism" as a moral ideal founded on the antithesis between self and other; on this model, pure concern for the other (altruism) will exclude any benefit to oneself. Taking this modern notion of the "pure" gift to its logical extreme, Jacques Derrida (1930–2003) insisted that a gift is only a gift if it does not, and cannot, come back: "For there to be a gift, there must be no reciprocity, return, exchange, countergift, or debt."[22] From Derrida's perspective, all that anthropologists describe as the circulation of the gift is something *other than* what is truly gift. But from the anthropologist's perspective, and from the perspective of most cultures, what Derrida describes as gift would be pointless, and would not count as gift at all!

We clearly need to be careful in our assumptions. What we associate with "gift," including its definition in our dictionaries, may be a product of modern cultural shifts, and it would be anachronistic to retroject these connotations onto the past or to take them for granted in our reading of Paul. Since Paul's discussion of (what we call) "grace" falls within the domain of gift, we should not rush to assume that we know what he meant. Perhaps he did, indeed, mean a gift without return, but perhaps that is our assumption about a "free" gift. Gifts are clearly complex, multidimensional, and culturally shaped. For the sake of clarity, we need some tools to analyze this complexity, and that is our task in the next chapter.

---

22. Jacques Derrida, *Counterfeit Money*, vol. 1 of *Given Time*, trans. Peggy Kamuf (Chicago: University of Chicago Press, 1992), 12.

CHAPTER 2

Perfections of Gift and Grace

What makes a gift *really* a gift, as opposed to a loan, a sale, or a wage? Is there something quintessentially "gift-like" about gifts? What would make a truly perfect gift? If God is perfect, and the giver of good gifts, we might learn from the gifts of God what constitutes a perfect gift. But what would that be?[1] Would gifts be perfect if they were given without limit or qualification? Or if they were given first, before anything is received? Or if they were given without our deserving them? Or if they expected nothing in return? Or would the perfect gift be all of these things—and others besides?

As we saw in the previous chapter, different cultures and times construct the ideal gift in different terms. In fact, we often push our definitions of gift to an extreme, and especially so in relation to divine gift or grace. We may call this the tendency to "perfect" a concept—to draw it out to its endpoint or extreme.[2] We speak of a "perfect" storm—when all that makes a storm "stormy" is combined in extreme form. People can be a "perfect nuisance"—a nuisance to the *nth* degree! But we can "perfect" a concept in other ways as well, without using the adjective "perfect." Philosophers speak of "pure gift" and theologians talk of "free grace," seeking the quintessence or perfection of these concepts, either for the purpose of definition or to clarify them by making the sharpest possible distinctions. This may also have rhetorical, even polemical aims. Disputes often arise within traditions when one side says it holds to the "true" and "proper" meaning of a central concept and attempts to disqualify the other on such terms. Once you have "perfected" a certain concept (X) in a particular

1. Cf. James 1:17: "Every good act of giving and every perfect gift is from above, coming down from the Father of lights, in whom there is no variation or shadow due to change."

2. I draw this notion of "perfection" from the literary critic Kenneth Burke, *Permanence and Change: An Anatomy of Purpose* (Berkeley: University of California Press, 1954), 292–94; cf. his *Language as Symbolic Action: Essays on Life, Literature, and Method* (Berkeley: University of California Press, 1966), 16–20.

form, you can claim that you alone have the proper understanding of X, and what your opponents mean by X is really non-X. Perfections therefore trade on antithesis, on pushing a concept into a form that excludes something else. Paul often uses antitheses, and sometimes speaks of "grace" in antithetical terms: "If it is by grace, it is not from works, otherwise grace would not be grace" (Rom 11:6). Formulations like this have encouraged Paul's interpreters to think of grace as a concept that should be perfected, in order to seek the genuine, "pure" understanding of grace, what it is that makes grace "totally gratuitous" and what ensures that salvation is "by grace alone." The pressure to perfect a concept also generates negatives: if God's grace is perfect, it is surely unmerited, unstinting, indiscriminate, unconditional, and unalloyed.

Not all gifts are "perfected" in such a way. In fact, the gifts we give to one another are rarely extreme; rather, they operate in moderation. What I give to another may be more than they deserve, but it is not wholly unmerited. It may surprise them by coming early, but it is not completely out of the blue. In everyday relations, gifts do not generally take extreme or radical forms. In fact, as we shall see, extremes may be problematic in some ways. But theologians naturally tend to portray the gifts of God in their sharpest form and purest profile. So, what would make a gift perfect in theological terms?

Six Perfections of Grace

It turns out that there is more than one way that a gift can be "perfected" and therefore more than one perfection of grace. Gift-giving has multiple ingredients, involving a giver, a gift, and a recipient, and each of these could be perfected in some way. A gift may be perfected in the attitude of the giver, for instance, or in the scale of the gift, or in the way the gift encounters its recipient. After observing how gifts were perfected in antiquity, and how grace has been perfected in the course of Christian theology, I have come to the conclusion that there are at least *six* possible "perfections" of gift/grace, particularly in depicting the giving of God:[3]

1. Superabundance

A superabundant gift is perfected in scale, significance, or duration: it is huge, lavish, unceasing, long-lasting, etc. Looking at the abundance of natural re-

---

3. Ideally, of course, there should be seven! I am open to suggestions . . .

sources, many ancient philosophers (Jewish and non-Jewish) took God's gifts to be superabundant, given lavishly from God's limitless resources, extravagant to the extent that the world was able to contain them and humans to receive them. Philo, for instance, speaks of God's grace as a treasure-store of "boundless and illimitable wealth," which God "pours forth from a continuous and inexhaustible spring."[4] We can see Paul "perfect" God's gifts in this way when he speaks of grace "abounding" or "super-abounding" (2 Cor 9:8, 14; Rom 5:15–20).

2. Singularity

Here attention shifts from the gift to the giver, and by "singularity" I mean that benevolence or goodness is the giver's *sole or exclusive* mode of operation. The giver is of such a character as only ever to give benefits: he/she would never do anything in a contrary mode, such as harm, punish, or judge. The lavishness of the gift is not here at issue: what matters is the singular devotion of this giver to do nothing other than what is beneficial. Some Greek philosophers were keen to attribute this perfection to God. Plato, for instance, insisted that God, as the highest form of being, was also morally perfect; being *purely* and consistently good, God does only what is beautiful and beneficial (not the capricious or harmful things attributed to gods in Greek mythology).[5] Since the Jewish Scriptures portray God quite frequently as judging, destroying, and causing suffering, this might be a perfection that Jews and Christians would *not* deploy; or if they did, they would have to find some way of handling that contrary impression. One might expect that God, as a *just* judge, would punish evil, and would *not* be singularly (i.e., exclusively) beneficial to everyone all the time. This is not, then, a necessary perfection of grace, and those who subscribe to other perfections might *not* subscribe to this. But one can see how it could be, and has been, attractive to many.

3. Priority

Priority concerns the timing of the gift, which is given before any initiative taken by the recipient. The prior gift is not a response to a request, and is thus spontaneous in its generosity; it is not obliged by a previous gift, and is thus

---

4. Philo, *Allegorical Interpretation* 3.163–64, my translation; *On the Posterity of Cain* 32, 127–28.

5. Plato, *Timaeus* 29c–d; *Republic* 379b–d.

(in this sense) "free." The greater the emphasis on priority, the greater appears the superiority of the giver as the initiator of the gift relationship. In antiquity God was commonly figured as the *first giver*, not least in the creation of the world as the first and original gift. In this sense, humans could never put God under any sort of debt; they were only ever respondents to previous divine gifts.[6] Christian theologians have spoken of the "prevenience" of grace and of prior election by grace as "predestination." Whatever its particular nuance, priority suggests the freedom or sovereignty of God in determining the operation of grace.

4. Incongruity

Incongruity concerns the relationship between the giver and the recipient, and maximizes the mismatch between the gift and the worth or merit of its recipient. To give lavishly and in advance is one thing, but it is quite another to give to unworthy or unfitting recipients. As we have noted, it was generally assumed in antiquity that gifts are best distributed to worthy recipients. "Worth" could be evaluated in many different ways, but discrimination in giving might be taken to be a necessary criterion of a *good* gift. However, discrimination creates limitation, and the perfection of incongruity figures the gift as given without condition, *without regard to the worth of the recipient*. The gifts of nature could be represented in this way: after all, the sun shines on the bad as well as the good.[7] Thus a supremely excellent gift might be figured as wholly incongruous, taking no account of worth, and given precisely to those who were undeserving. Again, this is a not a necessary perfection of a gift, and it might appear problematic: if the bad get the same as the good, that looks grossly unfair. Cosmic justice might require that God's gifts are *not* incongruous, but are distributed to those who deserve them. But for certain purposes, or in certain conditions, it is possible to perfect the incongruous gift.

5. Efficacy

Gifts that achieve something, that *change* things for the better, might be regarded as better than gifts with limited positive effect. The gift of life—giving

---

6. Philo, *On the Confusion of Tongues* 123; *Who is the Heir?* 102–24. For Philo's emphasis on this point, see Orrey McFarland, *God and Grace in Philo and Paul* (Leiden: Brill, 2015).

7. Matt 5:45; Seneca, *On Benefits* 1.1.9; 4.28. Seneca insists, however, that the gods would prefer to benefit only the worthy.

birth to a child, or rescuing someone from death—is in these terms a supreme gift, because it creates or enables all that follows. One might expect that God gives gifts that effect change, but this element can be perfected such that God alone is the effective agent at work. In ancient discussions of agency, philosophers were generally concerned to insist that humans retain moral responsibility for their action, so that the gods cannot be *exclusively* responsible for either the good or the bad that humans do.[8] However, God's grace might create the capacity to receive the seeds of virtue, or might aid the development of that virtue by instruction, example, and encouragement. And those wishing to perfect the efficacy of grace might take the role of God further: perhaps God's grace creates a newly configured self; perhaps this self can choose only the destiny determined by God; or perhaps grace replaces human agency such that God alone can be said to act in the performance of virtue.[9] Clearly, efficacy is another possible perfection of grace, and one that can be taken to various points of extreme.

6. Noncircularity

As we noted in the last chapter, Western modernity is inclined to perfect the gift as "pure" only when there is no reciprocity, no return or exchange. In antiquity, philosophers insisted that God/the gods *need* nothing in return for their gifts: they are not salesmen, trading their benefits for a monetary return.[10] Nonetheless, it was generally held that they did expect the return of gratitude or praise, just as higher-status humans wanted a return not of material benefit but of honor. In the modern era, as we have seen, there has been a persistent tendency to perfect gifts as noncircular and nonreciprocal: if they are truly "altruistic" and "disinterested," they should not be "tainted" by elements of return. Here, then, is another possible perfection of the gift, one clearly distinguishable from the others we have listed.

We should remind ourselves that it is not *necessary* to perfect gift-giving, human or divine. Most ordinary gifts are not particularly abundant, are mixed with other modes of behavior, are not clearly first in sequence, are given in accord with some element of worth, are not particularly efficacious, and involve

8. See Martha Nussbaum, *The Fragility of Goodness: Luck and Ethics in Greek Tragedy and Philosophy*, 2nd ed. (Cambridge: Cambridge University Press, 2001).

9. On the ancient discussion, see John M. G. Barclay and Simon J. Gathercole, eds., *Divine and Human Agency in Paul and His Cultural Environment* (London: T&T Clark, 2006).

10. See Philo, *On the Cherubim* 122–24.

some expectation of return. Even so, they may be good gifts! In fact, as we have noted, some of these perfections are potentially problematic, offending some principle of justice, responsibility, or friendship. However, gift-giving is always susceptible to one or more of these perfections, especially in relation to God, the ultimate Giver. In some cases, these perfections are matters of degree, and need not involve a total extreme, but this six-part taxonomy helps us to see the directions in which interpreters are liable to take the concept of divine gift or grace.

And *there is more than one* direction to go. To perfect one of these facets of gift-giving does not imply adopting any of the others—and certainly not all of them. Divine grace could be superabundant and prior without being incongruous with the worth of the recipient. It could be given without regard to worth but still expect a return. By separating out or disaggregating these six different perfections of grace, it becomes clear that they do not constitute a single "package." In fact, different interpreters of this concept have tended to operate with different clusters of perfection. Nonetheless, they have often regarded their interpretation as the "correct" interpretation of grace, such that any other is not just different but wrong.

We can now see how people can mean different things by "pure grace," and have taken grace to be "free" in more than one sense. "Pure grace" may mean its singularity (God is nothing but benevolent) or its noncircularity (God's grace seeks no return). Grace may be "free" in being given irrespective of the recipient's worth (incongruous), or in being given without subsequent expectations (noncircular), or in both senses at once. Even the word "unconditional" can be confusing: Does this mean without prior conditions (incongruous), or without resulting obligations (noncircular), or both?

This taxonomy can clarify some of the major disagreements on the topic of grace in the course of Christian theology, including those we noted in the prologue. Everyone likes to think that they have grasped the "real" meaning of grace in their particular cluster of perfections. Disagreements may arise, not because one side emphasizes grace *more than* the other, but because they perfect the term in *different ways*. You may think that divine grace is only properly grace if one strips away all notions of judgment or wrath (perfecting the singularity of grace). But another, equally sincere believer may hold that singularity is not an essential feature of grace: what is most important is that it is incongruous (undeserved). Another may hold that the only grace worthy of the name is one that guarantees the salvation of the believer (perfecting the efficacy of grace); but another believer may be suspicious of that perfection, while holding that grace, by definition, lays on us no demands (being noncircular). Pelagius, as we shall see, held firmly to the superabundance and priority of divine grace, but for theological reasons could not accept Augustine's perfection of the incongruity and efficacy of grace. Pelagius did not believe in grace *less than* Augustine; he simply believed in it *differently*.

SOME INFLUENTIAL FIGURES IN THE HISTORY OF INTERPRETATION

Almost all interpreters of Paul have agreed that grace is a central topic in his letters, but they have disagreed on what he meant by this term, and what connotations it bore. Our sixfold taxonomy of perfections helps us understand why they disagree, and before we come to read Paul himself it will be valuable to trace, in outline, some significant trajectories in the history of interpretation of this theme.[11]

One of the greatest admirers of Paul in the second century was the provocative theologian *Marcion*. Because he was considered heretical, his own work has not survived, and we know of him only from the polemical accounts of others. Even so, some features of his theology are reasonably clear.[12] It seems from Tertullian's response that Marcion warmed particularly to the antithetical features of Paul's letters (especially Galatians) and was struck by Paul's emphasis on God's favor or grace. In fact, Marcion believed that the gracious God revealed by Jesus and preached by Paul was incompatible with the Creator God of the Jewish Scriptures (the Old Testament). The Creator God was just, and in the cause of justice punished people and caused them harm; Marcion highlighted scriptural stories of God's anger, condemnation, and destruction. But the God revealed for the first time in Jesus Christ was wholly different. He was not only "good" but "supremely good," and that "primary and perfect goodness" was this God's sole mode of operation.[13] What Jesus taught and what Paul proclaimed was that this benevolent, merciful, and generous God

11. For a much fuller version of this matter, including figures not mentioned here, see my *Paul and the Gift* (Grand Rapids: Eerdmans, 2015), 79–182.

12. How much we can know about Marcion is a matter of scholarly controversy. See Judith M. Lieu, *Marcion and the Making of a Heretic: God and Scripture in the Second Century* (Cambridge: Cambridge University Press, 2014); and (with more confidence about the sources) Sebastian P. Moll, *The Arch-Heretic Marcion* (Tübingen: Mohr Siebeck, 2010).

13. Thus Tertullian reports in his treatise *Against Marcion*, which is available, with English translation, in Ernest Evans, *Tertullian: Adversus Marcionem*, 2 vols. (Oxford: Clarendon, 1972). The text cited here is from 1.23.3.

had emerged from hiddenness to save humanity, and to bid them respond not with fear but with love.

Using the terms of our taxonomy, Marcion perfected the singularity of grace, in a way that was easily understood and highly attractive in the ancient world. (And not only then: one may trace similar tendencies toward this perfection of grace in some strands of contemporary Christianity.) Other equally careful readers of Paul in the early church did not agree, but that is not because they neglected Paul's theology of grace. They just perfected it differently.

For a different way of perfecting grace, we may turn to *Augustine* (354–430), whose influence on Western theology has been enormous. Augustine took grace to be the central theme of Paul's letter to the Romans, but his interpretation developed over time as he wrestled with difficult texts and was drawn into controversy with other theologians.[14] For Augustine, Paul's theology of grace evoked the power and agency of God, and was crucial in combatting the central sin of pride, by which we attribute merit to ourselves. As Paul says in one of Augustine's favorite texts: "What do you have that you have not received?" (1 Cor 4:7). After abandoning his Manichaean views, with their tendency to determinism, Augustine initially maintained the free will of the believer in the act of faith, in response to God's call. That paralleled the emphasis of theologians in the Greek tradition, such as John Chrysostom, who, in interpreting the strong statements of Romans 9, took Paul to be speaking about God's *foreknowledge* of the believer's faith and virtue, not *predestination*.[15] However, when Augustine wrestled further with Rom 9:6–29 (as he prepared his *Letter to Simplicianus* in 396), his mind changed, and he began to think of faith itself as a gift from God.

Augustine had always been impressed by Paul's stress on the *incongruity* of grace: God justifies not the righteous but the ungodly (Rom 4:5). He now began to explore its *efficacy*, so that even our response to God's grace is not truly "up to us." He became convinced that God's grace was *prior* to our response, not just temporally (while we were still sinners) but also logically (it *brings about* our response). As he drilled down deeper into the human psyche and the motivations of the will (most famously in his *Confessions*), Augustine came

---

14. The literature is immense, but we may highlight Peter Brown, *Augustine of Hippo* (New York: Dorset, 1967); Carol Harrison, *Rethinking Augustine's Early Theology: An Argument for Continuity* (Oxford: Oxford University Press, 2006); J. Patout Burns, *The Development of Augustine's Doctrine of Operative Grace* (Paris: Études Augustiniennes, 1980).

15. Chrysostom's *Homilies on Romans* may be found in translation in vol. 11 of *A Select Library of the Nicene and Post-Nicene Fathers of the Church*, ed. Philip Schaff (Edinburgh: T&T Clark, 1996).

to think that even our will to delight in God must be "touched," "inspired," or "moved" by the grace of God. According to the verse he often quoted (in its Latin version), "God is at work in you both to will and to work for a good will" (Phil 2:13).[16]

Thus, Augustine combined the incongruity of grace with its priority and efficacy, the three woven tightly together. Because God's grace is effective and transformative, the initial incongruity of grace (given to sinners who were alienated from God) effects an eventual congruity, as good works merit their fitting reward, eternal life. But since it is *God* who works in a believer, "when God crowns our merits, he crowns nothing other than his own gifts."[17] These perfections became increasingly radicalized when Augustine got mired in bitter controversy with opponents. The most significant of these was the British monk Pelagius (c. 354–418), who was also an extremely close reader of Paul but was alarmed at the half-heartedness of elite Christians who made little effort to observe the strenuous commands of the gospel.[18] For Pelagius, God's grace is always prior and superabundant: God has already given us the ability to do the good and has graciously revealed to us how to do it, not least in the example of Christ. But the choice to do the good, and the action itself, is ours; otherwise we cannot praise people for their virtue or blame them for their vice. Pelagius exposed a weakness in Augustine's theology, if the powerful agency of grace reduced the human will to mere assent. But Augustine sensed in Pelagius a subtle form of self-congratulation, and an inadequate appreciation of the efficacy of grace. The human will, Augustine reasoned, is wounded and needs far more than instruction and assistance: it needs to be healed, liberated, and energized. Why else would we pray daily for divine aid: "Lead us not into temptation, but deliver us from evil"?

By melding his theology of grace with the piety of a believer, Augustine made his perfections of grace appear both necessary and irrefutable. But the polarizing tendencies of controversy (even with some of his admirers, such as John Cassian) led him to draw out his beliefs to ever greater end-of-the-line

16. Augustine was also impressed by Rom 5:5, reading "the love of God" (*amor Dei*) as "love for God": "Love for God has been poured into our hearts by the Holy Spirit who has been given to us" (my translations).

17. Augustine, *Epistle* 194.5.19 (my translation).

18. For Pelagius's reading of Paul, see Theodore de Bruyn, *Pelagius' Commentary on St. Paul's Epistle to the Romans* (Oxford: Clarendon, 1993). Augustine's counterarguments can be found in his treatises *On Nature and Grace* and *On the Grace of Christ*. For an analysis of these controversies, see P. Brown, *Augustine*, 340–75, and Gerald Bonner, *St. Augustine of Hippo: Life and Controversies* (Norwich: Canterbury, 1963), 312–93.

extremes. The more he stressed the efficacy and priority of grace, the more he was led to affirm the (inexplicable) *predestination* of believers, following some intriguing Pauline texts (e.g., Rom 8:28–29; Eph 1:4–5). If God's grace is effective in the human will, how could a true believer turn away from God? Must we not thus affirm "the *perseverance* of the saints"? Even more controversially, if God has already selected those who will believe, and none of God's intentions are fruitless, did Christ die only for the elect, and not for all? Centuries later, John Calvin (1509–1564) revived many of Augustine's arguments, such that the cluster of Augustinian perfections of grace has become a hallmark of the Reformed tradition. But these, we may note, are only one way of perfecting the theme of grace. Those who disagree do not necessarily deny or downplay grace: they might simply perfect it in other ways.

Our taxonomy of grace can also go some way toward explaining the difference between *Martin Luther* (1483–1546) and *Thomas Aquinas* (1225–1274) on this topic. Both in his *Summa Theologiae* and in his commentaries on Paul, Aquinas laid stress on the grace of God in creation and salvation—a grace that overturns the human deficit of sin and transforms its human recipients.[19] It is clear that God's grace is *initially* incongruous: Christ came to call not the righteous but sinners (Mark 2:17). But grace does not leave us as we were. It is "infused" into the human soul and does not destroy but elevates human nature, such that the believer is made righteous and rendered ultimately worthy of salvation. As a formative power (*gratia habitualis*), grace conducts the believer along a journey from forgiveness to sanctification and renders the believer fit for the final (but still threatening) day of judgment. Faith has a crucial part to play in this journey, but it must be completed and "formed" by works of love, and it is these that will be judged on the last day.

Luther's reaction to medieval theology and to its language of "merit" was visceral. Faith is, for Luther, not intellectual assent to propositions about God but *trust* in God's promises and in the benefits brought by Christ. He insists that in faith (and by faith *alone*) we have everything necessary for justification and salvation because we already have the gift of God, that is, Christ. To regard works as a *supplement* to faith necessary for salvation would suggest, to Luther, that we treat God's work in Christ as insufficient or incomplete—an act of hostile mistrust toward God that would be the height of impiety. Works

---

19. Philip McCosker, "Grace," in Philip McCosker and Denys Turner, eds., *The Cambridge Companion to the* Summa Theologiae (Cambridge: Cambridge University Press, 2016), 206–21. Cf. Joseph P. Wawrykow, *God's Grace and Human Action: "Merit" in the Theology of Thomas Aquinas* (Notre Dame: University of Notre Dame Press, 1995).

will properly follow from faith, but it is disastrous, in both theology and pastoral practice, to make them integral to salvation itself.[20] Grace, for Luther, is not a substance or a quality "poured into the soul" but a relation—God's free decision to pardon and to accept believers in Christ.[21]

For Luther it became essential to emphasize that the incongruity of grace—the mismatch between God's gift and the worth of the believer—is foundational not just at the start of the believer's life but as the permanent hallmark of the life of faith. Justification by faith (that is, trust) in Christ means that believers live not from their own righteousness but from the righteousness of Christ, an extrinsic or "alien" righteousness that they can never call truly their own. Luther sometimes spoke of this as the "imputation" of the righteousness of Christ but more often as the presence of Christ in faith, or as the believer's union with Christ: "Faith takes hold of Christ in such a way that Christ is the object of faith, or rather not the object but, so to speak, the One who is present in faith itself."[22] The important point is that, in themselves, believers remain deeply flawed: in their inmost souls there lurks a deep rebellion or resistance to God. But God looks on believers as if they are "glued" to Christ (and he to them), and in Christ he sees only righteousness, holiness, and goodness. There thus remains a lifelong incongruity in grace, such that Luther could coin the expression *simul justus et peccator* ("at the same time justified and a sinner").[23]

Luther challenged any theological structure that envisioned a meritorious return of good works to God. If the grace of God is given *gratis*, it is given not to elicit a return or benefit to God but for our sake alone: this selfless love is both in intent and motive nonreciprocal. As we noted in the previous chapter, the same applies to human gifts (arguably one root of the Western "pure gift"): they should be given purely for the benefit of the other. Luther thus radicalized the *incongruity* of grace and combined it with a presumption toward

20. Key treatises on this topic include *The Freedom of the Christian* and *Two Kinds of Righteousness*.

21. For the role of Melanchthon in this understanding of *charis*, and for a fine recent analysis of Luther's reading of Paul, see Stephen J. Chester, *Reading Paul with the Reformers: Reconciling Old and New Perspectives* (Grand Rapids: Eerdmans, 2017).

22. *Lectures on Galatians* (*Luther's Works*, 26:129). This theme has been emphasized and developed in the Finnish school of Lutheran interpretation: see Tuomo Mannermaa, *Christ Present in Faith: Luther's View of Justification*, ed. and trans. Kirsi Irmeli Stjerna (Minneapolis: Augsburg Fortress, 2005).

23. For discussion of this phrase, see Daphne Hampson, *Christian Contradictions: The Structures of Lutheran and Catholic Thought* (Cambridge: Cambridge University Press, 2001).

noncircularity: God's grace does not necessitate or demand a return. This is a powerful combination of perfections, which has long influenced Protestant thought. Lutheran polemics have insisted that this is the only proper meaning of grace, and of salvation "by grace alone." But as this brief survey has shown, it is not the only way one can think about grace.

Our six-part taxonomy of the perfections of grace can help us understand what these and other disputes are about, even if it cannot determine the "right" understanding of the term. The contemporary interpretation of Paul continues to be influenced by these long-running debates and the particular perfections they exemplify. Once we are aware of these, we can read Paul with more nuance and more self-awareness. We can no longer assume that we know what is meant by "grace" but can start with an open mind as to which, if any, of these perfections are truly present in his work. But before we get to Paul, there is one further step to take. Since Paul's theology is evidently Jewish, and since his relationship to the Jewish tradition in relation to grace has been the subject of important controversy, we must first investigate the significance of grace within Second Temple Judaism. We may understand that better as well, now that we are conscious of the different possible perfections of grace.

CHAPTER 3

Paul, Grace, and Second Temple Judaism

A revolution in the study of Paul took place in the wake of a famous book by E. P. Sanders, published in 1977: *Paul and Palestinian Judaism.*[1] Up to that point, the mainstream reading of Paul had been dominated by Reformation themes, which were given their most influential expression by the Lutheran New Testament scholar Rudolf Bultmann (1884–1976). On that mainstream interpretation, grace was at the heart of Paul's theology: salvation is not attained by human capacity or achievement but is given by the sheer, unmerited grace of God in Christ. Paul's insistence on justification by faith, not "works of the Law" (Gal 2:15–16), was taken to represent a contrast between the grace of the gospel and the "works-righteousness" supposedly characteristic of the Judaism of Paul's day. Jews, on this interpretation, hoped to gain merit by observing the Mosaic Law, through a system of recompense entirely contrary to the freely given grace of the gospel.

E. P. Sanders set out to overturn this reading of ancient Judaism, which he considered a gross caricature. He conducted a close reading of a range of Jewish texts from the Second Temple and early rabbinic periods (i.e., c. 300 BCE–c. 400 CE), and offered a counterimage of Judaism as a "religion of grace." On this reading, God's election of Israel was by grace, and the covenant was established *prior* to any requirement of Torah-observance.[2] Thus, whatever requirements were made regarding obedience and works, these were already founded on, and framed by, the grace of God.

Rather than selecting individual motifs, Sanders attempted to map the

1. E. P. Sanders, *Paul and Palestinian Judaism* (London: SCM, 1977).
2. Torah is a Hebrew term generally translated as "law," though it is wider in meaning (including what we might call instruction and revelation). I will use the terms Torah, Mosaic Law, and Law (capitalized) interchangeably. They refer to a specific textual and cultural phenomenon, since that is what Paul and his fellow Jews were talking about, not "law" or "obligation" in general.

entire "pattern of religion" to be found in Palestinian Judaism and in Paul. Crucial to this pattern is the matter of sequence: first one "gets in" to the community of the saved, and then one "stays in," and the difference between the two must be carefully preserved. As far as ancient Judaism was concerned, Sanders argued, "getting in" was always and only by grace, in the election of the patriarchs and in the gift of the covenant. Torah-observance was necessary for "staying in" the covenant but was not the means of "getting in." At most it was a condition for final salvation but not its cause. To capture this pattern of religion, Sanders coined the phrase "covenantal nomism," whose ingredients he summarized as follows:

> (1) God has chosen Israel and (2) given the law. The law implies both (3) God's promise to maintain the promise and (4) the requirement to obey. (5) God rewards obedience and punishes transgression. (6) The law provides for means of atonement and atonement results in (7) maintenance or re-establishment of the covenantal relationship. (8) All those who are maintained in the covenant by obedience, atonement, and God's mercy belong to the group who will be saved. An important interpretation of the first and last points is that election and ultimately salvation are considered to be by God's mercy rather than human achievement.[3]

Sanders wished to give proper weight to the demand for Torah-obedience in Jewish texts; nevertheless, he insisted that this "maintains one's position in the covenant, but it does not earn God's grace as such. It simply keeps an individual in the group which is the recipient of God's grace."[4]

In our terms, the element of grace that Sanders here highlights is *priority*: God's grace comes *before* human obedience. Sanders traced this pattern of covenantal nomism across almost all the Jewish texts he canvassed, noting special emphases in some (e.g., on predestination in the Dead Sea Scrolls). His results were sufficient to challenge and eventually overturn the misrepresentation of Judaism commonly found in Christian-influenced scholarship. It is no longer intellectually defensible to represent ancient Judaism as a religion of "legalism" or "works-righteousness," as if Jews sought to "earn" salvation by doing good works. That caricature must count as one of the many anti-Jewish tropes that have circulated in Christian-influenced scholarship but must now be strongly repudiated.

---

3. Sanders, *Paul and Palestinian Judaism*, 422.
4. Sanders, *Paul and Palestinian Judaism*, 420.

The New Perspective on Paul

What does this mean for the interpretation of Paul? The traditional reading of Paul, associating Paul with grace and Judaism with works, was no longer tenable in the wake of Sanders's work. Sanders traced a difference in Paul's "pattern of religion," but not at this point. Paul's soteriology, he argued, was based on participation in Christ, rather than covenantal nomism, but there was no difference with regard to grace and works: "On the point on which many have found the decisive contrast between Paul and Judaism—grace and works—Paul is in agreement with Palestinian Judaism ... salvation is by grace but judgment is according to works: works are the condition of remaining 'in,' but they do not earn salvation."[5] From this conclusion arose "the new perspective on Paul," which departed decisively from the traditional reading of Paul.

To speak autobiographically for a moment, I still remember the buzz of excitement when I started studying the New Testament as an undergraduate at Cambridge in 1979. My teachers, N. T. Wright and Morna Hooker, embraced Sanders's conclusions and approached Paul with new questions about faith, works, covenant, Judaism, and Paul's attitude toward the Mosaic Law. We pondered the work of Krister Stendahl[6] and eagerly awaited Sanders's next book.[7] It seemed clear that Paul did not entirely agree with his fellow Jews, but in what did that difference lie? Was it simply, as Sanders had it, that salvation is in Christ and therefore *not* in anything else? James D. G. Dunn, one of the architects of "the new perspective on Paul," posed the question as follows:

> The Judaism of what Sanders christened as 'covenantal nomism' can now be seen to preach good Protestant doctrine: that grace is always prior; that human effort is ever the response to divine initiative; that good works are the fruit and not the root of salvation. ... But if that is so, where does that leave Paul? And where does it leave his justification by faith?[8]

The answer offered by "the new perspective" was that the key issue for Paul was not the *structure* of salvation but its *scope*. Paul's theology was forged in

---

5. Sanders, *Paul and Palestinian Judaism*, 543.

6. Krister Stendahl, *Paul among Jews and Gentiles* (London: SCM, 1977), a book that contains his earlier, famous essay entitled, "Paul and the Introspective Conscience of the West."

7. *Paul, the Law, and the Jewish People* (Philadelphia: Fortress, 1983). He has written on Paul since, including his latest, *Paul: The Apostle's Life, Letters, and Thought* (London: SCM, 2016).

8. James D. G. Dunn, *The New Perspective on Paul: Collected Essays* (Tübingen: Mohr Siebeck, 2005), 193 (from his essay "The Justice of God," first published in 1991).

and for the sake of his mission to the gentiles, and the cutting edge of his theology lay in his insistence that gentiles do not need to adopt Torah-observance ("works of the Law") but are admitted to God's people by faith. In Stendahl's view, "The doctrine of justification by faith was hammered out by Paul for the very specific and limited purpose of defending the rights of Gentile converts to be full and genuine heirs to the promises of God to Israel."[9] Dunn pioneered an interpretation of Paul's phrase "works of the Law" that stressed that these were not works in general but works of the Mosaic Law, and in particular, he argued, the "boundary markers," such as circumcision, Sabbath regulations, and food laws, by which Jews were distinguished from gentiles. On Dunn's reading, Paul was not criticizing "salvation by works" but an overly "narrow" or "restricted" view of God's purposes, by which gentiles were being excluded or required to adopt ethnically specific, Jewish markers of identity.[10] N. T. Wright similarly identified Paul's target of criticism as Jewish ethnic privilege ("national righteousness"), by which Jews were distinguished from, and considered superior to, gentiles. Crucial for Paul was the fulfillment in Christ (the Messiah) of the Abrahamic promises to "the nations," throwing membership of God's people open to all, on the common basis of faith. The issue is not faith versus works in abstract terms but the establishment of the single, multiethnic family of the church.[11] On this reading, grace is not a distinctive or decisive element in Paul's theology because Paul says nothing on that subject that he did not have in common with his Jewish contemporaries.

Grace Is Everywhere, but Is It Everywhere the Same?

Sanders's rebuttal of then-current caricatures of Judaism has laid the foundation for most subsequent analyses of early Jewish soteriology. His notion of "covenantal nomism" has been nuanced in various respects,[12] but what we have discussed thus far in this book has taught us to ask a question that goes

9. Stendahl, *Paul among Jews and Gentiles*, 2. Note the use of the (modern) language of "rights," which signals a trend to explain Paul's theology, first and foremost, in sociopolitical terms.

10. See James D. G. Dunn, "The New Perspective on Paul," first published in 1983 and reprinted in his *New Perspective*, 89–110.

11. Wright's work on Paul is voluminous but is most accessible in his *Paul: Fresh Perspectives* (London: SPCK, 2005). Those wanting the long version may consult N. T. Wright, *Paul and the Faithfulness of God*, 2 vols. (London: SPCK, 2013).

12. Note especially, Simon J. Gathercole, *Where Is Boasting? Early Jewish Soteriology and Paul's Response in Romans 1–5* (Grand Rapids: Eerdmans, 2002), and D. A. Carson, Peter T.

to the heart of his project: What do we mean by "grace"? Because Sanders analyzed the pattern of religion in terms of sequence, he emphasized the *priority* of grace: God gives the covenant first, and Torah-obedience is a secondary phenomenon. He presumed that the priority of grace would also include its *incongruity* and made use of Augustinian and Protestant language about the "unmerited" grace of God.[13] Although he noted that some of the texts he studied spoke of "merit" and took God to be merciful to the *righteous*, he concluded that such texts were unsystematic or unclear.[14] But there is no reason to think that a *prior* grace will always be *incongruous*. As we have seen, priority is only one of the possible "perfections" of grace, and the presence of one does not entail the presence of any of the others. Each configuration of grace has to be treated on its own terms.

We may agree with Sanders that Judaism is "a religion of grace," but that claim lacks clarity and definition. To be sure, the Jewish texts speak frequently of the mercy, benevolence, and grace of God. But on the basis of our analysis of "perfections" in the last chapter, we are able to ask more precisely what they meant by such terms. Sanders's tendency to homogenize the Jewish texts on this crucial point should be resisted and replaced with a more penetrating set of questions regarding the dynamics of grace within each text. A simple binary question—do they speak of grace or not?—is too blunt. Perhaps there is diversity in the Jewish texts, and perhaps Paul's voice on this matter is neither simply "different" from, nor simply "the same" as, that of his fellow Jews but has its own tone and tenor within a complex Jewish debate. We cannot decide this in advance, only by careful reconsideration of the texts.

Four Second Temple Texts

In the Jewish Scriptures God is represented as full of grace, mercy, and "loving kindness" but also ready to execute judgment on the wicked: "a God merciful and gracious, slow to anger, and abounding in steadfast love and faithfulness, . . . yet by no means clearing the guilty, but visiting the iniquity of the parents upon the children" (Exod 34:6–7 NRSV; cf. Exod 20:5–6). If the universe is

---

O'Brien, and Mark A. Seifrid, eds., *The Complexities of Second Temple Judaism*, vol. 1 of *Justification and Variegated Nomism* (Tübingen: Mohr Siebeck, 2001).

13. See *Paul and Palestinian Judaism*, 394: salvation is "purely" by the mercy of God, "unmerited," and "groundless."

14. For fuller analysis and critique, see my *Paul and the Gift* (Grand Rapids: Eerdmans, 2015), 151–58.

morally ordered, God's grace could hardly undercut God's justice, even if God is patient and forgiving to an extraordinary degree. The election of Israel raised important questions about the relationship between justice and grace. God chose Abraham and the patriarchs and through them set the destiny of the chosen people. Was there some rationale for that choice, or not? The patriarchal narratives could be read in more than one way, but it was uncomfortable to believe that the choice was entirely arbitrary. If God loved the people of Israel not because of their righteousness but because of the promises to the patriarchs (Deut 7:7–8; 8:17–18), on what basis were they given those promises? Jews (including Paul) were bound to inquire into this matter, and they emerged with fascinatingly different answers.[15]

We will sample here just four texts from the end of the Second Temple period (c. 200 BCE–c. 100 CE) that discuss the mercy or grace of God, and the Scriptures that contain these themes, in varied contexts and in different ways. In each case, we will ask if there is evidence of a "perfection" of grace, and if so, which of the various perfections the text displays. Alert to possible diversity, we will resist assuming in advance what they mean when they describe God as the giver of grace. Even in our brief analysis, we may find quite a range of answers.[16]

Wisdom of Solomon

This text (from Alexandria in the first century CE) compiles a variety of materials to analyze how God's mercy and justice operate in a world where death and injustice seem to flout God's will.[17] From the start, the text emphasizes the goodness of God and the kindness of his Spirit/Wisdom (1:7), a benevolence that pervades the cosmos and extends to all people: "For you love all things that exist, / and detest none of the things that you have made" (11:24 NRSV). However, the world looks badly askew: the righteous suffer and some

15. For a discussion that covers a wide historical range of texts, see Jon D. Levenson, *The Love of God: Divine Gift, Human Gratitude, and Mutual Faithfulness in Judaism* (Princeton: Princeton University Press, 2016).

16. The rest of this chapter summarizes the full-scale textual analysis offered in part 2 of *Paul and the Gift* (194–328), where a fifth text (Pseudo-Philo, *Biblical Antiquities*) is also treated.

17. For recent analysis see especially Francis Watson, *Paul and the Hermeneutics of Faith* (Grand Rapids: Eerdmans, 2004), 380–411, and Jonathan A. Linebaugh, *God, Grace, and Righteousness in Wisdom of Solomon and Paul's Letter to the Romans: Texts in Conversation* (Leiden: Brill, 2013).

die young, while the powerful get away with murder (literally), and injustice reigns. Nonetheless, the author insists, God's justice will prevail: the righteous will live forever (5:15), and in the end God, armed with the powers of nature, will defeat his enemies and establish the proper order of the cosmos. The opening chapters thus affirm that God's kindness is also just: the ungodly will be punished in line with their own reasoning, while the godly will receive "the reward of holiness" (2:22, my translation). God's benevolence is not indulgence, and it is crucial that people get their just deserts. The structure of the universe would buckle if it were any other way.

The middle section of the text (chapters 6–10) describes the operations of Wisdom, which settled on Solomon as a gift, as befits the good soul that entered his body (8:19–20). Wisdom goes about seeking those worthy of her (6:16) and anticipates in grace the fitting recipients who search for her: "In every generation she passes into holy souls / and makes them friends of God" (7:27). A survey of biblical figures, from Adam to Joseph, illustrates this point (10:1–14). In every case, there is some congruity between the saving action of Wisdom and the worth of her beneficiaries: "Wisdom rescued from troubles those who served her" (10:9). Although Adam was sinful, his status as the "first-formed father of the world" justified his deliverance from transgression (10:1). All the others, from Noah onward, can be classified as "righteous" (even Jacob!). The survey makes clear that the order articulated earlier in the text is the blueprint of history. There is always a reason why some people perish and others are rescued; discerning that reason makes history comprehensible and hopeful.

The third and longest section (from the middle of chapter 10 to the end) retells the narrative of the exodus and the plagues, the paradigm of God's distinction between the righteous and the ungodly. The moral is clear: the wicked get their just deserts (often their punishment fits their crime), while "A holy people and blameless race / wisdom delivered from a nation of oppressors" (10:15).[18] The emphasis on God's judgment "by measure and number and weight" (11:20) does not mean that this text is heartless. In fact, in a moving analysis of the interaction between divine power, mercy, and justice (11:21–12:22), God is shown to exercise extreme patience, giving plenty of time for the ungodly to repent. But at the end of the day God has to punish those deserving of death (12:20), not as a limitation of God's goodness but as its ultimate proof. Because God is

18. There may be comfort here for Jews suffering political marginalization in Alexandria; see John M. G. Barclay, *Jews in the Mediterranean Diaspora from Alexander to Trajan (323 BCE–117 CE)* (Edinburgh: T&T Clark, 1996), 48–71; Erich Gruen, *Diaspora* (Berkeley: University of California Press, 2002), 54–83.

supremely and abundantly good, he guarantees a system of moral and rational symmetries, whereby the unrepentant get their deserts and the gifts of God reach their fitting beneficiaries. Wisdom of Solomon, we may say, expresses an emphatic theology of grace—which is fairly distributed to the worthy. God's grace is prior and superabundant but not incongruous.

Philo of Alexandria

Philo, the Jewish philosopher from Alexandria (c. 20 BCE–c. 50 CE), wrote a large number of treatises, mostly exegesis of the Greek translation of the Jewish Scriptures. Some of these treatises give a literal interpretation of the text, while others allegorize the persons in the text as various types of soul. The different kinds of treatise, audience, and philosophical leaning make it hazardous to generalize, but throughout these texts Philo deploys a rich range of gift-terminology and repeatedly speaks of God as "lover of gifts" (*philodōros*), who continually pours into the world an abundance of gifts (*charites*). These are seen primarily in the creation of the world and of each individual, and in the common blessings and benefits of life.

As a philosopher, Philo is especially careful in his claims about the gifts of God. We may detect, in particular, two ground rules:[19]

a) *God is the Cause of all good things.* Whatever else may be said regarding the world and our agency within it, God is the Cause. We should never attribute our virtues to ourselves, because both we and our virtues are ultimately attributable to God. Eve was mistaken to claim that she had acquired her son Cain "through God" (in the Greek of Gen 4:1–2): "through" suggests that God was just the instrument, but in truth all human existence, and all its qualities, are created *by God*, not just *through* him (*On the Cherubim* 125–30). There is an important qualification: God is the Cause only of what is good, not of what is evil. Like Plato, Philo thought that if God is perfect he must be *singularly* good: God does not cause harm but only what is beautiful and good.[20] A human response is expected: piety consists in thanksgiving (*eucharistia*), the return of *charis* for *charis* (*Who is the Heir?* 104).

b) *It is proper that God should give the best gifts to worthy or fitting recipients.* As we have seen, it was normal to think of giving well as giving gifts discrim-

---

19. For further discussion, see Orrey McFarland, *God and Grace in Philo and Paul* (Leiden: Brill, 2015).

20. *On the Creation of the World* 72–75. It was difficult for Philo to account for evil, but he suggests some blame can be attached to lesser powers to whom God delegated aspects of the creation of humanity (he notes the plural in Gen 1:26: "Let us make humankind").

inately, to those in some sense "worthy" of them. At times, Philo is nervous about such language. If "worth" suggests that the recipient is commensurate with God, then *nothing* is worthy of the gifts of God, not even the world as a whole (*That God is Unchangeable* 86–110). Moreover, "worth" language indicates only the *conditions* of God's giving, not the *cause*. But within these parameters, the notion of "worth" helps Philo to explain how God's best gifts are distributed unevenly in the world. In one notable passage (*Allegorical Interpretation* 3.65–106), he examines scriptural examples where God's giving seems to defy rationality or justice. This includes God's choice of Jacob over Esau even before they were born. How could that be fair? God must have known, says Philo, what their characters would be (he foresaw it in their names); on that basis, he chose the one who was worthy of his blessing.

There can be many sorts of worth, such as status, education, and gender (Philo thought men were more rational than women and therefore more worthy of the "higher" intellectual gifts). The covenants with Israel are gifts, and the choice is not arbitrary, since only the Jewish people properly acknowledge God (in refusing idolatry), while their laws inculcate the most rigorous form of piety. Israel is precious to God "because of the priceless righteousness and virtue of the founders of the nation" (*Special Laws* 2.181). Even such virtue, in the patriarchs and their descendants, must be traced to God so that, in a deep sense, God selects as objects of his giving only what he has already given. Blessings, external and spiritual, will be poured out in relation to the value of their recipients:

> These are the blessings of good people who fulfill the law by their actions, blessings which it says will be completed by the grace (*charis*) of the gift-loving God who dignifies and rewards what is excellent because of its likeness to himself. (*On Rewards and Punishments* 126, my translation)

Gifts to the worthy are still gifts of grace—unless, by prior decision, we limit the term "grace" to gifts that are unconditioned or undeserved. Philo thinks that God's gifts are singular, abundant, and prior, but it is not necessary that they are *also* undeserved. Christian interpreters are apt to think him confused because of their own assumptions about grace. But one perfection of grace need not entail the others, and by Philo's own logic it makes good sense for God to reward the excellence that, ultimately, he himself has created.

The Qumran Hymns

Among the texts discovered in the Dead Sea Scrolls is a fascinating set of "thanksgiving hymns" (*Hodayot*), best preserved in an anthology found in

Cave 1 (1QHᵃ).²¹ These hymns are spoken in the first person singular (some, perhaps, by a leader of the community) and address God with praise and wonder at the extraordinary generosity of his saving action on the speaker's behalf. They represent the spirituality of a group of pious Jews (probably the Qumran sect) who considered themselves specially chosen to gain knowledge of God's mysteries and to join in worship with the highest beings in creation.

The chief characteristic of these hymns is their sense of gratitude that God has performed such an extraordinary act of elevation, raising the worthless human speaker to such heights of wisdom and understanding. Here is a sample:

> I thank yo[u, O Lor]d, that you have instructed me in your truth and made known to me your wondrous mysteries, and (made known) both your kindness towards a [sinful] person and your abundant compassion for the one whose heart is perverted. For who is like you, O Lord? Who has truth like yours? Who can be righteous before you when he is judged? There is no utterance of the breath to offer in reply to your rebuke, and none is able to stand before your wrath. But all the children of your truth you bring before you in forgiveness to cleanse them from their transgressions through your great goodness, and through your overflowing compassion you station them before you for ever and ever.

(1QHᵃ XV.29–34; square brackets indicate reconstructions where the text is lost or unclear).

Here and frequently elsewhere, the hymns celebrate the abundant mercy, goodness, and forgiveness of God, a gift which shines all the brighter because its human recipient is sinful, perverse, and ignorant. Strikingly, the hymns persistently *denigrate* human beings, who are made out of low-grade material (merely dust, or clay mixed with water), who inhabit a weak, repulsive, and mortal body (they are like a "corpse-infesting maggot"), and whose sin and perversity fit them only for the wrathful judgment of God. It is God, and God alone, who can be responsible for the salvation of such shameful and polluted flesh.²² This is probably the most negative picture of the human condition in

---

21. For text and translation, see Hartmut Stegemann with Eileen Schuller (with translation of texts by Carol Newsom), *1QHodayotᵃ with incorporation of 1QHodayotᵇ and 4QHodayotᵃ⁻ᶠ* DJD XL (Oxford: Clarendon, 2009). For discussion of these hymns and their performative effects, see Carol Newsom, *The Self as Symbolic Space: Constructing Identity and Community at Qumran* (Leiden: Brill, 2004).

22. For the relation between God and human agents in these hymns, see Jason Maston,

Jewish literature of this time, making divine mercy all the more remarkable and praiseworthy. Of our six perfections of grace, here we find most clearly the perfection of *incongruity*, one not evidenced in the other two authors surveyed above.

This anomaly—the mercy of God shown to polluted and worthless humans—requires some explanation, which the hymns provide. The speakers belong to the "lot" of the sons of truth, chosen according to God's *razon*, his preference or favor. That favor represents a predestination embedded deep in the eternal design of God, decreed before their birth, indeed before the creation of the world. The hymns regularly comment on the order of the universe and posit a divine plan that has chosen this group for salvation (and the rest for damnation) as part of the primordial design of the cosmos. No further explanation is possible or required. It only remains for those who sing these hymns and find their identity within them to celebrate the immense kindness of God. Despite their utter worthlessness, both ontological and moral, God deigned to make them the privileged recipients of his truth, to lead them into the path of righteousness, and to grant them an eternal destiny that is wholly undeserved.

4 Ezra

Fourth Ezra (2 Esdras 3–16 in the Apocrypha) is a Jewish text from the end of the first century CE, which reflects the pain and soul-searching that followed the destruction of the Jerusalem temple in 70 CE. It is staged as a set of feisty dialogues between Ezra and the angel Uriel, who channels the perspective of God.[23] Large and serious questions run through this text, starting with the puzzle as to why other, sinful nations had proved more successful than the comparatively pious nation of Israel. If the world was made for Israel, why has Israel been given into their hands (3:28–36; 6:55–59)? Moreover, why has God allowed humanity, even Israel, to have an "evil heart," such that few, if any, can be called truly "righteous"? In a series of steps, the angel leads Ezra to understand God's plan in the form of two "worlds": this world is hopelessly corrupt, but God has planned another, to begin after the final judgment when evil will be destroyed and justice and truth will prevail.

Divine and Human Agency in Second Temple Judaism and Paul (Tübingen: Mohr Siebeck, 2010), 94–122.

23. The best recent commentary is by Michael E. Stone, *Fourth Ezra*, Hermeneia (Philadelphia: Fortress, 1990).

For our purposes, the most important section of this text is the long, third dialogue (6:36–9:25), where Ezra's dispute with the angel becomes most heated. When Ezra points out that God's plans for Israel have gone awry, the angel indicates that those who are righteous will inherit the world to come. In that case, Ezra complains, the vast majority of humanity will perish and only a tiny number will see the fulfillment of God's intentions. That, says the angel, is entirely fair: God gave everyone the chance to observe the Law and receive their reward, and if the majority have chosen to disobey God, they will get the punishment they deserve. "Empty things are for the empty, and full things are for the full" (7:25, NRSV). For Ezra, that notion of justice may be correct, but it has appalling consequences. Surely, he insists, God's nature is merciful and good. Echoing Exodus 34:6–7, he pleads,

> I know that the Most High is now called merciful, because he has mercy on those who have not yet come into the world; and gracious because he is gracious to those who turn in repentance to his Law; and patient because he shows patience towards those who have sinned, since they are his own creatures; and bountiful, because he would rather give than take away. (7:132–35, NRSV)

In support, Ezra cites cases when righteous people have pleaded for those who were sinful and hopes that the same will happen on the day of judgment (7:102–11). Surely God is "merciful" in having mercy on *sinners*: God's goodness would be evident in such an *incongruous* grace (8:19–36).

Uriel thinks otherwise. Within *this world*, certainly, mercy is exercised on sinners. But at the final judgment, after which the perfect world begins, there can be no bending of the rules of justice. If God's justice is not flawless in rewarding the righteous and condemning sinners, the future world would be corrupted from the start: justice is, and must be, the anchor point of the cosmos. Does that mean that very few will be saved? Yes, and properly so. The righteous are like gold dust in the common clay, very rare but all the more precious: "Many have been created, but only a few shall be saved" (8:1–3). Ezra resists this conclusion for a long time, but when he begins to see things the angel's way the world starts to make better sense (chapters 9–14). Indeed, he ends up concluding, with the angel, that mercy is properly exercised on those who rule their hearts in accordance with the Law (14:33–36).[24]

---

24. The final chapters of this text have received many interpretations; for an alternative reading, see Watson, *Paul and the Hermeneutics of Faith*, 475–503.

4 Ezra thus stages a profound debate about the relationship between God's mercy and God's justice, and whether incongruous goodness can be, or should be, the last word. Ezra's pleas are presented with such sympathy, and accord so well with our own hopes, that we are liable to find Uriel's view excessively harsh. But from Uriel's perspective, Ezra is pleading for a compromise of justice, which is ultimately unsatisfactory as a view of the world. The text poses a significant question: If grace is given to the undeserving, does that undercut the justice of the cosmos? This was clearly a live issue in the first century CE, and Paul was not the only Jew to reflect theologically upon it.

Conclusion

Even from this short review of four texts it is clear that grace is neither a simple nor an uncontroversial matter. The topic can be discussed using various terms (each with its own nuances), in different social circumstances, and in relation to a variety of other topics (creation, salvation, and eschatological judgment). How it is nuanced may reflect the influence of varying scriptural resources and philosophical traditions. But grace can also be "perfected" in different ways. All of these texts speak of the superabundance of grace, but none consider it devoid of expectations of return (i.e., noncircular). Some stress priority (even eternal predestination), while others do not consider this significant. Some insist that God is the cause of the virtue he requires, perfecting to some degree the efficacy of grace. And in one other respect they clearly differ among themselves: some stress the incongruity of grace (the *Hodayot* and Ezra in 4 Ezra), and others do not (Wisdom of Solomon; Philo; Uriel in relation to the final judgment). We might consider it obvious that the gifts and grace of God would be given without regard to worth, but it is clear that we cannot assume that to be so in all ancient texts, even those that engage closely with the Jewish Scriptures. Indeed, Philo and Uriel point to the problem that such a gift would seem arbitrary or unfair. The incongruity of grace is not absent among these Second Temple texts, but it is also not (for good reason) ubiquitous.

We may conclude: grace is everywhere in Second Temple Judaism, but not everywhere the same. Describing Judaism as a "religion of grace" helpfully counters some still-common caricatures, but the label is of little analytical value. Sanders's "covenantal nomism" is helpful in clarifying the *sequence* from election to obedience (the priority of grace), but it is conceptually incapable of grasping the differences we have noted, including the difference between congruous and incongruous grace. The voices we have been hearing, for all they have in common, are irreducibly diverse. And in some cases they evidence a profound theological debate.

Where should we place Paul within the diversity of Second Temple Judaism? If there is diversity and debate, we can avoid the temptation to place Paul *either* over against Judaism *or* in undifferentiated agreement with all his fellow Jews. In the midst of this diversity, and with the range of possibilities we have canvassed, we are free to ask afresh: What is Paul's particular configuration of grace? It is time to turn to his letters, starting with his letter to the Galatians.

CHAPTER 4

"I Do Not Reject the Grace of God" (Galatians 1–2)

Paul's letter to the Galatians is explosive. It is sharp-edged, polemical, and full of emotion. By turns Paul is surprised (1:6), frustrated (4:15), puzzled (4:20), and angry (5:12). He calls the believers in Galatia "foolish" (3:1) and wishes that his opponents there would use the circumcision knife to castrate themselves (5:12)! Such extremes of emotion indicate how high Paul reckons the stakes to be. From his perspective, what nearly happened in Jerusalem (2:4–5) and what began to happen in Antioch (2:11–14) constituted a betrayal of "the truth of the good news" (2:5, 14). And what he hears is happening now in Galatia is the same: the people who are troubling his converts are "twisting" the good news of Christ (1:7), such that the Galatians are turning to "another" gospel (1:6–7). As if there were another sort of good news (1:7)! Rescue from "the present evil age" (1:4), for the Galatians and for all humanity, depends on the one-and-only good news. To lose that is to lose everything.

This highly charged letter has had an enormous influence down the centuries. Its sharp antitheses have inspired many efforts to reimagine and reshape the world. Polemics can, of course, be dangerous, and this letter has been used in dismal ways to create negative caricatures of Judaism. But Paul's announcement of "new creation" (6:15) and his declaration that in Christ there is neither Jew nor Greek, neither slave nor free, no male and female (3:28) have also inspired a creative radicalism that has fostered new, unimagined possibilities. One of the watchwords of this letter is "freedom" (2:4; 5:1, 13), and Galatians has been a charter for Christian liberation of many different kinds.[1]

The situation to which Paul responds may be reconstructed in outline.[2] The addressees are "Galatians" (from central or southern Turkey), from a

---

1. For a fascinating analysis of the history of reception, see John K. Riches, *Galatians through the Centuries* (Oxford: Blackwell, 2008).

2. Despite some differences in nuance, scholars are mostly agreed on the essential facts.

non-Jewish (gentile or "pagan") background (4:8–10). They came to believe in Christ following a visit from Paul (4:12–20) but are now being influenced by new missionaries, to whom Paul is bitterly opposed. Whether these "troublers" were local or (more likely) from elsewhere, they considered that Paul had left his converts in Galatia only half-converted since he had not inducted them fully into the covenant with Abraham, with its implications of Torah-obedience. Paul devotes a lot of space to the figure of Abraham in Galatians 3–4, and it is likely that his opponents led the Galatians through the Genesis stories and pointed out that no males could be considered part of the Abrahamic covenant if they were not circumcised (Gen 17:10–14). The topic of male circumcision recurs at several points in this letter (Gal 2:1–10; 5:1–6; 6:12–15), and it was a well-known mark of Jewish identity, generally required of gentiles who wished to become "proselytes" and fully integrated into the Jewish community.[3] But in the Jewish tradition, circumcision marks the entry-point into a set of covenant obligations enshrined in the Torah, and Paul's Galatian converts are being persuaded that the practice of the Mosaic Law ("works of the Law") is a necessary supplement to their faith in Christ (3:1–5; 4:21). Paul's own authority was likely also under attack (1:10, 20): his opponents may have appealed over his head to the authority of Peter, James, and the mother-assembly in Jerusalem.[4]

For Paul's opponents, Jesus as Messiah was the fulfillment of the (Abrahamic-*cum*-Mosaic) covenant. They, too, had a mission to gentiles: since the Messiah had come, gentile believers should adopt the God-given, Scriptural, and time-honored patterns of Jewish practice. From a historical and sociological perspective, the issue was whether the Jesus-movement, as it spread into the non-Jewish world, was to remain a reform movement within Judaism, or whether it would allow non-Jewish believers to form communities that departed, in significant respects, from the Jewish tradition. What might

---

For fuller discussion, see John M. G. Barclay, *Obeying the Truth: A Study of Paul's Ethics in Galatians* (Edinburgh: T&T Clark, 1988), 45–60.

3. See John M. G. Barclay, *Jews in the Mediterranean Diaspora from Alexander to Trajan (323 BCE–117 CE)* (Edinburgh: T&T Clark, 1996), 438–39. Josephus has a story about the royal court in Adiabene in which it is clear that gentile males could be persuaded to accept circumcision if they wanted to adopt Jewish customs and be considered "assuredly Jewish" (*Jewish Antiquities* 20.17–96).

4. The Greek term *ekklēsia*, usually translated "church," means an assembly or gathering (especially a political assembly). Because our word "church" might have anachronistic overtones (referring to a building, or at least to a group that is clearly distinct from the Jewish community), I have opted in this book to keep with the translation "assembly."

seem a small dispute over circumcision determined, in fact, whether and in what ways the Jesus-movement would be able to adapt culturally as it crossed ethnic boundaries.

Paul, for his part, places the matter within a theological perspective. His question is what *God* has done in Christ, and what its implications are. It is striking how often Paul interprets this matter in the language of gift. "I do not reject the grace (*charis*) of God: for if righteousness were through the Law, Christ died in vain" (2:21). "You are disjoined from Christ, you who are justified in the Law; you have fallen from grace (*charis*)" (5:4). As elsewhere, Paul begins and ends the letter to the Galatians with an invocation of God's favor (*charis*) and peace (1:3; 6:18). But this gift-language is underlined by the fact that Christ "gave himself for our sins to rescue us from the present evil age" (1:4). A second reference to the self-gift of Christ occurs when Paul refers to "the Son of God who loved me and gave himself for me" (2:20), as if the Christ-event was, quintessentially, an event of gift. When Paul refers to the "calling" (i.e., conversion) of the Galatians, he speaks of God "who called you in the grace of Christ" (1:6); he then uses the same language of his own calling, "when it pleased God who had set me apart from my mother's womb and called me through his grace" (1:15; cf. 1 Cor 15:9–10). This language of gift or grace seems too prominent and too frequent to ignore. The question is: What does it mean, and how does it shape the rest of the letter?

Interpreters of the letter to the Galatians take their bearings from one or more of its striking polarities: slavery or freedom (2:4–5; 4:21–5:1); works of the Law or faith in Christ (2:16; 3:2, 5); humanity or God (1:1, 10–12); flesh or Spirit (3:3; 5:13–6:10).[5] In this and the following two chapters I will argue how these can be integrated best when we read the letter in light of Paul's conviction that the gift of Christ was the definitive act of divine grace and was an *incongruous gift,* given without regard to worth. Because this gift did not fit with previous criteria of value, the Christ-event has recalibrated all systems of worth, including the "righteousness" defined by the Law. Founded on this norm-breaking gift, new communities can take shape, whose patterns of life are significantly at odds with both Jewish and non-Jewish traditions of value. In other words, the Christ-event, as incongruous gift, is the basis of Paul's controversial mission to gentiles, in which Paul resists attempts to impose on believers preconstituted systems of worth, whether ethnic, social, or moral. Paul remaps reality in the wake of the unconditioned gift of God in Christ

---

5. For Paul's creative use of polarities, see J. Louis Martyn, "Apocalyptic Antinomies in Paul's Letter to the Galatians," *New Testament Studies* 31 (1985): 410–24.

and builds experimental, trans-ethnic communities that take their bearings from this singular event. The whole letter can be read afresh from this angle, and although we cannot engage here in every exegetical detail, we can chart in outline how Galatians makes sense along these lines.

THE CHRIST-GIFT AND THE RECALIBRATION OF NORMS (GALATIANS 1:1–2:10)

Paul uses the opening greetings of Galatians to focus his readers' attention on the gift of Christ, who "gave himself for our sins to rescue us from the present evil age" (1:4). This is the good news that undergirds his apostleship (by "the grace given to me," 2:9), which has come about in a peculiar way —"not from human beings nor through a human agent, but through Jesus Christ and God the Father who raised him from the dead" (1:1). The gift of God is here identified not with creation, nor with the gift of the Law, nor even with the long history of salvation, but with a singular event, the death and resurrection of Jesus. This has created a new dynamic of grace that has decisively altered the cosmos, effecting a rescue from a universal condition that Paul calls "the present evil age."[6] Paul bears witness here not to general truths about the nature of God or the structures of existence but to a historical event, a "singular universal" that has redivided history and redefined the whole of reality.[7]

Who are the "we" who have been rescued? And why them? Paul seems to include here both himself (a Jew) and his readers (non-Jews). But why should the Christ-gift be directed to these people, under the grip of the "present evil age"? One would expect a gift to be distributed fittingly, and the author of 4 Ezra, who was also pessimistic about the state of the world, thought that there must be some tiny minority of righteous individuals who were fitting recipients of God's mercy. But nothing in Galatians will indicate that the recipients of the Christ-gift were worthy to receive it. In fact, quite the contrary. The gentiles in Galatia, who were "called in the grace of Christ" (1:6), had no qualifications for this calling. Like other gentiles, they were "sinners" (2:15). They

---

6. For the apocalyptic tones of this letter, see especially the commentaries by J. Louis Martyn, *Galatians: A New Translation with Introduction and Commentary*, Anchor Yale Bible Commentary 33A (New York: Doubleday, 1997), and Martinus C. de Boer, *Galatians: A Commentary*, New Testament Library (Louisville: Westminster John Knox, 2011).

7. On the "universalism" created by an unconditioned event, see Alain Badiou, *Saint Paul: The Foundation of Universalism*, trans. Ray Brassier (Stanford: Stanford University Press, 2003).

have now received God's Spirit, but not because of some prior alignment to "righteousness" through practice of the Law (3:2, 5). They have come to know God, but not on the basis of their intellectual capacity or skill in inquiry: in fact, Paul makes a point of insisting that the initiative here was God's ("having come to know God, or rather having been known by God," 4:9). God's calling is qualified only by the phrase "in the grace of Christ" (1:6). In Paul's discourse, *charis* and other gift-terms appear to have acquired a particular perfection: this gift functions irrespective of the worth of its recipients, indeed in the absence of worth.

The character of this grace determines the shape of Paul's mission. The fact that the gift comes from God in this unconditioned way does not mean that human agency is bypassed: grace energizes its recipients into action (2:8). But the divine initiative in grace, and its sheer "otherness" in relation to human frames of reference, mean that those reconstituted by this grace march to a different tune. "Am I now persuading human beings, or God?" asks Paul (1:10). Whose normative criteria am I trying to match? "Am I trying to please my human audience?" (1:10). "I want you to know," he writes, "that the good news announced by me is not in accordance with human norms (*ouk estin kata anthrōpon*)" (1:11).[8] This negation is of central significance to the theology of this letter. It signals a relation of misfit, even contradiction, between "the good news" and the typical structures of human thought and behavior. The "good news" stands askance to human norms because its origin lies outside the human sphere: it was not received on human authority but came "through a revelation of Jesus Christ" (1:12). Jesus Christ is the content of the revelation and of the grace therein revealed. And because this cannot be "boxed" within preexistent traditions, it is capable of creating something completely new on the human scene.

The narrative that starts in 1:13 and runs through to 2:14 may be designed to refute alternative stories about Paul's origins and conduct, but it has other purposes besides.[9] Paul offers here a paradigm of the reorientation effected by an encounter with Christ (1:15; cf. 1:24). His former life within the Jewish

8. The standard translation, "is not of human origin" (NRSV), is mistaken (*kata* never refers to origin); the phrase *kata anthrōpon* is quite common in Paul (e.g., Gal 3:15; Rom 3:5; 1 Cor 3:3; 9:8) and refers to human patterns of speech or behavior. The question of origin is raised in the following verse (1:12).

9. See John H. Schütz, *Paul and the Anatomy of Apostolic Authority* (Cambridge: Cambridge University Press, 1975), 114–58; Beverly R. Gaventa, "Galatians 1 and 2: Autobiography as Paradigm," *New Testament Studies* 28 (1986): 309–26.

tradition ("in Judaism," 1:13–14) had two dimensions.[10] On the one hand, he was virulently opposed to "the assembly of God" and tried to destroy it (1:13, underlined in 1:23). On those grounds, he was the last person you would expect to be given the favor of God (cf. 1 Cor 15:9–10; Phil 3:6). On the other hand, he "advanced in the Jewish way of life" beyond his contemporaries and was outstanding in his zealous commitment to his "ancestral traditions" (1:14). Ethnicity, history, commitment, and moral excellence all contributed to Paul's seemingly superior cultural capital (cf. Phil 3:4–6). We might presume that, despite his error in persecuting "God's assembly," such capital would constitute Paul's worthiness to receive the divine call.

Not so. On Paul's account, what happened next was an event that bore no relation to the worth (either positive or negative) of his previous identity and conduct. It was not another stage in his development, a further step in his progress of zeal, but the effect of a divine decision: "When God was pleased . . . to reveal" (1:15–16). The change in the subject of the verb interrupts a string of verbs depicting Paul's agency (1:13–14, 17–22), and calls attention to the fact that this event originated from outside Paul's initiative. Moreover, this divine act had its roots in the fact that he had been "set aside from [his] mother's womb" (1:15). This phrase echoes descriptions of the calling of prophets that also speak of a mission to "the nations" (Jer 1:4–5; Isa 49:1–6). But for Paul, God's decision before a person's birth also signals that God circumvents any worth one might attribute to ancestry or behavior (cf. Rom 9:6–13). In fact, Paul describes his experience as a calling "through God's grace" (1:15), using language almost identical to his depiction of the calling of his gentile converts (1:6).[11]

These features of 1:15–16 indicate that what has reconstituted Paul's life is a divine act of grace without regard to his ethnicity, his tradition, or his excellence within it—and also without regard to his former opposition to God. Paul thus emphasizes the *incongruity* of God's intervention in his life. His transfor-

10. Scholars currently debate what is meant by the rare term *Ioudaismos*, which does not fully equate to our term "Judaism." It seems to mean something like the Jewish, ancestral pattern of life ("the traditions of my ancestors," 1:14).

11. Following Krister Stendahl, *Paul among Jews and Gentiles* (London: SCM, 1977), it has become common to insist that Paul's describes this experience as a "call," not a "conversion." It would certainly be misleading to describe Paul as converting from "Judaism" to another religion, but "calling" in Paul means much more than "vocation." He uses this term for all believers (Jews and gentiles; cf. 1 Cor 7:17–20), and it entails the "calling into being" of a new self (cf. 1 Cor 1:26–28; Rom 4:17). See Stephen J. Chester, *Conversion at Corinth: Perspectives on Conversion in Paul's Theology and the Corinthian Church* (Edinburgh: T&T Clark, 2003), 59–112.

mation was neither occasioned by his own action nor conditioned by his previous worth: it resulted from the unconditioned gift of God in the revelation of Christ. Paul does not criticize his former life for being blasphemously reliant on "good works," nor does he evoke negative stereotypes of Judaism as intolerant or exclusive. Paul had lived enthusiastically and well, within the norms and values of his tradition (cf. Phil 3:6: "in terms of righteousness within the Law, blameless"). But God's "calling in grace" had nothing to do with his success in those terms. It was given without regard to superior ethnicity, status, or cultural prestige, and without regard to the negative worth of the things he did in sinfulness or ignorance. Previously self-evident norms are suspended, relativized, or recalibrated, and Paul has to learn again what it means to "live to God" (2:19). In a life that is newly generated by grace, everything is now subordinated to a superior norm, "the truth of the good news" (2:5, 14).

The purpose of Paul's calling is "that I might preach him [Christ] among the nations" (1:16). As we have noted, what is radical is not so much that he takes the good news to gentiles but the terms on which he does so: he does not require them to "Judaize" (2:14), that is, to adapt their lives to practices marked as specifically Jewish.[12] Paul's policy is not a protest against "ethnocentrism": it is the disruptive aftershock of the incongruous gift of Christ. As a singular but unconditioned event, the Christ-gift belongs to no subset of humanity but is destined for all. Since no one is granted this gift on the grounds of their ethnic worth, no one of any ethnicity is excluded from its reach. This truth may have become increasingly evident to Paul as he experienced, time and again, the most "unlikely" people being called by God and receiving the gift of the Spirit. Practice and experience must have shaped his theology, as much as theology shaped his practice and interpreted his experience. But it is clear from what Paul says here and elsewhere (2:8–9; Rom 1:1–7) that his apostleship and his unconventional mission were constituted by a dynamic that arose from the unconditioned grace of God in Christ.

Paul's account of his early travels (1:16–24) indicates that he was not beholden to prior authorities ("I did not consult with flesh and blood," 1:16), and even the authority associated with the mother-city, Jerusalem, was not determinative for him. When he and Barnabas went up to Jerusalem, after many years, it was "according to a revelation" (2:2; i.e., not by some human in-

---

12. One might say that requiring gentiles to abandon idolatry (cf. 1 Thess 1:9–10) is to have them adopt a Jewish pattern of religion; so Paula Fredriksen, *Paul, the Pagans' Apostle* (New Haven: Yale University Press, 2017). But for Paul (as for Philo), to worship the one true God is simply to recognize the truth of the world, a truth that Jews had long recognized but not invented.

struction), and he laid his good news before "those of repute" (2:2), not because he needed their authorization, but because he was anxious to ensure that the ethnic diversity within the Jesus-movement did not tear it apart. The "pillar" apostles had a reputation (2:2, 6, 9), but what counts for them, as for everyone else, is how they are viewed by God, who "shows no partiality" (2:6). Despite the pressure of "false brothers" (2:4), Paul's Greek accomplice, Titus, was not required to be circumcised, and Paul won recognition in Jerusalem that "the good news" is not tied to a single cultural-ethnic tradition (2:7–10).

Male circumcision was a critical component of Jewish identity in antiquity, not least because it ensured that marriage and reproduction were (mostly) confined within the Jewish community. For Jews, the foreskin was a sign of inferior "otherness" and revulsion; for Greeks, it was the other way around, circumcision being viewed as a wholly unnecessary, even uncivilized, disfigurement of the body. At Jerusalem, it was agreed that the good news of Jesus Christ can be proclaimed and practiced without regard to circumcision; Paul even uses the shocking expression "the good news of the foreskin" (2:7). A central token of cultural capital within the Jewish tradition is here acknowledged to be disposable in the mission to gentiles—not because that mission is less important or because gentiles were of lower status but because *God is at work* as much in one mission as in the other (2:8).

As Paul puts it later in this letter, "Neither circumcision counts for anything, nor uncircumcision" (5:6; 6:15). Either may be practiced, where culturally appropriate (cf. 1 Cor 7:18–19), but neither constitutes a token of ultimate value, and so neither is to be insisted upon. Paul resisted in Jerusalem, and now resists in Galatia, the *requirement* that male believers be circumcised (note the language of "compulsion" in 2:3, 14; 6:12). To require circumcision would be to declare that this token of cultural identity was integral to the "good news." In that sense, "the truth of the good news" entails "freedom" (2:4), not in absolute terms (Paul declares himself a "slave of Christ," 1:10), but because it cannot be confined within the parameters of any one cultural tradition. To insist on the conformity of gentiles to the Jewish Law, or to any other preconstituted norm, would be to deny the essential character of the "good news" as an incongruous gift.

The Antioch Incident and the Redefinition of Value in Christ (Galatians 2:11–21)

The last event in Paul's narrative is the Antioch incident recounted in 2:11–14, where Paul describes how Peter came to Antioch, how he withdrew from his initial practice of eating with gentile believers, and how Paul confronted him because "he was not walking straight in line with the truth of the good news" (2:14). This is also the launch-pad for Paul's explanation of the "good news" as it applies both in Antioch and in Galatia: the final verses of this chapter (2:15–21), in which Paul first speaks of justification by faith in Christ, should not be separated from what comes before, since they expound what was at stake in Antioch. Paul's address to Cephas (Peter), which begins in 2:14 ("I said to Cephas before them all . . ."), continues in 2:15 ("We who are Jews by birth . . ."). That "we" continues in 2:16–17, before Paul reduces it to a paradigmatic "I" from 2:18 to the end of the chapter. Much of what seems confusing in 2:15–21 can be clarified if we take these verses to explain the logic of Paul's conflict with Peter at Antioch.

It is difficult to reconstruct exactly what happened at Antioch since Paul supplies minimal details. Why was Peter in Antioch? Why was he followed by "certain people from James" (2:12)? Who were they and how did they create "fear" (2:12)? All we can say is that a dispute arose over meals and that Peter withdrew from eating with gentile believers (2:12). The sharing of common meals, which included "the Lord's Supper," was central to the formation of Christian communities, as it expressed their common identity and their commitment to one another in shared allegiance to Christ. So Peter's withdrawal was a catastrophic breach of fellowship: it implied that these gentiles were not fully members of the assembly in Antioch. We know that Jews in antiquity were wary of eating meals regularly with non-Jews, especially if such meals created strong social bonds.[13] When Peter ate initially with gentile believers (2:12), his behavior constituted, in some sense, living "in a gentile fashion" (*ethnikōs*, 2:14).[14] When he withdrew and adopted a stricter Jewish line, Paul took that withdrawal as pressuring gentiles to conform to Peter's Jewish tradition: "If you, although a Jew, live in a gentile and not in a Jewish fashion, how is it that you are compelling gentiles to live like Jews (*ioudaizein*)?" (2:14).

13. Both pagan and Jewish sources take meal-separatism to be characteristic of Jewish life in the diaspora (e.g., Diodorus 34.1.2; Tacitus, *Histories* 5.5.2; Letter of Aristeas 139–42; 3 Maccabees 3:4; Josephus, *Against Apion* 2.173–74, 209–10, 234). What Jews regarded as culturally necessary, non-Jews misinterpreted as antisocial.

14. Scholars continue to debate whether, how far, or in what respects Peter might have strayed from conformity to Jewish norms. See James D. G. Dunn, *Jesus, Paul, and the Law* (London: SPCK, 1990), 129–82, and Magnus Zetterholm, *The Formation of Christianity at Antioch* (London: Routledge, 2003), 129–66. But we cannot ignore Paul's judgment that Peter was living, initially, "in a gentile fashion."

Since even Barnabas followed Peter (2:13), it appears that Paul was the only one at Antioch who objected to Peter's policy. Practices were crucial for Paul, and particularly practices that formed, or fractured, community. But his rationale was always theological as well as social. Peter, he says, was "not walking straight in line with the truth of the good news" (2:14). Paul's mission efforts were directed toward the formation of new communities, and it is impossible to form a community committed to the mutual responsibility of "bearing one another's burdens" (6:2) if its members cannot eat together. And if the terms on which they eat together are determined by Jewish ancestral traditions, or by anything other than "the truth of the good news," this is not just divisive but a denial of the truth. Because the Christ-gift was given without regard to ethnic distinctions, old ethnic rules of separation can no longer apply ("there is neither Jew nor Greek," 3:28). To reinstate a Jewish rule of sociality would be to add a condition to the ways that believers associate with each other, applying a differentiating norm that is not derivable from "the good news." In fact, the good news is good precisely in its disregard of the former criteria of worth that separated Jew from non-Jew. The gospel stands or falls with the incongruity of grace.

Many features of 2:15–21 are contested among interpreters, and it is easy to get lost in the thicket of exegetical issues. So let me start with a paraphrase, indicating how I read this passage, before I explain three exegetical decisions that underlie it. We can then return to the text to explore its argument in a little more detail. Here's my paraphrase:

You and I, Peter, are Jews, used to thinking of ourselves as categorically distinct from (and better than) "gentile sinners." But we know that a person is not considered righteous (of good standing) before God through observing the Mosaic Law, except through trust in Christ, and we have put our trust in Christ so as to be considered righteous in that way. But if we seek divine affirmation in Christ, and our resulting behavior (as in Antioch) makes us look like "sinners," has Christ led us into sin? No way! Only if I were to reinstate the Law as the measurement of righteousness would I make myself a "transgressor" by living non-Jewishly. The truth is: I have died to the Law (it is no longer for me the ultimate criterion of righteousness), in order to be aligned to God. My old self is dead, crucified with Christ, and my new self is reconstituted by the risen Christ, a life founded on trust in Christ and on his gift of himself for me. That is a divine gift I will not reject; for if the Law remains the normative standard and means of righteousness, Christ died to no effect.

47

Three decisions about the meaning of Paul's Greek are built into this paraphrase.

First, I take "works of the Law" (*erga nomou*) to refer to the observance of the Mosaic Law. Paul is not talking about "good works" in general but about practicing what the Torah demands, or as he put it just earlier, "living in a Jewish fashion" (2:14).[15]

Secondly, I interpret the verb *dikaioō* (usually translated "justify") as "consider someone righteous." In a social context, this means "consider someone to be in good standing" (socially acceptable), and in a legal context, "consider someone to be in the right" (vindicated in a lawsuit). This verb does not mean "make someone righteous" (or rectify their condition) but represents a judgment that someone is acceptable, honorable, and of value. Because of the theological battles that have raged over this word, it has sometimes been made to carry the wrong kind of freight, as if it means "forgive" or "make morally righteous" or "rectify." But it is best to respect its normal meaning in Greek, which expresses a judgment about someone's legal or social standing (not a change in their condition). God is the implied subject here (cf. 3:11), and when God considers people "righteous," they are being affirmed as acceptable, people of value or worth. In this case, that is because they have been reconstituted in Christ and draw their life and identity from him (2:19–20).[16]

Thirdly, I take the Greek phrase *pistis Christou* to mean "trust in Christ." "Trust" is a better word than "faith" since it evokes a relationship, and what Paul is talking about is not belief in a set of impersonal truths but personal dependence on what God has effected in the death and resurrection of Jesus.[17] In recent years, many Pauline scholars have interpreted this phrase as referring to the faith or faithfulness *of Christ*, either his faithfulness to God's purpose or his expression of God's faithfulness.[18] But Paul seems to spell out what he means by

---

15. Elsewhere, Paul refers to "works" in general (e.g., Rom 11:6), but in this context, as he explains his opposition to Peter (and with a view to Galatia), he is speaking specifically of Torah-observance. But there is no need to limit the reference, with Dunn, to certain "boundary-markers" (like Sabbath, food, and circumcision); see James D. G. Dunn, *The New Perspective on Paul: Collected Essays* (Tübingen: Mohr Siebeck, 2005), 23–28.

16. The discussion on this topic is immense. For helpful orientation, see Stephen Westerholm, *Perspectives Old and New on Paul: The "Lutheran" Paul and His Critics* (Grand Rapids: Eerdmans, 2004), 261–84; James B. Prothro, *Both Judge and Justifier: Biblical Legal Language and the Act of Justifying in Paul* (Tübingen: Mohr Siebeck, 2018).

17. For *pistis* as trust, see Teresa Morgan, *Roman Faith and Christian Faith: Pistis and Fides in the Early Roman Empire and Early Churches* (Oxford: Oxford University Press, 2017).

18. This view was championed by Richard B. Hays, *The Faith of Jesus Christ: The Narrative Substructure of Galatians 3:1–4:11*, 2nd ed. (Grand Rapids: Eerdmans, 2002), and Martyn,

this ambiguous shorthand when, in the middle of 2:16, he uses the phrase "we have trusted in Christ Jesus" (cf. Abraham's trust in God in 3:6). Trust is not some kind of achievement, since the act of God in Christ remains the event on which all else depends. By trusting in Christ, believers know themselves to live only as Christ lives in them (2:20), and they find their only worth in him.[19]

What Peter and Paul have discovered, through experience and reflection, is that the one thing that counts before God is being wrapped up into the death and resurrection of Christ. They previously thought that practicing the Mosaic Law was integral to their good standing before God, but they now realize, in the wake of the Christ-gift, that it is nonessential. That does not make Torah-observance wrong or inappropriate for Jews in all circumstances, but its value is contingent: appropriate for some and not others, in some circumstances and not all. It does not and cannot establish a person's worth or standing before God. The only thing that does, and thus the only thing of ultimate and noncontingent value, is trust in Christ—not because of the human act of trust but because of what is trusted, that is, Christ. The one thing that counts—counts for everyone, Jew and non-Jew, and counts invariably, in all circumstances—is "being considered righteous in Christ" (2:17), that is, being accounted of worth before God on the basis of the death and resurrection of Christ. In comparison with this, what Paul previously thought to be necessary, indeed essential, for a life lived "to God" (2:19) he now realizes is nonessential. He has "died to the Law" (2:19) in the sense that he no longer considers it the essential basis of his worth before God. It is not what constitutes his real worth, his proper "symbolic capital."[20]

This is the revolution that Paul traces through 2:15–21 (here expanding my paraphrase): "Peter," he says, "you and I now know that a person is counted

---

Galatians. The question is still disputed, as the Greek *pistis* can have a range of meanings, and the Greek genitive *pistis Christou* could have Christ as subject or object of *pistis*. For a range of views, see Michael Bird and Preston M. Sprinkle, eds., *The Faith of Jesus Christ: Exegetical, Biblical, and Theological Studies* (Milton Keynes: Paternoster, 2009).

19. To translate *pistis* as "faithfulness" or "allegiance" (cf. Matthew W. Bates, *Salvation by Allegiance Alone* [Grand Rapids: Baker Academic, 2017]) threatens to put the primary emphasis on the condition or action of the believer, whereas Paul seems at pains to insist that the (necessary) response of trust is always dependent on the primary promise or act of God (in Christ).

20. Our symbolic capital is what gives us value or worth within our cultural and social context—be that race/ethnicity, education, beauty, skill, wealth, social status, or whatever. This may be achieved by us or ascribed to us by others—and in Paul's theology, what counts is what is ascribed by God. Paul has undergone such a radical reconfiguration of his self and his worth that he can say, "It is no longer I who live, but Christ who lives in me" (2:20). We will consider the meaning of such a statement below, in chapter 10.

acceptable before God not on the basis of their practice of the Law but because of their trust in Christ—trust that signals absolute dependence on the gift given in Christ. The practice of the Law is not what counts before God in any absolute or complete sense. In making this total investment in Christ, our fellowship with gentile believers may require that we contravene the standard of 'righteousness' that we previously thought was integral to our good standing before God. By the Law's standards, that makes us 'sinners', but the Law is no longer the absolute or invariable criterion for pleasing God (2:17). 'Living in a gentile fashion' (in Antioch, for the sake of the good news) only counts as 'sin' if we have reinstated the Law as a noncontingent norm (2:18).[21] No, I have died to the Law, in order that I might live to God (2:19): I have distanced myself from its absolute claim, because my whole life is reconstituted by Christ, whose gift of himself is the only thing of absolute value (2:20). If I reject that gift, and reinstate the Law as the normative structure of value, I might as well treat Christ's death—for me—as a waste of effort (2:21)."

Trust in Christ is the acknowledgment that the only thing of true value is Christ himself. To invest in anything else is not just a distraction from what counts; it undermines that trust and empties Christ of value. Whatever else might be considered valuable, even the Law, is of value only if it serves the purposes of Christ and draws the believer deeper into connection with him. Ethnic identity, ancestral loyalty, cultural excellence, and all the preconstituted values that stand independent of Christ can no longer be counted as capital worth treasuring. And faith is not some alternative token of worth, a refined spirituality admirable in itself. To the contrary, faith *as trust in Christ* is a declaration of bankruptcy, a radical and shattering recognition that the only capital in God's economy is the gift of Christ, a gift given without regard to any other criterion of worth.

We shall consider later (chapter 13) the social and personal implications of this theology for our contemporary cultural context. But first we must follow the lines of his argument through the rest of the letter to the Galatians.

21. In this context, Paul would make himself a "transgressor" (2:18), not because it is impossible to live under the Torah without sin (although that is suggested in 3:10 and 3:22), but because "living in a gentile fashion" (2:14) is only "transgression" if the Torah remains the ultimate criterion of right and wrong.

CHAPTER 5

The Christ-Gift, the Law, and the Promise (Galatians 3–5)

Paul had the Galatians in mind all through the narrative of chapters 1–2 ("that the truth of the good news might be preserved for you," 2:5), but it is only at 3:1 that he turns to address them directly: "O foolish Galatians! Who has bewitched you, before whose eyes Jesus Christ was portrayed crucified?" The central section of Galatians runs through chapters 3 and 4 all the way to 5:12 and is framed by direct address to the Galatians, setting out their options in the starkest form (3:1–5; 5:2–12). Some paragraphs within that frame, with their intricate discussion of Law and promise, and their complex weave of Scriptures, might appear removed from this immediate crisis. But, in fact, each of the five subsections of these middle chapters (3:6–14; 3:15–29; 4:1–11; 4:12–20; 4:21–5:1) ends with an application to "you" (or "us"). Every part of the argument relates to Paul's effort to dissuade the Galatians from thinking that their worth can be secured or expressed by observing the Torah.

All the strands of this discourse amount to a single question: What is the ultimate value that shapes your lives and frames your other values and goals? Is it the Law? Or is it the gift of Christ and of his Spirit? The radical claim of this letter is that the Christ-gift does not just modify traditional values and categories, adding new content or stretching their meaning. It installs a new center of orientation and meaning for the whole of life, such that Paul can say, "May I never take pride in anything except in the cross of our Lord Jesus Christ, through whom the world has been crucified to me and I to the world" (6:14). That reconfiguration of life has far-reaching implications for all cultures and contexts, but Paul thinks it through here with respect to his own "ancestral traditions" and to what God, he now sees, had signaled right from the start.

Paul's rivals in Galatia likely placed the Christ-event on a narrative line that featured the Law as the ultimate expression of God's will, given through Moses, confirmed by the Messiah Jesus, and fulfilled in the Law-observance of believers, both Jews and gentiles. That is what one would expect: in the rich tapestry of Second Temple Judaism, it is hard to find any strands that do not identify the Law as the definition of virtue or righteousness.[1] Of the texts we surveyed in chapter 3, 4 Ezra takes the gift of the Law to be the central moment in the history of the covenant (3:12–19), of eternal significance: "Let many perish who are now living, rather than that the Law of God that is set before them be disregarded" (7:20 NRSV). Wisdom of Solomon celebrates the people of Israel "through whom the imperishable light of the Law was to be given to the world" (18:4). Philo took the Law to define what is true and right universally and across all time, corresponding to the unwritten law of nature.[2] Thus the missionaries in Galatia could draw on any number of strands in the Jewish tradition to take pride in the Law as the centerpiece of God's revelation to Israel and to the world. It was entirely natural that they should place God's gift of Christ and of the Spirit within this Law-configured frame.

What was *unnatural* for anyone reared in the Jewish tradition was to de-center the Law, to limit its role in history to an interlude, and to distinguish it categorically from "covenant" and "promise." But that is what Paul does in Galatians 3–4. He interprets history from the vantage point of the Christ-event, not the Christ-event within the frame of a Law-shaped history. It is not that the Christ-gift comes out of the blue. It is the fulfillment, Paul insists, of God's promises to Abraham. But it does not match the worth or capacity of its recipients, and at the human level it is marked by discontinuity and misfit, giving blessing to the cursed and freedom to the enslaved. We will trace here how Paul reconfigures history and Scripture in the light of the incongruous gift of Christ, first in the frame passages, at the beginning and end of this discussion, and then in the main content of these central chapters of Galatians.

THE FRAME PASSAGES (GALATIANS 3:1–5; 5:2–12)

When he addresses the "foolish Galatians" (3:1), Paul refers at once to "Jesus Christ . . . crucified" in order to place at the center of all that follows the one who "gave himself" (2:20). The new life arising from this gift has been active and powerful among them in the form of the Spirit (3:2, 5). This also is a gift, "supplied" by God (3:5) and "received" by the Galatians (3:2)—not a second gift, independent of the Christ-gift, but "the Spirit of God's Son" (4:6) and

---

1. E. P. Sanders, *Judaism: Practice and Belief, 63 BCE–66 CE* (London: SCM, 1992).
2. Christine Hayes, *What's Divine about Divine Law? Early Perspectives* (Princeton: Princeton University Press, 2015).

thus the presence of Christ in the "hearts" of believers (4:6) and experienced in their everyday lives.[3] Everything may be reduced to a single question (3:2): Did the Galatians receive this gift on the basis of their practice of the Law, and thus within its frame, or as a result of the message to which they responded in trust?[4] The Galatians are who they are, children of God gifted with the Spirit of Christ (4:5–7), not because they had adjusted their lives to the values and practices of the Law but because the good news of Jesus Christ, given for them, had elicited their trust in the one thing of value, in which they had invested everything.

The logic here is like that of the narrative concerning Cornelius in Acts (Acts 10–11; cf. Acts 15:8–11): when Jewish believers witness the gift of the Spirit to gentiles, they are shocked into recognition that the Christ-event cannot be confined within the parameters of their own tradition. For Paul this is confirmation of his conviction that the Christ-event is an incongruous gift. The Spirit has been given without regard to the Torah, which was for Jews the most significant bearer of symbolic capital or worth. To repackage this gift would be to lose it (Gal 3:4). A Law-conditioned Spirit is no Spirit at all, only flesh (3:3).[5]

The frame at the end of the central chapters (5:2–12) also emphasizes these stark alternatives. If the Galatian men adopt the rite of circumcision, they are buying into a whole-life orientation to the Jewish Law (5:3). This would not be an add-on to their trust in Christ. It would demote Christ to the status of a supplement, an assistant to the project of Law-observance. But that would be to lose the whole value of Christ and of the gift given without condition: "You have been disjoined from Christ, you who would be considered righteous in terms of the Law; you have fallen out of grace (*charis*)" (5:4). To set the Christ-gift within a commitment to the regulative authority of the Law is not to protect or enhance it but to lose it altogether.

3. The Spirit is thus the form in which believers experience the gift of Christ, and the new "life" by which they now live (5:25); see Gordon D. Fee, *God's Empowering Spirit: The Holy Spirit in the Letters of Paul* (Grand Rapids: Baker Academic, 2011).

4. Paul's shorthand phrase, *akoē pisteōs*, is ambiguous, and has been interpreted in several ways (in NRSV: "believing what you heard"). *Akoē* could mean the act of hearing, or the message heard, while *pisteōs* could refer to what is heard or its mode of receipt. Paul's use of *akoē* in 1 Thess 2:13 and Rom 10:16–17 suggests that this word refers to the good news he proclaimed, while *pisteōs* ("of trust") probably refers to the means of its receipt: thus, "the message received in trust."

5. This potent polarity between Spirit and flesh will reemerge in 5:13–6:10 as the frame for two alternative patterns of life: you either invest in ("sow to") what God has started in the Spirit, or you sow to your own flesh (6:8). See chapter 6 below.

Why so? Paul does not consider circumcision an evil or inferior practice; he does not expect Jewish believers to attempt to reverse their circumcision (1 Cor 7:17–19). But to *require* circumcision of gentile believers is to place the Christ-event within the parameters of worth defined by the Jewish ancestral tradition and the Law, and thus to make ethnicity and Law the conditions for the gift. Not that Paul thinks *uncircumcision* (literally, "the foreskin") to be in any sense superior. Certainly, in the Greek tradition (adopted by the Romans), the foreskin was a mark of the noble, unblemished male, while circumcision was considered a barbaric disfigurement of the body.[6] But the Christ-gift was given without regard to this (or any other) physical distinction. It was given to circumcised Jews *and* uncircumcised gentiles, and thus shows both traits to be of no ultimate significance. To make either trait essential for *all* believers would be to install a principle of value as high as, or higher than, Christ himself. "In Christ Jesus," Paul insists, "neither circumcision is worth anything (*ti ischyei*) nor the foreskin" (5:6; cf. 6:15). One is not superior to the other. What matters now is "trust operative through love" (5:6), because the Christ-gift elicits a trust that wagers *everything* on Christ and is caught up in the love that issues from "the Son of God who loved me and gave himself for me" (2:20).

Christ, Promise, and Law (Galatians 3:6–5:1)

The terms "promise" and "Law" are interspersed through Galatians 3–4, not to coordinate them but to make them clearly distinct (3:18). It matters to Paul that the Christ-gift is the fulfillment of God's promises, articulated at the beginning to Abraham; as *promises* they are received by trust. But he has come to regard the Law as another matter altogether—not antithetical to the promises but time-limited and, most of all, unable to deliver the blessings that were promised. Indeed, what he brings out here is that, even under the Law, humanity remains at an impasse—under a curse, under sin, and enslaved. If there is to be any solution to this impasse, it will need to come via a creative gift that makes the impossible possible, that frees, gives life, and grants blessing. That promised blessing, Paul argues, comes into existence only in Christ, and as believers are taken up into this countermovement of God they find themselves wholly remade and realigned.

6. See the critiques of circumcision echoed in Josephus, *Against Apion* 2.137; Philo, *Special Laws* 1.1–3. Roman satirists often made jokes about this Jewish custom (e.g., Juvenal, *Satire* 14.96–106; Martial, *Epigrams* 7.30.5; 7.82).

The opening discussion of the Abrahamic promises (3:6–14) looks to the past, the origin of the story of God's people, because the past "looked forward" to the present (3:8). There are many scriptural stories about Abraham (the migrant, the circumcised forefather, the one who offered Isaac, his only son), but Paul picks out one key text, when God made impossible promises to Abraham regarding his heirs: "Abraham believed [or, trusted] God and it was reckoned to him as righteousness" (3:6, citing Gen 15:6). The vocabulary of this verse (*pisteuō; dikaiosynē*) was one source for Paul's earlier statement about "justification" and "trust" in 2:16. What is happening now in Christ turns out to have been exactly what Scripture envisaged all along. Just as the promises to Abraham envisaged blessing for all the nations (3:8, echoing Gen 12:3 and 18:18), so the "blessing of Abraham" is now being experienced among gentiles ("the nations") through the presence and power of the Spirit (3:14).[7]

But was not the Law the means of that blessing? Sadly not, says Paul (3:10–12). According to the Law itself, a curse falls on those who do not adhere to the whole Law (Deut 27:26), and Paul finds that curse tragically applicable to all whose lives are framed by Law-observance (3:10). He seems to assume here the kind of pessimism about the human condition we find in several Jewish texts of his time, which consider humans to be hopelessly flawed and the Law unable to cure their "evil hearts" (see, e.g., the Qumran hymns and 4 Ezra, discussed in chapter 3). We had a clue to this already in Paul's reference to "the present evil age" in 1:4. So, the Law brings curse, not blessing! And if the narrative is shaped in this way, the Christ-event is not a climactic blessing following a series of partial blessings. It is the reversal of curse into blessing (3:13–14); it does not supplement an incomplete positive but turns a negative into a positive. How so? Christ, it seems, participated in the curse (on the cross, 3:13), entering all the way into the human disaster, so that those now in solidarity with Christ ("in Christ") are taken all the way out, into God's intended blessing. Paul outlines here (and in the parallel passage in 4:4–6) the profound drama of the Christ-event, whereby Christ participates in the human condition so that believers may participate in his.[8] What is striking is that those thus "rescued" and "blessed" are not the righteous few, the gold-dust in the clay (4 Ezra), but the cursed.

7. The Spirit is not mentioned in the promises to Abraham, but it was bound up with Jewish expectations for the fulfillment of God's promises to Israel (especially in Isaiah and Ezekiel); see Rodrigo J. Morales, *The Spirit and the Restoration of Israel* (Tübingen: Mohr Siebeck, 2010).

8. For the pattern of "interchange," see Morna D. Hooker, *From Adam to Christ* (Cambridge: Cambridge University Press, 1990). See further, chapter 10, below.

The next section (3:15-29) also moves from the origin of the promises to their present fulfillment, but now the relation between the promise and the Law is spelled out. The promises were given 430 years before the Law was "ordained" (3:17, 19). The Law, Paul insists, is not an eternal but a contextual phenomenon, and it does not supplement, still less alter, the original "covenant" of promises (3:15, 17). Those promises were pitched toward the future, but what they envisaged was not the Law of Moses but the "seed," first and foremost Christ himself (3:16).[9] In this bold reading, Paul sees all the forward-thrusting elements of Scripture converging on Christ. But at the same time he marginalizes the Law, comparing it to a *paidagōgos*, a slave who disciplined and protected children but had a time-limited period of authority (3:23-25).[10] The Law is not opposed to God's promises (3:21), but it is not the rubric of history, nor the centerpiece in God's ordering of the world. Try reading any Second Temple Jewish text to see what a radical claim that is!

What, then, is the centerpiece in God's ordering of the world? If the Law is unable to "make alive" (3:21), and if all things are "shut up under sin" (3:22), this "ordering" will have to be a radical *reordering*, creating something that was hitherto impossible. Everything is oriented to the arrival of Christ, which is also the arrival of humanity's proper orientation in "trust" (3:23, 25). This takes ritual expression in baptism (3:27) because there the believer is reconfigured in solidarity with Christ ("baptized into Christ"), remade through the resurrection life of Christ ("It is Christ who lives in me," 2:20), or, to use Paul's metaphor, "clothed" with Christ (3:27).

Paul here adapts a baptismal formula to show how this new location of believers scrambles the dominant systems of social classification: "There is neither Jew nor Greek, neither slave nor free, no male and female: for you are all one in Christ Jesus" (3:28). This is a staggering statement, which empties normal systems of differentiation of their evaluative freight. All the pairings cited by Paul carry connotations of value. For Jews, to be Jewish is not only different from being Greek but also self-evidently superior (cf. 2:15). Everyone in Paul's context considered free people worth more than slaves. And it was commonly presumed in the ancient world that men were superior to women (on various, spurious, grounds). The differences indicated by these categories

9. God's promises to Abraham's "seed/offspring" (e.g., Gen 22:17-18) were combined in Jewish tradition with the promises to the seed of David (2 Sam 7:12), and Paul identifies Jesus with both (Gal 3:16, 19; Rom 1:3-4), although he knows that "seed" can be interpreted as both a singular and a plural entity (Gal 3:16, 29).

10. Paul's term *paidagōgos* is sometimes translated "tutor" or "disciplinarian." No other Jewish text known to us applies to the Law this image of a time-limited role.

are not erased. Paul and Peter remained Jews in Christ (2:15; cf. Titus, a Greek, 2:3), and Paul was still masculine and free. What is altered is the *worth* associated with these labels. What counts ultimately and fully—the only true symbolic capital—is not one's ethnicity, gender, or legal status but one's solidarity with Christ. Paul is free, but *more importantly,* a slave of Christ (1:10); his body is masculine and circumcised, but *more importantly,* associated (via his scars) with the cross of Christ (6:17; cf. 5:11). All forms of symbolic capital that are not derived from belonging to Christ lose their ultimate significance, even if they are significant at a secondary level or in an instrumental sense (in service of Christ). Baptism "into Christ" thus provides a new foundation for communities that are freed from traditional, hierarchical systems of distinction. As Paul found, this is hard to put into practice. But what we find throughout his letters, and often in his practice, is the attempt to rethink human identity and worth on the basis of a singular, unconditioned gift, which undercuts all other reckoning of worth and *gives* the only worth that counts.[11]

For a third time (4:1–11) Paul traces a narrative arc from promise to fulfillment in Christ, this time focusing on the category "sons of God." The variation in pronouns in 4:1–7 between "we" (4:3) and "you" (4:6) is confusing, but it probably represents the juxtaposition of Jewish history with the history of non-Jews. "We" (Jews) have been in the situation of children waiting to come into our inheritance; the promises have been spoken but await their fulfillment "at the time set by the father" (4:1–3). "You" (gentiles in Galatia) share in the adoption that we have now received (4:5–7). This metaphor of heirs and inheritance might give the impression that all that is required is the passage of time, as children wait to mature. But Paul interprets what happens in Christ not as a process of maturation but as a transformation, created by an *interruption* of time. The condition of these "children" is actually one of slavery (4:1–3): they need to *become* children of God by an act of liberation and *adoption* (4:4–6). Up until now, Paul says, "we" have been enslaved to the "elements of the world" (*stoicheia tou kosmou,* 4:3).[12] Paul probably refers here to the physical elements

---

11. Exegetes have rightly found in Gal 3:28 a revolutionary subversion of hierarchical values; see, e.g., Elisabeth Schüssler Fiorenza, *In Memory of Her: A Feminist Theological Reconstruction of Christian Origins* (New York: Crossroad, 1992). But Paul's understanding of liberation and worth in Christ does not match entirely the expectations that we bring from Enlightenment philosophy or critical theory.

12. The phrase (echoed in 4:9) has been translated in various ways, but most scholars now think it refers to the physical elements that constitute the world; see Martinus C. de Boer, *Galatians: A Commentary,* New Testament Library (Louisville: Westminster John Knox, 2011), 252–56.

of the cosmos, to which all religious calendars (Jewish and non-Jewish, cf. 4:9) were aligned, inasmuch as they were regulated by movement of the sun, moon, and stars. Humanity has found itself determined by these "elements" rather than sovereign over them (cf. 1 Cor 3:22–23; 15:20–28). These "elements" provide no power to alleviate the human condition: they are "weak." They bring no benefit or gift: they are "destitute" (4:9).

What is needed is not that children should come of age, in some natural process of maturation, but that God should intervene to change the conditions of the possible. That is what Paul traces in 4:4–6, which (like 3:13–14) summarizes the Christ-event as the participation of Christ in the human domain (and specifically "under the Law") so that believers might participate in the privileges of the Son. The metaphor of adoption makes clear that "sonship" can come about only through *receiving* a new status and a new identity, as granted by God.[13] If they have come to know God, that is only because they have *been known* by God (4:9). This sense of dependence on a divine initiative is experienced in the Spirit, whose operation in the lives of believers alerts them to the fact that their existence is derived from outside themselves (4:6). Paul thus reminds the Galatians that the most important thing about them is not inherited nor humanly ascribed or acquired: it is *received* as an incongruous gift (4:5). "So, you are no longer a slave, but a son; and if a son, then an heir—*through the agency of God (dia theou)*" (4:7).

Paul next rehearses his relationship with the Galatians (4:12–20), and it might appear that he has wandered off into a digression. But in fact this clarifies on an existential level what it means to receive an unconditioned gift.[14] Paul wants them to "become like me, as I became like you" (4:12). He is probably referring to the way that he was prepared to live in their midst "in a gentile fashion" (2:14), because his value-orientation had been reset by Christ, the source of his new life (2:19–20). Initially they had understood the point: they had received him "as Christ" (someone whose self is wholly identified with Christ) and had suspended their normal code of honor and shame by welcoming him, despite his apparent worthlessness (4:13–14). They could have disdained him, even spat at him (4:14)—an expression of fear or disgust in the face of physical deformity. But he mattered to them because the Christ he proclaimed came to matter to them more than anything else, and instead of

13. See John M. G. Barclay, "An Identity Received from God: The Theological Configuration of Paul's Kinship Discourse," *Early Christianity* 8 (2017): 354–72.

14. On this paragraph, see especially Susan Eastman, *Recovering Paul's Mother Tongue: Language and Theology in Galatians* (Grand Rapids: Eerdmans, 2007), 25–61.

shunning him they displayed generous friendship (4:15). If that friendship has now waned, or turned into hostility, that can only be because the good news is losing its grip in Galatia (4:16–18).

Thus Paul yearns that the Galatians may be shaped again by the gift that reset their identity and their values: "My children, with whom I am again in labor until Christ be formed within you . . ." (4:19).[15] The echo of 2:19–20 is strong: "It is no longer I who live, but Christ who lives in me" (2:20). As Paul diagnoses the Galatian condition, they need to be "rebirthed" such that Christ becomes both the source and the measure of their lives. Their reconstitution by the good news once revolutionized their honor code and its associated system of values. They need to show the same freedom by refusing the demand to submit to the "yoke" of the Law (4:21; 5:1).

In the final thread of the central chapters (4:21–5:1), Paul returns to the Abraham story, which set the tone of all that has followed in the history of God's people. Those who appeal to Scripture to urge circumcision and Law-observance, can be met on their own terrain (4:21). The "allegorical" reading that Paul offers here (4:24) does not abstract the text from history but matches the past time ("then") with the present time ("now," 4:29) in a "figural" reading that discovers more in the past (in the light of the present) than had previously been seen.[16] The story of Abraham, Hagar and Sarah, and their sons (Ishmael and Isaac) is here taken to figure two patterns of people-formation ("two covenants"). One is based on natural, physical descent ("according to the flesh") and the other on a miraculous, promise-created birth ("according to the Spirit," 4:29). The Hagar-Ishmael line is associated with slavery (in the biblical story, Hagar and her children were slaves), which evokes the condition of entrapment within "the present evil age" (1:4) under "the elements of the world" (4:3), a condition applicable to "the present Jerusalem" (4:25). By contrast, the Sarah-Isaac line is associated with freedom, and its life and liberation are externally sourced, from "the Jerusalem above" (4:26). The spatial imagery ("above") is a common apocalyptic figure for what derives from God and God alone. Thus, Paul associates Sarah with another initially barren mother, Isaiah's barren woman made fertile (a figure for Jerusalem in Isa 54:1, cited in Gal 4:27).[17] Both can attribute their fertility only to a powerful intervention by God.

---

15. Paul's maternal imagery is striking; see Beverly R. Gaventa, *Our Mother Saint Paul* (Louisville: Westminster John Knox, 2007).

16. J. David Dawson, *Christian Figural Reading and the Fashioning of Identity* (Berkeley: University of California Press, 2002).

17. See Martinus C. de Boer, "Paul's Quotation of Isa 54.1 in Gal 4.27," *New Testament Studies* 50 (2004): 370–89.

The familiar Abrahamic stories make new sense in the light of Christ. A new event has changed the canons of the interpretation of Scripture, which now resounds with echoes of the good news.[18] What Paul traces in the Abraham story is the creative work of God, who gives life to the barren and creates a human impossibility, people here labelled "children of the promise" (4:28). This is the operation of the Spirit, a sign of the "new creation" (6:15). The "mother" metaphor concerns the *source* of life and sharpens the question: Are events on the stage of history of human origin, and thus humanly limited and culturally determined, or are they "ex-centric"—derived from a divine initiative that breaks through human boundaries?[19] Paul is driven by the good news of Jesus Christ to found new communities, social experiments on the urban landscape, where old values are superseded and new relationships created. He is convinced that this is not just a human invention, a product of skill or cultural innovation. What he sees at work is, rather, a divine activity that creates new human agents, a phenomenon as fruitful and miraculous as the birth of Isaac (4:28). Because this derives from *elsewhere*, all kinds of new possibilities emerge on the human stage.

This Sarah-Hagar passage has often been taken, in the history of interpretation, as a sign that Paul "disinherits" Jews, that he regards those who belong to "the present Jerusalem" as excluded, like Ishmael, from the covenant line, and that (in schematic terms) the church has superseded the synagogue. As we shall see, Romans 9–11 should be enough to convince us that Paul does *not* see things that way (see below, chapter 9), but even here in Galatians there are hints that those Jews who have not (yet) believed in Christ are objects of God's continuing commitment. Paul supports Peter's mission to the "circumcised" (Jews, 2:7–8) and surely hoped it would be fruitful. If the child-heirs of 4:1–3 are a reference to the Jewish people (see above), they constitute a special category in the plan of God. And at the very end of the letter Paul may anticipate Romans 11 when he pronounces "mercy also on the Israel of God" (6:16). The syntax of that blessing is unclear, and it may be read in more than one way, but the echo of traditional prayers for Israel, the label "Israel *of God*," and (crucially) the prayer for *mercy* (a central motif in Rom 9–11) might suggest that Paul prays here for the people of Israel.[20] Paul speaks of Jews who are yet to be transformed by the arrival of the Messiah in double tones: as enslaved

18. See the seminal work of Richard B. Hays, *Echoes of Scripture in the Letters of Paul* (New Haven: Yale University Press, 1989).

19. See Eastman, *Recovering Paul's Mother Tongue*, 127–60.

20. Susan G. Eastman, "Israel and the Mercy of God: A Re-Reading of Galatians 6.16 and Romans 9–11," *New Testament Studies* 56 (2010): 367–95. But other readings are possible:

yet heirs, as in Hagar-like slavery yet objects of a prayer for mercy. That should caution us against reading Galatians as "supersessionist." However, in what sense Israel has been and remains special becomes clear only in the letter to the Romans.

CONCLUSION

The central chapters of Galatians weave together such a variety of motifs in such small compass that readers are often left bewildered. Some features of these chapters (such as the power of sin) are only hinted at here and will be explained further in Romans. However, we have traced a common pattern that takes a recognizable form. At every point, the fulfillment of the promise in Christ alters and interrupts the human story: it brings blessing to the cursed, freedom to the enslaved, life to the barren. Where one might expect a different pattern—of heirs who naturally mature and so acquire their inheritance—Paul reframes the heirs as *slaves*, who require not time to mature but liberation and adoption. Like the revelation that interrupted Paul's life and changed its coordinates (1:13–17), the Christ-event has realigned history, not by adding one further chapter but by a cross-cutting incongruity that is "not in accordance with human norms" (1:11). The incongruous gift of Christ is mapped across the story of Israel and the world, and is manifest in the Galatians' experience of the Spirit and of baptism.

This Christ-shaped reconfiguration of reality governs Paul's interpretation of Scripture, separates promise from Law, and makes all history pivot around the gift of Christ. That event fulfills the plan and promise of God but is incongruous with the conditions of human history. The continuity at the divine level is evidenced *in* human history but does not operate *according to* human patterns of continuity. Pauline scholars who stress the "covenant faithfulness" of God are right to insist that the Christ-event does not come out of the blue but pulls together the threads of God's promises.[21] But Israel's history does not progress in stages, and "the fullness of time" (4:4) is an irruptive event, not a matter of chronological development. Conversely, those who stress the "apocalyptic invasion" of God into the human story are right to highlight

---

see the discussion in de Boer, *Galatians*, 405–8 (who sees a reference to Jewish believers in Christ).

21. See, especially, N. T. Wright, *Paul and the Faithfulness of God*, 2 vols. (London: SPCK, 2013).

the incongruity of the Christ-event and the newness of the "new creation" (6:15).[22] But because this is a gift "from above" (4:26), it is not bound by the rules of time, which operate by sequence, and its newness is consistent with what God had announced and started from the beginning. What matters for Paul is that the Galatians should recognize how deeply the world has been reformulated by the gift of Christ. That should alter their expectations and values. Old normative structures have been undercut or decentered, including Paul's ancestral traditions "under the Law." The good news is good only if it is an *unconditioned* gift and is recognized to be so. Since this grace constitutes God's counterstatement to the possible, new communities may be created, and new relationships formed, as is spelled out next in the exhortations that follow (Gal 5:13–6:10).

22. See, especially, J. Louis Martyn, *Galatians: A New Translation with Introduction and Commentary*, Anchor Yale Bible Commentary 33A (New York: Doubleday, 1997), and his *Theological Issues in the Letters of Paul* (Edinburgh: T&T Clark, 1997).

CHAPTER 6

The New Community as the Expression of the Gift (Galatians 5–6)

The section of Galatians that runs from 5:13 through to 6:10 concerns the ethos of communities that live out of the gift of Christ, that is, out of the new "life" given through the Spirit (5:25). Following the modern distinction between "theology" and "ethics," scholars typically label this "the ethical section" and treat it as a supplement to the theological heart of the letter.[1] Moreover, because the material is necessarily quite general (Paul is writing to a circle of Galatian assemblies, not just one, 1:2), it has sometimes been treated as "general exhortation" (or "paraenesis"), only loosely connected to what precedes.[2] Paul certainly deploys here several types of material (lists of vices and virtues, direct commands, warnings, and declarations of fact), but they are unified by their focus on what creates, or shatters, the life of a community. The key theme has already been announced in 5:6: what counts in this community is not a particular ethnic or cultural frame of reference but "trust operative through love." In disregarding previous criteria of distinction, the Christ-event has released a new creative energy, a quality of social commitment sourced in the Spirit and summarized as "love." It is not surprising that love is prominent both explicitly (5:14, 22) and implicitly (e.g., 6:1–2) throughout this section of the letter.

Social practice is, for Paul, the necessary expression of the Christ-gift. As the Antioch incident made clear (2:11–21), the dispute about the Law is not an abstract question of "soteriology," nor does it concern only the individual's relationship to God. It concerns the frame within which the communities of God's people are to operate in the wake of the gift of Christ and the associ-

---

1. The distinction is rightly questioned by Philip F. Esler, *Galatians* (London: Routledge, 1998).

2. On the character of this section and its close relationship to the rest of the letter, see John M. G. Barclay, *Obeying the Truth: A Study of Paul's Ethics in Galatians* (Edinburgh: T&T Clark, 1988).

ated gift of the Spirit. The "truth of the good news" (2:14) is ineffective unless it "takes place" within communities whose behavior instantiates its novelty. Thus, the social life of the assemblies formed by the gift is not just the consequence of the gift but its necessary, practical expression. Two pithy sentences in 5:24–25 sum up the break with normality that this entails: "Those who belong to Christ Jesus have crucified the flesh with its passions and desires. If our life derives from the Spirit, it is with the Spirit that we should keep in step." Paul articulates here a dynamic that moves from death ("crucified the flesh") to new life ("if our life derives from the Spirit")—the same dynamic that was operative in 2:19–20 ("I have been crucified with Christ; it is no longer I who live but Christ who lives in me"). A decisive break with the past has been effected and accompanied by a new orientation. The new life is not humanly generated: it derives from the Spirit. But it is humanly expressed: believers, as reconstituted agents, "crucify the flesh" and "keep in step" with the Spirit. Without this practical expression, it is hard to see in what sense the transformation of believers is real. To live from the Spirit is at the same time to walk by its norms. The options in the matter are simple: the only alternative is to "sow to the flesh" (6:7–8), which would mean to deny one's identity in Christ. Moreover, life in the Spirit is not limited to "personal morality" but is worked out on the public stage, in the creation and development of communities governed by new values and norms.

FREEDOM, FLESH, AND SPIRIT

"You have been called for freedom," declares Paul (5:13), evoking the "calling in grace" highlighted at the start of the letter (1:6; cf. 5:8). This freedom is the product of the newly creative work of God. The constraints of former patterns of life and systems of evaluation are suddenly lifted, and a whole new set of possibilities arises (cf. 2:4). But this is not an absolute freedom, as if another set of human options could take the place of the old: "Only do not let your freedom turn into an opportunity for the flesh" (5:13). When he declared himself free from human systems of evaluation, Paul simultaneously announced himself a "slave of Christ" (1:10). If the unconditioned gift of Christ jolts believers out of their standard expectations and values, it also shapes them anew. They are not "free" to adopt whatever practices they want.

We have noted the antithesis between "flesh" and "Spirit" before (3:3; 4:29), but it is in this section of the letter that Paul uses these terms most extensively to redraw the map of the cosmos.[3] "The flesh" is not limited to physical appetites, as we might think; even the list of the "works of the flesh" in 5:19-21 includes social and "religious" phenomena, not merely what we might call "sins of the flesh." In fact, "flesh" has become a label for the whole realm of activity, power, and meaning *outside of the Christ-event and its Spirit-created consequences.* Paul is not turning here to a different issue, a problem of "libertinism" distinct from the focus of the rest of the letter. The camera is not panning across to a different topic but pulling back to reveal the larger context in which the whole Galatian dispute is situated. That is why in the midst of this discussion of "flesh" Paul insists that "you are not under the Law" (5:18), and why earlier he had associated the program of his opponents with "the flesh" (3:3). As Paul was aware, circumcision was known in his tradition as "the covenant in your flesh" (Gen 17:13, NRSV), and he echoes this phrase with criticism of those who "take pride in your flesh" (Gal 6:12-13). But he is not objecting to circumcision because it is a physical (as opposed to a "spiritual") phenomenon. By labeling it "flesh" he is placing it within the sphere of ordinary, unreconstructed life, where human relations and practices have not been reordered in Christ. If "flesh" takes on here an active, semipersonified role, as in the struggle between flesh and Spirit in 5:17, this is because the misaligned goals and deceptive values of life outside of the Spirit have the capacity to shape human lives at a level deeper than humans generally realize.

According to this new taxonomy, life "under (the regime of) the Law" (5:18) does not counter the power of the flesh (as one might expect) but represents only another option within its sphere. We should not miss what a radical claim this is for someone of Paul's Jewish heritage—parallel to his claim that in making the move to Law-observance, the Galatians are going back to the "weak and destitute elements" (4:9). Paul has completely redrawn his inherited map under the impact of the "new creation" (6:15). That does not mean that the Law is evil or misleading, only that it is inadequate as a basis of worth, trapped within the conditions of "the present evil age," and no longer the supreme norm for those in Christ ("Through the Law, I have died to the Law," 2:19). Paul is now oriented fully and exclusively to Christ, or as he puts it in 6:2, his goal now is to "fulfill the law of Christ."[4] Christ and all that he has effected

---

3. On the Spirit-flesh dualism, see Barclay, *Obeying the Truth,* 178-215.

4. Scholars continue to debate what Paul means by "the law of Christ" (*nomos tou Christou*); for a survey of options, see Barclay, *Obeying the Truth,* 125-35. The closest parallel in Paul's letters is his claim to be *ennomos Christou* ("under lawful obligation to Christ," 1 Cor 9:21), which is there, as in Galatians, distinguished from being "under the Law."

have become the unique, noncontingent, first-order source of authority and value (cf. 2:14: "walking in line with the truth of the good news"). Under the illumination of the Christ-event, some aspects of the Mosaic Law fall into the shadow (as nonessential, contingent, and thus not required of all believers), while others are heightened in significance and profile. What stands out in this context is the command, "You shall love your neighbor as yourself" (Lev 19:18; cited in Gal 5:14). Paul was not alone among Jews in finding here a particularly significant statement that could be taken to summarize "the whole Law." But he uses the (rare) language of "fulfillment" to indicate that what has happened in "the fullness of time" (4:4) is the completion of the goal of the Law, although in a form and at a level beyond its own frame of reference. It is only when believers have their identities refounded and their goals remolded by the love enacted in the Christ-gift that they are able to perform what the Law had in mind. In other words, it is those whom Paul calls "spiritual people" (6:1), those reshaped by the Spirit, who bear love in its fullest form, as the first of the fruits produced by the Spirit (5:22).

"Fleshly" Competition and Its Antidote

Because urban life in the Roman world was a face-to-face social sphere, within crowded space, the opposite to love and mutual support is not isolation or indifference but mutual harm. "But if you bite and devour one another, watch out lest you be consumed by one another" (5:15). A few verses later, Paul portrays the alternative to walking in the Spirit in equally negative terms: "Don't be vain, provoking one another and envying one another" (5:26). In fact, as many have noticed, the list of the "works of the flesh" (5:19–21) includes, alongside standard characterizations of the gentile world (idolatry, sexual impurity, magical practice), an extensive catalogue of socially destructive behavior: "acts of hostility, strife, jealousy, outbursts of anger, selfish aggression, dissensions, factions, fits of envy, inebriated loutishness, drinking parties, and the like" (5:20–21). The heavy concentration of such items here reflects not a particular issue in the Galatian assemblies but the perennial threats to social cohesion and wellbeing in a society where honor is aggressively pursued and zealously maintained.

As recent research has emphasized, almost all social relations in Paul's cultural context were governed by competition for honor. In many modern cultures, some measures of worth are regarded as "objectively" secure—educational qualifications, for instance, or status within public institutions: if one has a degree from a high-ranking institution, one does not need to fight all the time to establish one's educational credentials. But in the ancient world, almost every aspect of worth was dependent on one's public reputation, which was insecure and perpetually contestable at almost every point. To maintain your worth, you had to keep asserting it and defending it, in the awareness that others could at any moment make a claim by which your worth would be undermined or outclassed. The rumor mill was the Romans' social media, and they were ever anxious to make it clear that by one criterion or another—wealth, ancestry, education, legal status, physique, ethnicity, or character—their honor could be established, in comparison with others'. As Cicero put it, "By nature we yearn and hunger for honor, and once we have glimpsed, as it were, some part of its radiance, there is nothing we are not prepared to bear and to suffer in order to secure it" (*Tusculan Disputations* 2.24.58).

In this competitive atmosphere, pride, hostility, envy, and revenge become dominant characteristics of social interaction. A slight injustice is quickly inflated: "Every tiff is a tumult, every wrangle a war."[5] The brazenness with which honor was advertised was a sign of the insecurity of this precious commodity, and the ferocity with which it was attacked indicated the critical spirit which pervaded society. Paul's warning against vendettas (5:15) is neither empty nor unusual: the lust for honor which might inspire great feats of heroism could just as easily destroy a whole community.

Paul's antidote to this social poison has two ingredients. On the one hand, those who have been reconstructed by the Christ-event are no longer invested in the forms of "capital" in which most people find their worth. Since ethnicity, status, and gender are no longer criteria of superior worth (3:28) and since God pays no regard to the "face" (2:6) but distributes his grace without regard to worth, the normal grounds for competition have lost their significance. The believer's true and only worth is constituted by his/her identity "in Christ," a gift received, not a status inherited or achieved. Within the new community there stand out those whose lives are most marked by the new ethos created by this gift, those, for instance, who are "spiritual" and given responsibility insofar as they are attuned to the Spirit (6:1). But—and this is the second ingredient in Paul's antidote—the hallmark of this alternative system of value is that it is specifically directed *against* rivalry: the greatest honor is reserved for those who work against the competitive spirit of the quest for honor! All the characteristics of "the fruit of the Spirit" (5:22–23) are directed toward the

5. Carlin A. Barton, *Roman Honor: The Fire in the Bones* (Berkeley: University of California Press, 2001), 66.

construction of community, from love onward. "Spiritual" people are so designated because they work with sensitivity to repair the community (6:1–2). What counts among believers, according to Paul, is precisely the antithesis to arrogance and competition.

The items listed among the "fruit of the Spirit" (5:22–23) are not so much individual virtues as the social characteristics that enhance and maintain a community. Their practice is spelled out in 6:1–10. "Gentleness" (5:23) is required in the restoration of an errant member (6:1). "Love" (5:22) is to be expressed in "bearing one another's burdens" (6:2), the practice of costly mutual support that Paul earlier described as "being enslaved to one another through love" (5:13). Individuals should take care not to trumpet their work before others (6:3–4), applying "self-control" (5:23) for the benefit of others.[6] "Goodness" (5:22) is not an abstract quality but labels acts of beneficence and kindness, "doing good to all" (6:10), including solidarity with those who teach the word (6:6). And where these practices seem poorly reciprocated or ineffective, believers should persist with "patience" (5:22), not flagging or giving up (6:9). Thus, the fruit that springs from the Spirit's life is operative in the delicate negotiation of communal relations, in behavioral qualities that are fostered over time. If faith is operative in a love like this (5:6), it has implications wider than an individual's relationship to Christ.

Paul's striking phrase "So fulfill the law of Christ" (6:2) has caused considerable discussion. The language echoes talk of "fulfilling" the Law in 5:14, so does Paul have in mind some Christological redefinition of the Mosaic Law? Or is he thinking of a new law, based on the teaching of Jesus? The phrase reflects Paul's linguistic creativity, his ability to coin new expressions, and the link with 5:13–14 suggests that what he means by "the law of Christ" is, primarily, love.[7] That should not surprise us. The story of the good news is the story of one who "gave himself for our sins" (1:4) and who "loved me and gave himself for me" (2:20). The momentum of the Christ-gift is a momentum of love, which enters into the depths of the human situation (3:13; 4:4–5) in order to rescue and redeem. That momentum is represented and continued by "the Spirit of

---

6. 6:4 is often translated: "All must test their own work; then that work, rather than their neighbor's work, will become a cause for pride" (NRSV). But the Greek is better read another way: "Let each person test his own work and then keep his sense of pride to himself alone and not direct it toward others" (Barclay, Obeying the Truth, 160; J. Louis Martyn, Galatians: A New Translation with Introduction and Commentary, Anchor Yale Bible Commentary 33A [New York: Doubleday, 1997], 550).

7. See above, note 4.

[God's] Son" (4:6), whose prime fruit is love (5:22).[8] In other words, to live by faith is to have "Christ formed in you" (4:19), and that formation has a specific ethical and social shape. Believers do not just imitate the Christ-gift, admiring it from a distance as an external example. Their new selves and identities are created by it, and in "putting on Christ" (3:27) they inhabit the purpose of his self-giving, in the practical form of love.[9]

Here, as elsewhere in his letters, Paul understands love to be expressed best not as one-way service (giving but receiving nothing back) but in reciprocal relationships: "Through love be slaves *to one another*" (5:13), and, "Bear *one another's* burdens, and so fulfill the law of Christ" (6:2). Paul envisages communities where no one is self-sufficient. In these communities, believers are not expected to bear their own burdens by themselves and also to carry the burdens of others. Neither is everyone to look after themselves, leaving everyone else to do the same.[10] Rather, members will freely contribute to one another but also receive from one another, so that each helps the other to carry their burdens. "Burden" often has, for Paul, economic overtones (cf. 1 Thess 2:7; 2 Cor 11:9), and the motif here is not confined to psychological or emotional difficulties but includes the regular, mostly unspectacular ways in which those in fluctuating economic circumstances help each other out and support one another materially in times of crisis.[11] The goal is what Paul calls "partnership" or "solidarity" (*koinōnia*; cf. Phil 2:1; 2 Cor 8:4), illustrated here by the mutual give-and-take between the learner and the teacher of the word, who "share" (*koinōneō*) in all good things (6:6). In such conditions of mutual dependence, friction is bound to arise, and strong doses of love are required to keep the benefits flowing in all directions.

Love, then, does not mean self-sacrifice in the sense of negating oneself for the sake of others and expecting nothing back. The Scriptural citation—"You shall love your neighbor as yourself" (Lev 19:18, cited in 5:14)—could be understood in a number of ways, but it seems to include, not exclude, the self in the good that one shares with another in love (perhaps: "you shall love your neighbor as if he/she were integral to yourself"). In other words, the self is not

---

8. See Richard B. Hays, "Christology and Ethics in Galatians: The Law of Christ," *Catholic Biblical Quarterly* 49 (1987): 268–90.

9. See Grant Macaskill, *Living in Union with Christ: Paul's Gospel and Christian Moral Identity* (Grand Rapids: Baker Academic, 2019).

10. In context, the advice that "each will bear his own load" (6:5) is about the responsibility of each person before God, not about the "burdens" of everyday life (6:2).

11. See Ryan S. Schellenberg, "Subsistence, Swapping, and Paul's Rhetoric of Generosity," *Journal of Biblical Literature* 137 (2018): 215–34.

given *away* in love but given *into* a relationship with others, a relationship in which all parties will benefit and flourish.[12] Christ himself, we may recall, was not finally obliterated in his self-gift: he gave himself *into* the human condition so that humans may enjoy blessing and life, not instead of him or without him, but in him and with him (2:20; 3:14).

Finally, we may note the paradox in the expression "Be slaves to one another" (5:13). This is a remarkable expression since it adjusts an inherently hierarchical relationship (slavery), not by cancelling it, but by making it reciprocal, a hierarchy that turns both ways. "One another" converts a one-way relationship of power and superiority into a mutual relationship of reciprocal deference, where *each* seeks to promote the interests of the other (cf. 1 Cor 7:4). Thus, submission to the interests of others does not become a charter for the crushing of the weak: it is turned both ways, such that service and honor are continually exchanged. This perpetual inversion of hierarchy (a form of "reciprocal asymmetry") has an equalizing effect since no one is in a stable or comprehensive position of superiority.[13] Since, in Paul's notion of the body, resources are differentially distributed and all are bound together by their need of the others (1 Cor 12:12–28), each will have the responsibility to serve the others and the opportunity to be served by the others (see below, chapter 11).

The Christ-gift thus enters into human relations, by the operation of the Spirit, equipping new patterns of social relationship where people are no longer treated by reference to the old hierarchies of worth (which have been bypassed by the gift of Christ), nor by competitive jostling for honor. These are communities that stand at odds with normal configurations, as they are released from the typical criteria by which worth is differentially distributed and acclaimed. Although Paul's instructions provide only the outlines of a new communal ethos, they fit the formation of communities where the Christ-event has had transformative effect. Here "the household of faith" (6:10) is given house rules that are neither "under the Law" (5:18) nor subject to the competitive spirit that governs the surrounding culture. What gives each new assembly the inspiration and strength to conduct this new social experiment, which is in principle open to all (6:10), is the sense of a newly gifted life, whose incongruity is expressed in social terms. If "keeping in step with the Spirit"

12. I owe this way of putting things to Logan Williams, whose Durham University dissertation ("Love, Self-Gift, and the Incarnation: Christology and Ethics in Galatians, in the Context of Pauline Theology and Greco-Roman Philosophy") offers profound reflection on this theme.

13. See Alain Badiou, *Saint Paul: The Foundation of Universalism*, trans. Ray Brassier (Stanford: Stanford University Press, 2003), 98–106. This does not quite fit our modern notions of "flat" equality because it concerns a more dynamic sense of "equalization."

(5:25) breaks fresh ground, that is because the Christ-gift has instantiated a new regime that not only may but *must* take expression in the formation of countercultural communities.

THE NEW CREATION (GALATIANS 6:11–18)

The final paragraph of the letter, written with highly personal emphasis (6:11), sums up its challenge by again presenting the Christ-event as subversive of normative systems of worth. Here it becomes apparent that Paul places the particular Galatian crisis on an enormously broad canvas, in which the Christ-event shatters the systems of meaning that constitute "the world" (6:14). At issue is not simply the adoption of this or that Jewish practice but the capacity of the Christ-gift to reground and reorient the whole of life by a logic that challenges every other attribution of value.

Paul warns the Galatians against those whose only motives (in his view) are "to make a good showing in the flesh" (6:12) or "to take pride in your flesh" (6:13). "Taking pride" (*kauchaomai*) is not wrong in itself (as the usual English translation, "boast," might suggest): Paul is about to take pride in the cross of Christ (6:14). What is at issue is not "bragging" but the object in which you take pride, since you are confident of its value. In other words, the question is: What is your "symbolic capital"? What do you think is of ultimate worth? If others want to "make a good showing," they are bound by public systems of honor, and for Paul "the flesh" should never be the object of pride or confidence (Phil 3:3–5), only, at best, the arena in which something more significant is played out (cf. 2:20: "the life I now live in the flesh"). It is like taking pride in the football stadium and not in the quality of the football played there (and which could be played elsewhere equally well). Those who insist on circumcision in Galatia are investing in the wrong thing, giving significance to something that, in the light of the Christ-event, is "neither here nor there." The *uncircumcised* state ("the foreskin") is not inherently better: neither state counts in any ultimate sense (6:15; cf. 5:6). What has undermined the value that Jews would give to one and Greeks would give to the other is an event that has recalibrated every cultural norm.

It is worth pausing here to note that Paul does not seem to be attacking "works" as such, as if human agency were a problem for him. He expects believers to "walk" by the "rule" of the new creation in an active and engaged way (6:16). Nor is the issue exactly the gaining of salvation by self-reliance. Paul discounts *both* circumcision *and* uncircumcision (5:6; 6:15), and while the former might be figured as a work, it is hard to see how leaving oneself *uncircumcised* is a "work" in any sense. Neither is the issue the "nationalistic imperialism" that "restricts" the covenant to Jews alone, as some in "the new perspective" suggest.[14] Again, why does Paul discount *uncircumcision* as well? It seems that Paul's target is neither ethnocentrism nor the false opinion that good works can gain benefit from God. The power of the good news is to subvert *any* form of symbolic capital that operates independently of Christ: "I [have been crucified] to the world" (6:14).

"The world" is a potent term, associated in the ancient world with order, design, and a "natural" structure of values. To be "crucified to the world" is not to demonize nature nor to downgrade creation (as Marcion thought) but to declare that there is nothing in all the world, natural or culturally constructed, that can compare in value to the event of Jesus Christ, from whom all meaning and value derive. The language of "crucifixion" (cf. 3:1) is deliberately brutal (cf. 1 Cor 1:18–25): it is form of death that epitomizes the very opposite of what counts as dignified and noble (see below, chapter 10). In *form* (as unconditioned gift), in *content* (as death), and in *mode* (in the shame of crucifixion), the cross of Christ breaks the allegiance of believers to preconstituted notions of the honorable, the civilized, and the proper. This single and particular event is of universal significance because it is beholden to no precalculated system of distinction and privileges no subset of humanity. It is a radically unconditioned event.

To take pride in a death announcement (6:14) would be unbearably paradoxical were it not for the fact that precisely in this death there emerges the creativity of God. "For neither circumcision counts for anything, nor foreskin, but new creation" (6:15). Scholars continue to debate what Paul means here by "new creation" (cf. 2 Cor 5:17). Does he speak of the reconstitution of the individual, as earlier he had said of himself, "It is no longer I who live, but Christ who lives in me" (2:20)? Or does he mean "new creation" on a cosmic scale, as God's reordering and remaking of all reality, in contrast to "the present evil age" (1:4)?[15] Paul's phrase may resonate right across this spectrum, but its meaning certainly includes new communities who are governed by this "rule" (6:16). If the new creation is indifferent to traditional regulative norms, it generates new patterns of social existence, new communities which chart a course

14. Despite James D. G. Dunn, *The Epistle to the Galatians* (London: Black, 1993), 265, 267.

15. For the options, see Moyer V. Hubbard, *New Creation in Paul's Letters and Thought* (Cambridge: Cambridge University Press, 2002); T. Ryan Jackson, *New Creation in Paul's Letters: A Study of the Historical and Social Setting of a Pauline Concept* (Tübingen: Mohr Siebeck, 2010).

"at a diagonal" to normal evaluations of worth (neither aligned nor contrary because reset in an altogether different orientation). The shock of the new world that began with the resurrection refounds each individual believer, but it also reorients every community of believers, who are required to discover new patterns of behavior in line with the truth of the good news (2:14).

The "grace" benediction in the final sentence of Galatians (6:18) forms a bracket with the opening blessing (1:3) and invites us to look back over the letter as Paul's reflection on the Galatian situation in the aftermath of a gift-event that has changed the conditions of reality. Throughout I have emphasized the *incongruity* of grace enacted in the Christ-event and experienced in the Spirit, since this undergirds Paul's reconfiguration of reality. Other "perfections" of grace (see chapter 2) may be present, but they seem less prominent. In this letter Paul puts no particular emphasis on the *superabundance* of grace, nor does he perfect God's beneficence as *singular*, in the sense that it excludes divine judgment (see 5:21; 6:7). The *priority* of grace is presupposed behind the "call" of believers, but it is not developed in the language of "predestination," as in other Pauline letters. One may certainly find elements of the *efficacy* of grace, in the sense that all believer-agency is founded and energized by the presence and power of the Spirit, but this does not mean that divine agency occludes or suppresses the agency of believers.[16] As depicted in this letter, the grace of God is *unconditioned* (without prior considerations of worth) but not *unconditional*, if we mean by that the *noncircular* perfection of grace that expects nothing in return. Grace, for Paul, is not a gift from a disengaged benefactor who would rather be left alone; it is not a donation "with no strings attached." To the contrary: personal and social practice aligned to the good news is integral to what Paul means by "faith" or "trust." But the emphasis lies on the *incongruity* of grace—its mismatch with the worth of its beneficiaries in ethnic, cognitive, moral, or any other terms. There are no criteria, negative or positive, that limit that grace or qualify its recipients. Because this unconditioned gift, given in Christ, cannot be mapped onto prior configurations of worth, it subverts old cultural norms, it refounds individual subjectivity, it justifies new patterns of mission, it reconfigures history, it retunes the voice of Scripture, and it creates new communities on the landscape of the Roman Empire.

This letter has repeatedly gripped the imagination of Christian radicals for

---

16. For reflection on the noncompetitive relation between grace and the agency of the believer, see John M. G. Barclay, "Introduction," in *Divine and Human Agency in Paul and His Cultural Environment*, ed. John M. G. Barclay and Simon J. Gathercole (London: T&T Clark, 2006), 1–8.

a reason. It realigns all reality to the singular event of Christ and to the Gift that creates and grants the only worth that counts. Down through the ages this theology of grace has challenged patterns of thought and practice that do not take their bearings from the gift of God in Christ, and it has undercut the ways we order society with our inherited assumptions of worth. Its radical voice continues to reverberate today, and we will note just some of its implications in the final chapter of this book.

CHAPTER 7

The Incongruous Gift and Its Fitting Result (Romans 1–5)

Paul's letter to the Romans is extraordinary—in its length, in its theological depth, and in its impact on two thousand years of Western thought. Like his other letters, Romans begins and closes with remarks about Paul's relationship with his addressees; but unlike the others, the bulk of the letter is not explicitly addressed to any particular situation. Paul is very conscious of writing to believers whom he has never visited (Rom 1:1-15), and the letter seems designed to prepare for his intended visit to Rome once he has taken to Jerusalem his collection for "the poor among the saints" (Rom 15:14-33). Writing from Corinth (in about 57 CE), Paul is about to go east, before coming west to Rome, with the aim of going even further west, to Spain, with the support of the believers in Rome (Rom 15:24). But how will they receive him, and why should they support him? Who is Paul to them? Paul's claim to be an apostle was contested and his message controversial, and it was not at all clear what sort of reception he would be given in Rome.

Scholars have been disputing "the reasons for Romans" for nearly two hundred years, and the debate continues to this day.[1] Some view the letter as largely unrelated to circumstances in Rome itself, others as subtly responding at every turn to this or that issue in the Roman churches. We have very little evidence about the origins of the Jesus-movement in Rome, and what we have is unclear. Judging from the number of people greeted in Romans 16 (a chapter omitted in some manuscripts but an original part of the letter), Paul had a lot of contacts in Rome. But it appears that his main purpose in writing was not to resolve their issues (except with regard to shared meals, Rom 14–15) but

---

1. For a collection of the main opinions, see Karl P. Donfried, ed., *The Romans Debate: Revised and Expanded Edition* (Grand Rapids: Baker Academic, 2011). Cf. Alexander J. M. Wedderburn, *The Reasons for Romans* (Edinburgh: T&T Clark, 1988) and, more recently, Andrew A. Das, *Solving the Romans Debate* (Minneapolis: Fortress, 2007).

to introduce himself and the good news he proclaimed. He presents himself carefully as an "apostle to the gentiles" (Rom 1:1–5, 13–14) and signs off in that capacity (15:14–16; cf. 11:13). Because he did not found the assemblies in Rome, his approach is nonintrusive (1:11–12; 15:14–15), but the most pressing issue, which will become urgent when he visits, is whether they understand and embrace him as *their* apostle.

This specific reason for writing explains why Paul here covers many of the general themes in his theology. Because he writes as an "apostle to the gentiles," what is most relevant is the meaning of his ministry: God's calling of gentiles, on the basis of the death and resurrection of Jesus, which were God's gracious answer to the corrupting power of Sin.[2] The canvas is huge—as wide as the destiny of all creation (Rom 8:18–39)—because Paul wants the Roman believers to understand where they stand within God's purpose to redeem the world and to fulfill the scriptural promises to Israel. Although Paul's visit to Rome did not go to plan (when he eventually arrived there, it was as a prisoner), we are fortunate that he felt the need to explicate the good news in such a comprehensive way.

In comparison with Galatians, the Christ-event is here placed within a wider historical and theological frame. Christ, "the seed of David," constitutes the fulfillment of the prophetic promises (Rom 1:2–4). He confirms God's faithfulness by his messianic role on behalf of "the circumcision" (Jews), while drawing gentiles, as predicted, into shared worship of the one God (15:7–13). The power unleashed in the Christ-event is also portrayed here more fully in its capacity to overcome the devastating effects of Sin. Galatians referred briefly to "the present evil age" (Gal 1:4) and to the confinement of all things "under sin" (Gal 3:22), but the depth and range of Sin is spelled out in Romans; this is done in three different ways (Rom 1:18–32; 5:12–21; 7:7–25), indicating both the impotence of the Law (Rom 8:1–3) and the superior power of grace (5:12–21). If Galatians stresses the value of God's grace *irrespective of worth*, Romans clarifies that it operates *in the absence of worth*: it is given to "the ungodly" (4:5; 5:6), to those who are utterly unworthy.

In this light Paul finds it necessary to be clearer about "the Law"—that it is not evil, but holy, righteous, and good (Rom 7:7–13), even if it is, nonetheless, powerless against Sin. And, notably, the hints in Galatians concerning the significance of Israel are hugely expanded, with analysis of God's commitment

---

2. I use here the capitalized "Sin," to reflect the way that sin is represented in Romans as an agent with power. For analysis, see Matthew Croasmun, *The Emergence of Sin: The Cosmic Tyrant in Romans* (Oxford: Oxford University Press, 2017).

in mercy to his people (Rom 9–11). Paul here indicates on scriptural grounds why Israel is special, even while he names Jews and gentiles alike as recipients of God's grace (1:16; 10:10–12; 11:28–32). So, has Paul found in Israel some preexistent element of worth that justifies its special place? Or is its specialness itself the product of the incongruity of grace?

The language of "grace" in Romans is clustered in strategic places and is mixed with related terms ("love" and "mercy") that indicate further aspects of the benevolence of God. Paul introduces the Christ-event with a combination of gift terms ("as a gift, by his favor," 3:24), and these are expanded in the macro-contrast between Sin and grace (5:12–21), where near-synonymous gift-terminology (*charis; charisma; dōrea; dōrēma*) occurs eight times in the space of three verses (5:15–17). In between, Paul declares that "we have access . . . to this grace in which we stand" (5:2), which is glossed as the "love" of God, displayed in Christ and poured out by the Spirit (5:5–11; cf. 8:31–39). The gift language continues in Romans 9–11 (e.g., 11:5–6, 29) but is supplemented there by reference to the "mercy" of God (9:16, 18, 23; 11:30–32; cf. 12:1). God's grace and mercy are not identical, but, as we shall see, they overlap in meaning and character, both being unconditioned and undeserved.[3] The good news can be summed up in the one word "grace" ("Where Sin increased, grace superabounded," 5:20), but it can also be characterized as "the power of God" (1:16).[4] The resurrection of Jesus constitutes, for Paul, that explosive moment when the power of the Spirit was let loose (1:3–4), creating the dynamic of life-out-of-death on which the believers' trust is pinned (4:24–25) and in which their identity is formed (6:1–12; 8:9–11). This resurrection power is the hallmark of grace in Romans, in its capacity to create out of nothing, despite the weakness and worthlessness of its object.[5]

In this reading of Romans, I will highlight the ways in which Paul perfects the incongruity of grace and its efficacy, its capacity to overcome Sin and human powerlessness. Romans also demonstrates the superabundance of grace—a theme Paul underlines in multiple ways in Rom 5:12–21. But, as we noted, the presence of one or two perfections does not imply the presence

3. For their semantic fields and cultural resonances, see the appendix in my *Paul and the Gift* (Grand Rapids: Eerdmans, 2015), 575–82, and Cilliers Breytenbach, *Grace, Reconciliation, Concord: The Death of Christ in Graeco-Roman Metaphors* (Leiden: Brill, 2010), 207–38.

4. For a highly readable guide through Romans, with attention to its focus on God and power, see Beverly R. Gaventa, *When in Romans: An Invitation to Linger with the Gospel according to Paul* (Grand Rapids: Baker Academic, 2016).

5. See J. R. Daniel Kirk, *Unlocking Romans: Resurrection and the Justification of God* (Grand Rapids: Eerdmans, 2008).

of the rest, and we still have to determine whether, for instance, this letter perfects the singularity of grace (that God is gracious *and not* punisher or judge) or its noncircularity (that grace expects nothing in return). I will argue, in fact, that these two perfections are *not* evidenced in Romans and that the letter evinces a theology that might appear paradoxical, but only to those who have confused the incongruity of grace with its noncircularity. Paul expounds in multiple ways the incongruity of grace, unconditioned by the worth of its recipients and unlimited by their sinfulness and hostility to God. But the purpose of this grace is to *remake* its recipients, to transform them as they draw new life out of a reality that is not their own but in which they share. By this gift, always undeserved, they are molded into a holiness that accords with the will and character of God, such that the *unfitting* gift is designed to create a *fitting* outcome. In this chapter, we will trace how this pattern emerges in the first five chapters of Romans.

Human Sin and the Creative Power of God (Romans 1:16–3:20)

When Paul announces the "good news," what he highlights is "the power of God for salvation to everyone who believes, both the Jew—first—and the Greek" (Rom 1:16). The peculiar way in which Paul interrupts his "both . . . and" by interjecting "first" indicates that in one sense this good news affects everyone alike, but in another, there is something distinctive and special about "the Jew." That formula is repeated in 2:9 and 2:10, and echoed in 3:1–2 ("What is special about the Jew?"), as pointers toward the full discussion of Israel in chapters 9–11. This story of grace and power has special resonance with the story of Israel, even if it now takes effect among all peoples. "The righteousness of God" (1:17) is revealed in this good news. That phrase has multiple senses, but it here connotes a divine act: it is not only that God is consistent or correct but that God puts the world to right and corrects what is wrong (cf. 3:5, 21, 25).[6] It thus entails a power that, as Abraham found, "gives life to the dead and calls into existence the things that do not exist" (4:17). This power is not a supplement

---

6. "The righteousness of God" has many connotations in Romans and cannot be limited to one meaning only; see the overview of scholarly debates in E. P. Sanders, *Paul and Palestinian Judaism* (London: SCM, 1977), 523–42. "Covenant faithfulness" is not its primary sense, *pace* N. T. Wright, *Justification* (London: SPCK, 2009). For its connotations of power, see Ernst Käsemann, "'The Righteousness of God' in Paul," in *New Testament Questions of Today*, trans. W. J. Montague (Philadelphia: Fortress, 1969), 168–82.

to human capacity, an enhancement added to partial human achievement: it operates precisely where humanity has reached the end of the road.

The material running from 1:18 to 3:20 starts (1:18–32) and finishes (3:9–20) with depictions of human sinfulness but is not confined to that topic. History is here viewed from the perspective of the ultimate judgment of God (2:1–11), and when seen from that end point it includes not only those who "do what is wrong" and receive judgment but also those who "do what is good" and receive "glory and honor and peace" (2:10). The inclusion of both types of people suggests that these chapters do not only describe human sin. Rather, while breaking down a common stereotype of "Jewish righteousness" and "gentile sin" (2:9–10), Paul remaps humanity and anticipates what he will expound later: that God will remake and reorient those (both Jews and gentiles) whose lives are transformed by the Spirit (2:13–15, 29; 7:4–6). If the topic here were only human sinfulness, these would be a purely hypothetical category, or a blatant contradiction of Paul's main point. But Paul is already juxtaposing judgment with salvation because he is eager to display that God is already at work to remake the world—but not on the lines or by the means that one would expect.[7]

The foundational analysis of human unrighteousness (1:18–32) most obviously concerns the idolatry and immorality of the gentile world. Many Jewish texts of this time draw similar portraits of gentiles, but there is a particularly close relationship between Romans 1–2 and Wisdom of Solomon.[8] But there is a twist. In Wisdom of Solomon, after a lengthy diatribe against gentile idolatry (chapters 13–14), the author addresses God and insists that "we" (Jews) know better: "For even if we sin, we are yours, knowing your power; but we will not sin because we know that you acknowledge us as yours" (Wis 15:2). Paul tracks Wisdom of Solomon some of the way but then diverges dramatically (Rom 2:1–11).[9] For Paul, there can be no equivocation: those who judge others but

---

7. Many interpreters have struggled to make sense of Romans 2, and some have reached for extreme solutions. E. P. Sanders considered it a synagogue sermon that had little to do with Pauline theology, *Paul, the Law, and the Jewish People* (Minneapolis: Fortress, 1983), 123–35. Douglas Campbell treats it as the viewpoint not of Paul but of Paul's opponent, *The Deliverance of God: An Apocalyptic Reading of Justification in Paul* (Grand Rapids: Eerdmans, 2009).

8. On the relation between these texts, see Jonathan A. Linebaugh, *God, Grace, and Righteousness in Wisdom of Solomon and Paul's Letter to the Romans: Texts in Conversation* (Leiden: Brill, 2013).

9. Francis Watson, *Paul and the Hermeneutics of Faith* (Grand Rapids: Eerdmans, 2004), 405–11.

do the same cannot be exempt from God's judgment (2:1–4). The impartiality of God allows no ethnic distinctions: God judges all, both Jew and gentile, on the same terms (2:5–11).

The author of 4 Ezra hoped that there might be a tiny number of "the righteous" who would fulfill the criteria for salvation because they knew and kept the Law (see chapter 3). For Paul, knowing the Law is one thing, keeping it is quite another (2:12–13; cf. 3:20). Such is the power of Sin that even those Jews who take pride in the Law and teach it to others are tragically confounded by their inability to keep it (2:17–25).[10] But there are some, even gentiles, who do (2:14–16, 26–27). How so? Although some scholars see these gentiles as a purely hypothetical entity, Paul probably anticipates here what he will clarify later, that those whose hearts are transformed by the Spirit are able to "bear fruit for God" (2:29; 7:4–6).[11] Thus, when Paul speaks of gentiles who have the Law "written on their hearts" (2:15), we should think of Jeremiah 31 ("I will put my Law within them, and I will write it on their hearts," Jer 31:33), a text that Paul applies elsewhere to gentile converts (2 Cor 3:2–6). And when he speaks of Jews whose circumcision is "hidden," "of the heart," and "by the Spirit" (2:28–29), we should think of key passages in Deuteronomy (Deut 29:29; 30:6, "The LORD your God will circumcise your hearts"), which Paul takes to be fulfilled by the Spirit (Rom 7:6). In other words, Paul is speaking of believers—Jews and gentiles—whose Spirit-transformed lives create the fruit that God will judge "in accordance with their works" (Rom 2:6).

For those (in the Protestant tradition) who find Paul's language of grace and justification hard to square with "judgment according to works," this passage (together with Rom 14:11–12; 2 Cor 5:10, etc.) is a serious stumbling block.[12] But that arises from a confusion between different "perfections" of grace. God's grace is indeed incongruous with the worth of its recipients: it is unconditioned by their ethnic or moral worth since no one of any ethnicity has grounds to claim righteousness fitting for salvation. But it does not leave recipients as they were. By the transformative power of God, those previously

---

10. Since Augustine, this text has been wrongly interpreted as a critique of Jewish arrogance; in fact, it depicts the tragedy of those who find that the Law is not an effective antidote to Sin.

11. The reading I follow is expounded by Francis Watson, *Paul, Judaism and the Gentiles: Beyond the New Perspective*, 2nd ed. (Grand Rapids: Eerdmans, 2007), 205–16, and Simon J. Gathercole, "A Law unto Themselves: The Gentiles in Romans 2:14–15 Revisited," *Journal for the Study of the New Testament* 85 (2002): 27–49.

12. See discussion in Kent L. Yinger, *Paul, Judaism, and Judgment according to Deeds* (Cambridge: Cambridge University Press, 1999).

disobedient will exhibit "the obedience of faith" (Rom 1:5), and those who bore fruit for death will bear fruit for God (7:4–6). Thus, God's incongruous grace creates congruity—people who "under grace" are committed to serve righteousness and holiness (6:12–21). This obedience is not the product of merely human effort: it is "written on the heart" (Rom 2:15) and Spirit-formed (2:29), the product of the newly created self. As becomes clear in Romans 6, that new self is ever dependent on the resurrection life of Christ: for that reason, it remains incongruous with the worth and capacity of the believer, even when it produces this congruous result. For the judgment that Paul depicts in Romans 2 is not God's decision to allocate a new, second, and finally decisive gift but the recognition and reward of the work produced by the single, incongruous gift of life in Christ. It is unimaginable for Paul that a Spirit-circumcised heart will *not* produce work that is pleasing to God: in that sense, the works evidenced here are necessary for the fulfillment of salvation. But they are not its root or cause: that is the powerful work of God that is and remains utterly undeserved.

Paul is aware of the delicate balance he maintains here (cf. 6:1–2). In 3:1–8 he insists that God's faithfulness is not dependent on the faithfulness of his people: in the midst of Sin, God's righteousness will prevail and will be manifested as God's (3:3–5). But if this righteousness is incongruous—given where there is no worth—has God abandoned his values? Are his gifts indiscriminate and unjust (3:5–7)? This is not an artificial question. It exposes the *problem* of the incongruous gift and the reason why Paul's contemporaries might consider this perfection of grace dangerous since it seems to subvert the moral order of the cosmos. Does a God who gives without regard for worth retain the moral authority to judge the world (3:6) and the sinner (3:7)?[13]

As Paul knows, his argument has taken us to the edge of theological good sense. That it does not take us *over* that edge is indicated by the fact that the final judgment *will* distinguish between good and evil, with the praise of God accorded to "good work" (2:6–11). But this is Paul's essential point: *the basis for that fit, the foundation and frame of the patient good work that leads to eternal life, is an act of divine power,* an incongruous gift to sinful humanity whose transformative effects will be evident at the judgment. This incongruity (God's faithfulness to the faithless) is the ground for Paul's hope, in a world corrupted by the universal effects of Sin. But the purpose of the unfitting gift is to create a fit, to turn lawless gentiles into those who keep the Law (2:12–15) and tres-

---

13. Paul's logic in these highly compressed verses is notoriously difficult to follow; for fuller discussion, see *Paul and the Gift*, 471–74.

passing Jews into Spirit-circumcised servants who bear fruit for God (2:28–29; 7:4–6; 8:1–4). All this is yet to be expounded in the following chapters, but the basic structure is already clear. By the power of God that effects the humanly impossible, something new is being formed in Christ, something that will bring about the fulfillment of both gentiles and Jews by orienting them to God in trust, thanksgiving, and obedience.

THE CHRIST-GIFT (ROMANS 3:21–26; 5:1–11)

As in Galatians, the good news announces an event of divine grace enacted in Jesus Christ (3:21–26). The language of gift suddenly clusters at this point (3:24), and the incongruity with the condition of its recipients could not be clearer: "All have sinned and lack the glory of God, being justified as a gift by his [God's] grace, through the redemption that is in Christ Jesus" (3:23–24). God's action in Christ is not a calibrated reward for the godly, nor merciful protection of the faithful few, but an utterly incongruous gift, given despite the universal worthlessness of its recipients. Like the Qumran *Hodayot* (see chapter 3), Paul finds *nothing* in the state of humanity that could explain the miracle of salvation. But whereas the authors of the *Hodayot* find an explanation in the predestined blueprint of creation, Paul points to an event in history that has altered the conditions of the world.

The dense depiction of the "redemption" effected in Christ in 3:21–26 is punctuated by references to "the righteousness of God" (3:21, 22, 25, 26), the last of which is expanded by the statement that God himself is "righteous" (or "just") in considering righteous the person who lives "by trust in Jesus" (*ek pisteōs Iēsou*, 3:26). As in Gal 2:16 (see above, chapter 4), Paul clarifies what he means by this shorthand expression by referring to "those who believe/trust" (*hoi pisteuontes*, 3:22).[14] Thus, despite recent arguments that Paul refers here to "the faith/faithfulness of Jesus," I think it best to read *pistis* as a reference to the faith (or trust) of those whose new mode of existence is dependent on what God has done in Christ.[15] What do believers trust? That in Christ God has displayed and enacted his "righteousness"—his realignment of a distorted cosmos—and that he has done that "justly" through decisively dispensing with

14. See R. Barry Matlock, "The Rhetoric of πίστις in Paul: Galatians 2.16, 3.22, Romans 3.22 and Philippians 3.9," *Journal for the Study of the New Testament* 30 (2007): 173–203.

15. For an alternative reading, see Douglas Campbell, *The Rhetoric of Righteousness in Romans 3:21–26* (Sheffield: JSOT Press, 1992). In Romans 4, it is Abraham, not Christ, who exemplifies *pistis*, and what he displays is not faithfulness but trust (4:5, 17–20).

Sin in an act of atonement (*hilastērion*, 3:25). Paul does not spell out the "mechanism" of this atonement (cf. 8:3: God "condemned Sin in the flesh") because his concern is only to indicate that Sin has been dealt with (not brushed under the carpet) and that those whose existence is derived from this saving act are properly considered in the right ("justified") by God. God's "righteousness" thus both overcomes what has corrupted the world and establishes its proper realignment, starting with those who are liberated and remade through the Christ-event in which they trust (cf. 8:18–25).

This "grace in which we stand" (5:2) is the product of God's unconditioned love (5:1–11; we will return to Rom 4 shortly). Paul goes out of his way to underline the *absence* of worth on the human side. While "we" were *weak*, Christ died on behalf of the *ungodly* (5:6); God proves his love in that "Christ died for us while we were still *sinners*" (5:8); we who were reconciled to God were *enemies* (5:10). The variety of terms underlines that the conditions for the gift were anything but positive. This is not a gift to the worthy: no fitting features can be traced in the recipients of God's love, not even in their hidden potential. And this is the costliest gift imaginable. Christ did not give some*thing*, he gave himself: the gift takes place in his *death* and concerns his *blood* (5:6–10).

Paul himself notes the oddity of such an incongruous gift: "Rarely will anyone die for a righteous person, though perhaps for a good person someone might be courageous enough to die" (5:7). One might presume that good gifts would be given to the worthy, and the costlier the gift, the more discrimination should be applied. One would hardly give one's life to an undeserving cause. Yet Christ died for the worthless, as an expression of unparalleled love. This is no throwaway donation: it is the costliest gift, given with the deepest sentiment to those who had nothing to render them fitting recipients. It is this strange, even nonsensical phenomenon that Paul parades in 5:1–11, but on this basis he has the highest hopes for the future. If God has gone to such lengths to reconcile his enemies, how confident can they be that his love will endure through all the vicissitudes they face (5:3–5), all the way to complete salvation (5:10)!

Paul has clearly thought deeply about what sort of gift was given in Christ, in the light of ancient sensibilities about the proper distribution of the gift. It was a gift to the utterly unworthy, but it was neither unjust nor thoughtless, neither impersonal nor trivial. Instead it was an act of costly, personal love that both met its recipients where they were and altered their condition. In this sense, the Christ-gift is the ultimate incongruous gift that creates a new possibility, arising from the "life" now given in Christ (5:10).

THE ABRAHAMIC FAMILY TRAIT (ROMANS 4)

As in Galatians, the figure of Abraham forms the bedrock of God's purposes in history, since he stands at the origin of the covenant story of Israel (Genesis 12–26). As we have seen (in Gal 3:8–9), one reason why Paul is drawn to Abraham's story is that it contains the original promise of blessing to all the nations. This promise is the scriptural foundation for Paul's mission to the gentiles, and a significant part of Romans 4 is taken up with clarifying that Abraham is, indeed, the father of both Jews and gentiles (4:9–17). But that is not all. Paul here returns to Gen 15:6 ("He trusted God and it was reckoned to him as righteousness" [my translation]), which forms the base text for the whole of Romans 4. Paul knows the context of this verse: what Abraham trusted was a promise that God would do the impossible, that Abraham and Sarah would have an heir. What interests Paul is *how* Abraham became the father of this Jew-and-gentile family. The answer is: by trust (faith). This is not some special spiritual achievement but absolute dependence on the God who gives where there is no human achievement or capacity. Thus, while some scholars have stressed that Abraham stands at the origin of the Abrahamic family, and others have taken him to be the paradigmatic believer, Paul sees him in both roles. Or better, Abraham has a *programmatic* role: his story not only starts the history of the Abrahamic family but sets its tone. He indicates that to belong to this family is to trust in the incongruous gift and power of God.[16]

The opening verses of Romans 4 zero in on Gen 15:6 and its connection between trust and righteousness. Paul picks out an absence in the text of Genesis: although there is talk of "reward" (Gen 15:1), nothing is said about what Abraham had done to deserve it. There are no works here rewarded with "pay," only a promise, received in trust. This, for Paul, is the foundational character of the Abrahamic story: it concerns not pay/reward but gift, and gift not to the worthy but to the "ungodly" (4:4–5). Once again, Paul perfects *charis* (gift/grace) as an *incongruous* gift, so startling that God is here described as one who "justifies the ungodly" (4:5).[17] God does not reward the righteous Abraham: Abraham had no recorded worth. Similarly, David functions as the spokesman of those who are blessed only because their sins are forgiven (4:7–8).

16. Compare the discussion by N. T. Wright, "Paul and the Patriarch," in his *Pauline Perspectives: Essays on Paul 1978–2013* (London: SPCK, 2013), 554–92. In my view, Wright gives insufficient weight to the opening verses of the chapter and thus to the *mode* in which the Abrahamic family is formed.

17. For the biblical (but also universal) definition of the just judge as the one who does *not* declare the guilty "righteous," see Exod 23:7; Isa 5:23.

This incongruity between divine action and human status is the Abrahamic family trait; it is the rationale for God's calling of gentiles, as well as Jews, into this family. God's unconditioned blessing is clear in the reckoning of Abraham's righteousness (in Genesis 15) *before* he was circumcised (in Genesis 17). That shows, Paul insists, that circumcision is not a mark of differential worth, setting one ethnic group above another (4:9–12). Rather, it is a "seal" of something more basic (the righteousness reckoned by God), which is shared by both gentiles and Jews who trust in God (4:11). That does not mean that circumcision should be abandoned by Jews (cf. 3:1–2): it is not a negative factor and can continue to play its (subsidiary) role, inasmuch as Abraham was the father of both the circumcised and the uncircumcised who trust in God (4:11–12). Paul is not downgrading circumcision (or the circumcised) as somehow mistaken or superseded by noncircumcised gentiles. But he does want to clarify that the difference between Jews and non-Jews is not basic to the Abraham story. From the beginning, the Abrahamic blessing was blind to this significant token of differential worth.

By extension Paul argues in 4:13–22 that it is trust in God, not the Law, that is the medium of the Abrahamic story. This is not because trust is easily or universally accessible but because it is the stance of those who look to God—and only to God—in the absence of human capacity.[18] God's promise to Abraham, that he would be the father of many nations, was made at a time when Sarah was barren and Abraham was "as good as dead" (4:19). That Abraham would have *his own* children *with Sarah* was a complete impossibility. But he trusted in "God who gives life to the dead and calls into existence the things that do not exist" (4:17). *That* is what it means to be Abrahamic, to call Abraham "father" and to be part of his family—to trust in the God who creates "out of nothing" (*ex nihilo*). Paul finds a deep connection here between the gift of God in the absence of human worth and the power of God in the absence of human capacity: both are features of the God who "calls into existence the things that do not exist." This is the ultimate justification for Paul's mission to the gentiles and for his delight that, despite the universal power of Sin, God has acted with a still greater power to create righteousness and life (5:12–21).

This life-creating power, with its promise of God's intentions for the world, has been demonstrated in the resurrection of Jesus. Thus, Abraham's trust is

---

18. Cf. Benjamin Schliesser, *Abraham's Faith in Romans 4* (Tübingen: Mohr Siebeck, 2007). To take Abraham's faithfulness or "trusting loyalty" as a condition of God's grace turns this chapter on its head; see Stanley Stowers, *A Rereading of Romans: Justice, Jews, and Gentiles* (New Haven: Yale University Press, 1994), 241–44.

fulfilled in the form of the believer's trust "in him who raised Jesus our Lord from the dead" (4:24). To believe in the resurrection is, for Paul, to believe in the God who does the impossible and to trust that the gift of new life to the dead is what God wills for everyone and everything. It is not just to believe a past fact but also to trust in a present and future reality that wraps believers into its miraculous momentum, since Jesus's death was "because of our trespasses" and his resurrection "for our justification" (4:25). Believers find that what was written about Abraham was written "for us" (4:23–24) because they live by an identical trust that the God who raises the dead has created *their* "newness of life" through the resurrection of Jesus (6:1–6).

CONCLUSION

The opening chapters of Romans confirm that, as in Galatians, Paul figures God's grace as incongruous with the worth of its recipients and consciously develops this perfection. Paul parades not the match but the mismatch between the gift and power of God, on the one hand, and the worth or capacity of the human, on the other. Indeed, such noncorrespondence is characteristic of the Abrahamic family from the very beginning. As in Galatians, this theology is at the service of the gentile mission and undergirds Paul's conviction that the traditional distinction marked by circumcision is not of definitive significance. This mission is central to Paul's identity and it has a distinctive theological rationale, deeper than any political ideal of "equality." Paul's gentile mission reflects his understanding of the Christ-event as God's fulfillment of the Abrahamic promises in the mode of incongruous gift.

Paul does not set himself here in opposition to other, contemporary Jews. Although he criticizes any Jewish pride in the Law that is not matched by practice (2:17–29), and although he may be aware that the Abraham story could be read differently (4:1–2), he does not present the Jewish tradition or his fellow Jews as wedded to a soteriology of "works" in contradistinction to "grace." As we saw in chapter 3, Paul was part of a contemporary Jewish debate about the operation of divine mercy or grace. What is distinctive about Paul is not that he believed in the possibility of God's incongruous grace but that he identified this phenomenon with the love of God *in Christ*, that he developed this perfection of grace in the context of the gentile mission, and that he rethought his Jewish tradition in this light, going all the way back to Abraham.

This gift of God is, and remains always, incongruous—*a gift created out of human nothingness* and received in trust. But it is designed to produce obedient lives that, by a transformative heart-inscription performed by the Spirit, produce what is pleasing to God. This grace justifies the ungodly but its purpose is not to leave them that way. In this sense, the grace of God is *unconditioned* (given in the absence of merit or worth) but not *unconditional*, if by that we mean without expectation of alteration in the recipients of the gift. It is free in the sense that it is without prior conditions; and it remains always a miraculous, unconditioned gift, forged out of human incapacity. But it is not free (or "cheap") in the sense that it expects no transformative result. Viewed in this way (that is, distinguishing between different "perfections" of grace) we can understand why the opening chapters of Romans emphasize *both* the grace given without regard to works (4:1–5) *and* the expectation that those who have been transformed by the gift will have something to show for it on the day of judgment, something described in outline as "doing the good" (2:10).

Viewed in this light, some of the longstanding disputes between Protestants and Catholics, and among Protestants themselves, concerning Paul's theology of grace and works can be reduced or even resolved. We will return to that matter in chapter 12, but we can perhaps already sense how Paul puts together what we often artificially divide. The following chapters of Romans will make clearer still how grace can be both liberative and transformative, both free and demanding, and it is to those chapters that we now turn.

CHAPTER 8

New Life in Dying Bodies (Romans 5–8 and 12–15)

In Romans 5–8 Paul parades both the incongruity of grace in a world dominated by Sin and death (5:12–21) and its powerful effect in forming heart-obedience and holiness (6:15–23). Paul describes this double-sided phenomenon at some length, with the event of baptism at its center (6:1–14), and this enables us to see how the incongruous grace of life in Christ in an important sense *remains incongruous* with the condition of believers even while they "bear fruit for God" (7:4) and please God through the Spirit (8:1–13). We will discover here the importance of the body as the site of the believer's obedience and the significance of practice as the expression of the gift of life.[1] And since talk of the "presentation" of the body links chapter 6 (6:12–14, 19) with the beginning of chapter 12 (12:1–2), we will follow the thread of Paul's thought into chapters 12–15, which spell out how the new embodied allegiance of believers takes shape in communal life.

UNDER THE REIGN OF GRACE (ROMANS 5–6)

In the second half of Romans 5 (5:12–21), Paul maps the event of Christ onto the whole human story by a series of comparisons (and contrasts) between Adam and Christ (cf. 1 Cor 15:20–28). On the Adam side is a story of Sin leading to death, where the Law proves less than helpful because it cannot counteract the power of Sin (5:12–14, 20). On the Christ side is an event of gift or grace: with an extraordinary compilation of terms (*charis, charisma, dōrea, dōrēma*), Paul underlines in every way possible that the divine response to Sin is not (as one might expect) judgment but the grace event of Christ: "If

---

1. For a rich collection of essays on Romans 5–8, see Beverly R. Gaventa, ed., *Apocalyptic Paul: Cosmos and Anthropos in Romans 5–8* (Waco: Baylor University Press, 2013).

the many died through the one man's trespass, much more have the grace of God and the gift in the grace of the one man, Jesus Christ, abounded for the many" (5:15). The language of abundance serves to show not just the greatness of God's grace but its capacity to overpower a vast negative phenomenon by the more-than-matching surplus of its opposite: "Where Sin increased, grace hyper-abounded" (5:20). What occurs in Christ is a great reversal. Judgment from one man's sin led to condemnation (5:16), and out of many sins one expects that more condemnation will result. But the gift, out of many sins, leads to justification (5:16)! The relentless momentum of Sin, with its inexorable consequence in condemnation and death, is not just stopped in its tracks; it is *reversed* by a counter-momentum that leads out of Sin into life (5:17). This is the dynamic of re-creation, the hallmark of grace (cf. 4:17), which creates life out of its opposite, death (5:21).[2]

Because of this strange incongruity, there arises the question of 6:1: If grace abounds not as the reward for righteousness but in response to Sin, should we maximize its operation by continuing in Sin? The more Paul's theology emphasizes the power of grace in the midst of Sin, the more it might be heard to encourage sinning. Normal gifts would not evoke that suggestion, but an incongruous gift, given where there is no element of desert, certainly might.

In fact, Paul has already hinted that this is not so since he describes the superabundance of God's grace as "reigning through righteousness" (5:21). Far from offering a license for sin, the Christ-gift establishes an alternative regime of power. In baptism (6:1–14) a new life is formed, sourced in the resurrection life of Christ, and this "newness of life" (6:4) has a new structure of allegiance and obligation. Those who owe their life to Christ are not to let Sin reign in their mortal bodies, to obey its desires (6:12), because there is an alternative power now at work in their lives, the power of grace. "Sin will not rule over you, because you are not under the Law, but under grace" (6:14). Grace is a gift with power: it is no accident that the following verses (6:15–23) use the language of "slavery" and "obedience," signaling that everyone is under one power or another, Sin or Righteousness. Paul's cosmos has no neutral zone, no pocket of absolute freedom, no no-man's-land between the two fronts. The gift of God in Jesus Christ has established not liberation from every kind of authority but a new allegiance, a new responsibility, a new "slavery" under the rule of grace.

The ancient world—as well as most cultures today—recognized that gifts

---

2. For fuller treatment, see Martinus C. de Boer, *The Defeat of Death: Apocalyptic Eschatology in 1 Corinthians 15 and Romans 5* (Sheffield: Sheffield Academic, 1988).

convey power. A gift expects reciprocity, and the recipient is obliged to make a return, in one form or another. None of Paul's hearers would have been surprised to learn that, as recipients of the divine gift, they were placed under obligation to God. The notion of a gift "without strings attached" was practically unimaginable in antiquity; it is, as we have seen, a product of the modern era (see chapter 2). Even if Paul's language of "slavery" may seem overly strong to us (and Paul may be aware that it sounds extreme, 6:19), the sense that the gift of grace carries obligations is basic to the structure of Paul's theology (cf. 12:1–2).

But for Paul there is something more. The gift in this case is the grace of Christ (5:17), and the believer's new identity is formed in the tightest possible connection to Christ, the risen Lord. What grace conveys is not a thing but a person; it establishes a relationship where the gift cannot be separated from the person who gave it. Grace is not an object passed from Christ to believers or a quality infused into them: it is, first and foremost, a transformative relationship with the Giver. Thus, as Ernst Käsemann once put it:

> The gift which is being bestowed here [in salvation] is never at any time separable from its Giver. It partakes of the character of power, in so far as God himself enters the area and remains in the arena with it. Thus personal address, obligation and service are indissolubly bound up with the gift.[3]

In the modern West, we are culturally attuned to think of obligation as the opposite of gift: surely, we say, gifts should be absolutely "free," putting no pressure on the recipient. That, however, is a modern notion, and even for us a bit of a fantasy: as we know deep down, "There is no such thing as a free lunch." For Paul, as for all his contemporaries, gifts combine elements of voluntariness and obligation: they are not coerced or coercive, but they do carry expectations, even obligations of return. In fact, Romans 5–6 illustrates particularly clearly that a perfection of grace in one dimension (incongruity: without regard to the worth of the recipient) does not entail the perfection of noncircularity (expecting nothing in return). There is no possibility here of "cheap grace." Paul contrasts the gift (*charisma*) of God with the wages (*opsōnia*) of sin (6:23): unlike wages (or soldiers' rations, as the term sometimes means), the Christ-gift does not correspond to the worth or work of the recipient. But, at the same time, the gift leads toward a life of holiness and

---

3. Ernst Käsemann, "'The Righteousness of God' in Paul," *New Testament Questions of Today*, trans. W. J. Montague (London: SCM, 1969), 168–82, at 174.

righteousness (6:22). This holiness is not figured by Paul as a gift that believers give back to God; nor is it instrumental in winning a second, final gift from God at the last judgment. It is the necessary product of the one gift—necessary in the sense of inevitable, inseparable, and indispensable. The incongruous gift is entirely undeserved but strongly obliging. If that sounds peculiar to us, the problem is in our mentality, not Paul's.

Newness of Life: Ex-centric Existence in Christ

Paul has a distinctive way of understanding the life of believers: he matches it to the death and the resurrection of Jesus. For him our selves are constituted not by "substance" or "essence" but by relationship: who we are is forged out of our relationships.[4] Thus, in Pauline terms, you may be "alive to" something or "dead to" it (in Greek, this is expressed with the dative case): that is, your relationship to that thing/person may be formative or it may be broken. In Galatians, it was a case of being "dead to the Law" so that one might "live to God" (Gal 2:19) or of the world being "crucified to me and I to the world" (Gal 6:14). In Romans 6, it is about being "dead to Sin" and "alive to God" (Rom 6:10–11). In both texts, the language of death and life comes from the narrative of the crucifixion and resurrection of Jesus, but this is applied to believers not just by analogy but by a form of solidarity, even *participation*. Believers do not just die *like* Jesus, they die *with* him; they do not just live a life *similar to* his resurrection life, they live *from* and *in* that life.[5] Baptism constitutes, for Paul, simultaneously death and life—the death of the "old self" (6:6) and a "newness of life" (6:4)—and this life is no ordinary existence but the product of an impossibility, the resurrection of Christ. Because Paul associates the word "resurrection" with the reconstitution of bodies (cf. 8:23), and because this new life is present within bodies that are still mortal (6:12), participation in resurrection in the fullest sense remains in the future tense ("We *will* be united with him in a resurrection like his," 6:5).[6] But this does not lessen the sense in which everything that may be said about the believers' new mode of

4. See Susan G. Eastman, *Paul and the Person: Reframing Paul's Anthropology* (Grand Rapids: Eerdmans, 2017).

5. See Grant Macaskill, *Living in Union with Christ: Paul's Gospel and Christian Moral Identity* (Grand Rapids: Baker Academic, 2019); Michael Gorman, *Cruciformity: Paul's Narrative Spirituality of the Cross* (Grand Rapids: Eerdmans, 2001).

6. In Colossians (2:12; 3:1) and Ephesians (2:5–6) there is talk of already "being raised" with Christ, but Romans 6 uses a different pattern of language.

existence—their allegiances, dispositions, emotions, and actions— is attributable to the miraculous life of Christ himself. As Paul had put it in Galatians: "It is no longer I who live, but Christ who lives in me" (Gal 2:20).

Because this new life is sourced elsewhere, outside of human resources and in the life of the risen Christ, Paul does not figure salvation as a reformation of the human person, like some newly discovered technique in self-mastery. Believers live a life derived from elsewhere, in a kind of "ex-centric" existence (an existence whose center is outside of oneself) that draws on Jesus's life from the dead. They are, as it were, walking miracles, all the more evidently miraculous because this new creation life begins while they still inhabit bodies destined for an earthly death. In Romans 6–8, Paul repeatedly emphasizes the mortality of the body: "Let not sin reign in your mortal bodies" (6:12); what you inhabit presently is "a body of death" (7:24); the Spirit will finally vivify "your mortal bodies" (8:11). Whereas Christ has finished with death (6:9), believers have not: they are dead to Sin (6:11) but not dead to death. This puts their lives into a state of permanent ontological incongruity: in one respect they are heading toward death (8:10), but in another they are alive, in a "newness of life" (6:4) that in source and character is the life of Christ.

Many interpreters have noted that Paul presents the believers' lives in these chapters as double-sided in some paradoxical way, but it is important to be clear about the paradox. The Protestant Reformers, following the later Augustine, thought that Romans 7 (the frustration of the self by Sin, 7:7–25) described one aspect of the believer's life, and Romans 8 (life in the Spirit) the other. Thus, in Luther's famous tag, the believer is simultaneously justified and a sinner (*simul justus et peccator*).[7] Most modern interpreters (myself included) do not now read Romans 7 this way: it is better understood as Paul's retrospective view of an unbeliever's life in captivity to Sin, not as a description of the believer's frustration by Sin. In other words, it is better to read Romans 7 and 8 as a "before" and "after" story (as suggested by the introduction in 7:4–6).[8] Nonetheless, there is another kind of paradox that does run through these chapters, concerning the presence of new life in dying bodies (we might dub this *simul mortuus et vivens*, "at the same time dead and alive"). Believers

---

7. For exposition, see Stephen J. Chester, *Reading Paul with the Reformers: Reconciling Old and New Perspectives* (Grand Rapids: Eerdmans, 2017).

8. Nearly all the recent commentators on Romans follow this line, with the exception of Dunn and Cranfield. See, however, the recent treatment by Will Timmins, *Romans 7 and Christian Identity: A Study of the "I" in Its Literary Context* (Cambridge: Cambridge University Press, 2017).

are at one and the same time dying (in a body bound by mortality) and alive. They are the site of an impossible new life whose origin lies in the resurrection of Jesus and whose goal is their future resurrection (8:11). This paradox is the sign that God's grace is permanently at odds with the natural (post-Adamic) condition of the human being, however much believers may (and should) grow in holiness.

If the normal human condition (life "in the flesh") is unable to keep the Law and to please God, the new self is constituted by a life lived in and from the Spirit (8:1–9). In Romans 8 Paul speaks most fully about the Spirit—a more precise and personal way of speaking of the "newness of life" (6:4) that is at work in believers, who are joined to the resurrection of Christ. The Spirit is the Spirit of Christ (8:9), such that Paul can speak of both the Spirit and Christ indwelling the believer (8:9–10). The Spirit does not *take the place* of the believer, as if one agency overrides the other. Paul can give instructions to believers (here in 8:12–13, and much more in later chapters), who are not merely puppets on a string, controlled by the Spirit. But their agency is enabled and sourced in the agency of the Spirit.[9] What Paul expects of believers is not that they create a new existence but that they express what has already been created in and by Christ. The primary reality is what is true of Christ and present in the Spirit. The believer's new self is a secondary reality, derived from Christ, and it exists in a form that is contrary to its surrounding habitat: life in the midst of death, hope in the midst of suffering (8:18–39). But such a life subsists to the extent that it is active. To "present yourselves to God as alive from the dead" (6:13) and to "put to death the deeds of the body" (8:13) are the positive and negative poles of a demand to practice the new life that has been given. Indeed, that new life cannot be said to be active *within* believers unless it is also demonstrably acted out *by* them.

THE BODY AND THE CONSTRUCTION OF A CHRISTIAN HABITUS

What does it mean for believers to "consider themselves dead to Sin and alive to God in Christ Jesus" (6:11)? The following two verses spell this out in four clauses that put notable emphasis on the body:

9. One of the best theological analyses of this dynamic is by Karl Barth. See the illuminating discussion by John Webster, *Barth's Ethics of Reconciliation* (Cambridge: Cambridge University Press, 1995).

> So, do not let Sin rule *in your mortal body* to make you obey its
>   desires,
> nor present *your limbs* as weapons of unrighteousness to Sin,
> but present yourselves to God, as people alive from the dead,
> and *your limbs* as weapons of righteousness to God. (6:12–13)

It is striking that to present "yourselves" to God is given very physical expression, by reference to the body and its limbs.[10] The self here is not something anterior to, or separable from, the body; to the contrary, the body is the site where the self is identified and defined.

Scholars have long disputed what Paul means by "the body" (*sōma*) and why it seems so important to him, but it is now commonly recognized that physical embodiment is an essential component of Paul's understanding of the human self.[11] Through the body we participate in relationships and are connected to spheres of influence that go beyond our individual particularity. Indeed, in Paul's perspective, we express here, in the body, our solidarity with powers that hold sway across the cosmos, divine or anti-divine. The body belongs to Sin or to God. As Ernst Käsemann put it, the presentation of the body to God is where God lays claim to "that part of the world that we are in our bodies," raising the flag of God's sovereignty over territory that has been liberated from Sin.[12] And since God intends to vivify the mortal body (8:11), here the future is promised in the present.

What is demonstrated in the body of the believer is that overlap between the present reign of death and the new life of grace that springs from the resurrection of Christ. It is in the body that the believer is both visibly on the path to death and is required, visibly, to display the presence of the risen Christ, in the service of righteousness and holiness. Paul rightly speaks of the body with the military language of "weapons" (*hopla*, 6:13, 19; cf. 13:12), since it is the site of resistance to Sin. The body was once appropriated by Sin but is now reappropriated by Christ. The very place where Sin once had most visible sway, and where its grip still draws believers' bodily selves toward death, is now the location where the "newness of life" breaks through into sight. In this tug-of-war between death and life, Christian obedience *in the body* displays the fact

---

10. So again in 6:19; note the reference to the limbs in relation to Sin in 7:5, 23 (x2).

11. See Dale B. Martin, *The Corinthian Body* (New Haven: Yale University Press, 1995).

12. Ernst Käsemann, *Commentary on Romans*, trans. Geoffrey W. Bromiley (London: SCM, 1980), 177–78; cf. his essay "On Paul's Anthropology," in *Perspectives on Paul*, trans. Margaret Kohl (London: SCM, 1971), 1–31.

that a miraculous counterforce is already at work, "putting to death the deeds of the body" by the superior power of the Spirit (8:13).

Paul outlines what we call "ethics" in Romans 6–8 in a way that anticipates Romans 12–15, but without the specificity of the later chapters. Here he is concerned with the ethic-structuring orientations, allegiances, and dispositions that undergird particular practices. At issue is what he calls "the mindset" (*to phronēma*) which governs the body—a mindset either of the flesh or of the Spirit (8:6–8). This is expressed in ethical practices, but it operates at a deeper and more comprehensive level.

The best way to articulate what this means is to use the concept of the *habitus*, as developed by the anthropologist Pierre Bourdieu. He suggested that, at a level deeper than specified rules, cultures operate by "a system of lasting, transposable dispositions" which shape the way we view the world and ourselves. These are expressed in practices and are shaped by practices but are so taken for granted that they are rarely spelled out.[13] "Behave yourselves," we say to children, as if they and we just knew what that meant—it has been inculcated countless times by the way we behave and speak. For Bourdieu, it is essential that this *habitus* is embodied, written into all kinds of bodily habits and behaviors (like standing up to greet someone or looking them in the eye when you thank them); these express our values in simple bodily actions. The body, as it were, "learns" our values and is also crucial to how we perceive, order, and practice the reality we inhabit.

Paul also links the body with the mind in a way that makes the body crucial to the expression of one's whole life-orientation: "Present your bodies as a living sacrifice. . . . Be transformed by the renewal of your minds" (12:1–2). Even the emotions, which are both bodily and cognitive phenomena, are part of this matrix: the old life was a slavery to fear (8:15) and the new life is characterized by peace, both relational and emotional (8:6; cf. 5:1). Although the Law is good and holy (7:12) it could not avoid "bearing fruit for death" (7:5) because it was powerless (8:3) and received by a body "inhabited" by Sin (7:17, 20), that is, with a deeply inculcated *habitus* of Sin. What is needed is rescue from this "body of death" (7:24), a new mindset operative in new patterns of behavior, appetite, and practice.

The physical rite of baptism is a highly effective demonstration of this "rescue," a transition from death to life performed on and with the body. Because the *habitus* is so deeply engrained, it takes time for a new set of allegiances

---

13. Pierre Bourdieu, *Outline of a Theory of Practice*, trans. Richard Nice (Cambridge: Cambridge University Press, 1977), 72–95.

to take full bodily effect, but the baptismal act of "putting on Christ" (13:14; cf. Gal 3:27) requires a change of habits that will alter the whole repertoire of bodily actions (Rom 13:12–14). And because the body is affected by its social interactions, this will never be a solo affair. The new "mind" will require new collective practices, a new communal life—as outlined in Romans 12–15.

A COMMUNITY CONSTRUCTED BY GRACE (ROMANS 12:1–15:13)

Paul skillfully begins his more detailed ethical instructions by appeal to "the mercy of God" (12:1; literally, "mercies," but the plural is a Hebraism). "Mercy" is the gift-term he had used extensively in Romans 9–11 (to which we will return in the next chapter), where it became clear that mercy bears no relation to the preceding status, achievement, or worth of its recipients (9:6–18; 11:32). To live on this basis is to allow one's values and norms to be recalibrated—a "transformation of the mind" that will newly determine what is "good and acceptable and perfect" (12:2). This transformation will not clash at every point with the modes of behavior found in the Roman world: there will be some overlap in the understanding of what is "good" and "bad" (12:17), and no *inevitable* clash with the interests of the governing authorities (13:1–7).[14] But the new orientation to the Lord (12:11) will involve a mindset whose assumptions and priorities are newly configured, in distinction from "this age" (12:2).

If all are received in Christ on the basis of "the mercy of God," there is no room for individual boasting or the carryover of hierarchical assumptions from the social environment. As in Galatians (see chapter 6), a high premium is here placed on a communal spirit that counters the competitive quest for honor. Each person is to view themselves with modesty and not to inflate themselves (12:3); as Paul puts it elsewhere, "What do you have that you have not received?" (1 Cor 4:7). Paul can speak only because of the grace given to him (12:3), and each member of the body has their place in the community, and their unique contribution toward it, only on the basis of "the grace given to us" (12:6). The *charis* (grace) of God distributes gifts (*charismata*) by which

14. Romans 13:1–7 undercuts readings of this letter as a subtle attack on the Roman Empire, although Paul, of course, would consider the worship of emperors a form of idolatry. For my response to N. T. Wright (and others) on this matter, see "Why the Roman Empire Was Insignificant to Paul," in John M. G. Barclay, *Pauline Churches and Diaspora Jews* (Grand Rapids: Eerdmans, 2016), 363–87. For a discussion of method, see Christoph Heilig, *Hidden Criticism? The Methodology and Plausibility of the Search for a Counter-Imperial Subtext in Paul* (Minneapolis: Fortress, 2017).

the members of the body support one another (12:5–8). Developing the body-motif (cf. 1 Cor 12:12–31), Paul envisages a community so interdependent that all are figured, individually, as limbs of one another (12:5), everyone essential to everyone else.

Within this community, honor does not have to be sought: all the honor that counts has already been given, or will be given, by God (2:29; cf. 1 Cor 4:1–5). Believers are freed from the need to *establish* their honor through competition or in retaliation against those who harm them (12:14, 17–21), and they can afford to grant honor without reservation to others. In fact, in 12:10 Paul outlines a paradoxical inversion of the normal honor-quest: in loving one another, believers strive to take the lead not in claiming honor but in giving it to one another (12:10). Because this is done in a reciprocal way, no one is left demeaned, but all are supported within a community where every member matters.

What this means in practice is given outline shape in the instructions of 12:9–21. "Sibling love" involves moral and emotional support ("Weep with those who weep," 12:15) but also financial commitments to "share the needs of the saints" in the kind of economic support that Paul assumes will be present in all his churches (12:13; cf. Gal 6:2, 6, 9–10; 1 Thess 4:9–11).[15] This communal generosity is also to be extended to outsiders (12:14, 17–21), since the love of Christ knows no boundaries. In their new social relationships in Christ, those of higher social status are required to shed their snobbery in associating, on a level, with "the humble" (12:16). Since their only true worth is that given in Christ, the old social pecking order, with its differentials of worth and honor, is now seen to be hollow, and new relationships are founded on the sole ground of love (13:8–10).

Paul applies this in the greatest detail in relation to meals (14:1–15:6), because meals were where Christian community was most obviously formed or deformed (cf. 1 Cor 11:17–34), and (probably) because there were cultural clashes around meals in the Roman assemblies. Paul addresses here disputes about food and "days"—and his use of the language of clean/unclean (14:14, 20) suggests that this concerns Jewish traditions concerning food and Sabbaths.[16] Those whom Paul calls "weak in faith" are inclined to refuse all meat at the assembly's common meals, lest it be tainted by uncleanness (they eat only

---

15. See Bruce W. Longenecker, *Remember the Poor: Paul, Poverty, and the Greco-Roman World* (Grand Rapids: Eerdmans, 2010). See further chapter 11 below.

16. For analysis, see "Do We Undermine the Law? A Study of Romans 14.1–15.6," in my *Pauline Churches and Diaspora Jews*, 37–59.

vegetables, 14:2), while "the strong" (among whom Paul counts himself, 15:1) believe that anything can be eaten since nothing is unclean in itself (14:14). The "weak" thus condemn the "strong" for their laxity, while the "strong" despise the "weak" for their scruples (14:3). In addressing this dispute, Paul's first move is to re-present the believers to each other as "welcomed" by God (14:3; cf. 15:7). To judge or despise a fellow believer is to impose on them an evaluation of worth, but the first thing to say about them is that God has welcomed them, according them worth that no human evaluation can overturn. What is at stake is what God has created ("the work of God," 14:20), people whose value is based on the fact that Christ died for them (14:15). They are to be welcomed because they stand before God on the basis of Christ's welcome (15:7). To recognize one another in that light is already to dissolve the presumption that traditional criteria of judgment can be transferred into the community of believers.

With the new status comes a new allegiance: welcomed by Christ, each believer is also beholden to Christ, as a slave is beholden to no one other than his/her master (or "lord" [*kyrios*]; 14:4–12). Paul emphasizes this at length because he wants to orient all moral decisions to Christ. Whether eating or not eating, whether observing or not observing special days, the action is justifiable only if it is done "to the Lord" and "with thanks to God" (14:6–9). The final criterion here is allegiance to Christ, and whatever believers do must spring from trust in him (14:22–23). Believers may practice that orientation to Christ in various cultural forms, Jewish and non-Jewish, just as Paul himself does in the course of his mission (1 Cor 9:19–23). One might keep kosher, or one might eat anything, so long as one's eating is in honor of Christ. Both patterns of behavior are legitimate if they are forms of service to the Lord.

Paul wants the "weak in faith" to be welcomed, since their faith is genuine and their desire to keep kosher is integral to their commitment to honor Christ as Lord (14:6). Their faith is labelled "weak" not because it is timid, but because it is vulnerable, attached to a set of cultural traditions that they cannot abandon without abandoning Christ. If they were pressured by fellow believers to discard their way of honoring Christ, they would be "destroyed" (14:15, 20). Paul will do anything to avoid that outcome (cf. 1 Cor 8:1–13). The "strong" are also expected to act at all times from faith, but kosher customs are not integral to their faith: they can keep kosher or not, both in honor of Christ. Their "strength" is the degree to which they have been able to uncouple their faith in Christ from norms that are not derived from the good news itself.[17]

17. For further analysis, see John M. G. Barclay, "Faith and Self-Detachment from Cul-

Thus Paul can require them to accommodate their eating at communal meals to the scruples of the "weak" without any danger to their faith. Their priority is to walk in love (14:15), the love that "builds one another up" (14:19); nothing they do must end up causing harm.

For Paul, there is only one supreme, nonnegotiable, and all-pervasive good: serving Christ. One can do that in various ways, in this cultural tradition or that; and for the sake of love one may need to adjust one's behavior to accommodate (even adopt) others' traditions. Our tendency to view our own cultural traditions as somehow superior makes forming a mixed community difficult. Mutual welcome will require the members to relativize their traditions—not necessarily to abandon them but to subordinate them to the higher goal of serving Christ, or what Paul calls here "the kingdom of God," whose values include love, righteousness, peace, and joy in the Holy Spirit (14:15, 17). What matters above all is people: because they have been valued and welcomed by Christ, one must do all one can to secure and support them. Once again, the values of the community are recalibrated by the good news that every member has received an unconditioned welcome by Christ.

Conclusion

Paul's careful handling of disputes over food indicates how important it is that the "newness of life" arising from the Christ-event is expressed in practices that are reframed in allegiance to Christ. The new *habitus* of believers can become effective only in bodily practice. It is no accident that the practice discussed here concerns communal meals. As in Antioch (Gal 2:11–14) and Corinth (1 Cor 11:17–34), shared meals may make or ruin a community. At times, Paul's focus is strongly individuated: *each* believer has a responsibility and a *charisma* within the body (12:3–8), and *each* is answerable to Christ for the practice of his/her faith (14:12, 22). But that responsibility to Christ is expressed in, and for the sake of, the community, where every member depends on others for their growth and "upbuilding" (14:19). As they form a community, Jew with non-Jew (15:7–13), socially superior with socially inferior (12:16), "strong" with "weak," believers recognize and embed in practice the worth of others who are "welcomed" by Christ (15:7). Because this grace is unconditioned, it undercuts the normal systems of differentiation—as can be demonstrated only in a com-

---

tural Norms: A Study of Romans 14–15," *Zeitschrift für neutestamentliche Wissenschaft* 104 (2013): 192–208.

munity which self-consciously crosses ethnic, social, and cultural lines. (We shall explore what this might mean in contemporary terms in chapter 13.)

However, life "under grace" (6:14) has its own structure of obligation. As we have seen, Paul figures believers as "slaves" both in Romans 6 and in Romans 14. This allegiance results from receiving the "welcome" of Christ or the "mercy" of God. The Christian life is a peculiarity, a "newness of life" active within a mortal human body. Everything in this new life refers back to its source in the Christ-gift and forward to its eschatological fulfillment in resurrection. Everything that can be said about Christian action, obedience, and obligation arises from this generative basis, because this new life is created and sustained by the resurrection life of Christ. Hence, the obligation on believers is not to win a further installment of grace or to "gain" salvation. A single *charisma* of eternal life (6:23) runs from the Christ-event to eternity (8:39), not a series of graces won by this or that increase in sanctification. Paul certainly believes that the *moral* incongruity at the start of the believer's life will be reduced over time, as they are drawn toward holiness (6:19). When they come before the judgment seat of God to give an account of themselves (14:10–12), he expects that they will evidence a life lived in light, not darkness (13:12; cf. 2:6–16). But this does not reduce the essential *incongruity* of grace, since the life from which this holiness and light arise is an ex-centric creation, sourced in the resurrection life of Christ. Baptism enacts and dramatizes this transition, but believers never progress "beyond" this truth: from first to last they are saved in, and only in, the life of Christ (5:10).

Thus, the gift is entirely undeserved but strongly obliging, unconditioned but not unconditional. It is circular but only by remaking the human agent who responds to the gift. The "obedience of faith" is not instrumental toward acquiring an additional gift, but it is integral to the gift itself, as newly competent agents express in bodily practice their freedom from Sin and slavery to Righteousness. Without this obedience, grace is ineffective and unfulfilled.

CHAPTER 9

Israel, Christ, and the Mercy of God
(Romans 9–11)

For long periods of Christian history, Romans 9–11 has been interpreted as a treatise on divine predestination and human free will, with scriptural illustrations. We now recognize that the subject is Israel, its past, present, and future—not as an illustration of something else but because Israel itself is important to Paul. We noted earlier the striking formulation in 1:16 ("to both the Jew—first—and also the Greek"; cf. 2:9–10), and it was clear already in 3:1–8 that Paul had more to say on this subject. Even so, Romans 9–11 has often been treated as an appendix, after the main argument of the letter is over (chapters 1–8), as if we could stop reading at 8:39 and lose nothing essential. But that will not do. Even as an "apostle to the gentiles" (in fact, especially in that role), Paul understands the purposes of God in history to be irrevocably tied to the calling and destiny of Israel. He cannot do theology without thinking about Israel, both because Israel's Scriptures constitute his primary resource and because he takes the story of Israel to be central to all God's dealings with humanity. In these chapters Paul is most self-consciously Jewish and most creative, and in that creativity, induced by the Christ-event, he rethinks the identity of Israel. Scholars have often had difficulty finding coherence in these chapters, but we will trace a single pattern of incongruity that is basic to God's calling of Israel, by which Paul makes sense of the strange reversals of the present, and in which he finds hope for the future.

THE CRISIS OF ISRAEL

Romans 9–11 is full of emotion, the product of grief and shock. Paul's deep sorrow (9:1–2) and his earnest prayer for the salvation of Israel (10:1) arise from his self-identification with fellow Israelites (9:3–4; 11:1), whom he perceives as standing at a moment of crisis. The cause of that crisis is the failure of "some" (in fact, most) to believe in the Messiah Jesus (cf. 3:3), an unbelief that jeopardizes their salvation (9:32; 10:1) by severing their connection to the "root" that sustains them (11:17, 20). Echoing Moses (Exod 32:32), Paul contemplates discarding *his* salvation for the sake of theirs (9:3). What makes this crisis shocking is that Israel's unbelief concerns nothing less than the Messiah himself (9:5), who has become, paradoxically, a stumbling-block (9:32–33). But to trip up here is to miss the goal of Israel's history (9:4–5; cf. the *telos* of the Law, 10:4).

Paul's first response to this crisis is to recount God's promises and Israel's privileges: "They are Israelites, and to them belong the adoption, the glory, the covenants, the giving of the Law, the (temple) worship, and the promises; theirs are the patriarchs, and from them springs the Messiah, in terms of human descent" (9:4–5). These are for Paul, as for other Second Temple Jews, irrevocable privileges: the only question is how their promise will be realized. "It is certainly not the case that the word of God has fallen" (9:6). Has God rejected his people? "No way" (11:1–2). At the end of Romans 8, Paul had made the resounding declaration that "nothing can separate us from the love of God in Christ" (8:39), and it has sometimes been suggested that Romans 9–11 is an example, from the story of Israel, that God will not discard those he has chosen. But it would be better to put this the other way around. Gentile believers are to find in God's dealings with Israel not a *parallel* story of divine reliability but the *root* of their own experience of grace (11:17–24). What has happened in Christ can only be understood as the definitive expression of God's incongruous mercy to his people, right from the start (Rom 9) and right to the end (Rom 11). This discussion of Israel is not an illustration of something else: if Paul cannot make sense of what is happening to Israel, he cannot make sense of history, Scripture, or Christ at all.

As we have seen (chapter 7), in preparing for his arrival in Rome, Paul needs to portray his message and his role as "apostle to the gentiles" on a large canvas. He here speaks about himself with a rare intensity (9:1–3; 10:1–2; 11:1, 13–14), perhaps to counter the impression that some have gained, that he no longer cares about Israel. But the mission to gentiles does not make sense, for Paul, without the larger context of Israel. If some gentile believers thought (as many have done in the centuries since) that Israel was a relic of the past, that idea was wholly impossible for Paul. From Paul's perspective, there can be no salvation of gentiles *without Israel*. The surprising "wealth" of God's mercy to gentiles (11:12) is a sign not that God has abandoned Israel in favor of gentiles but that God will have mercy on *all* and that the presently "hardened" Israel will be saved (11:11–32).

In Romans 9–11 Paul makes sense of Scripture, of the present crisis, of the gentile mission, and of God's purposes for Israel by finding in all these inter-linked phenomena *the paradoxical operation of God's incongruent grace*. In recent decades, scholars have puzzled long and hard over these chapters, with many conflicting results. Some consider that when Paul says "all Israel will be saved" (11:25–26), he envisages Israel's salvation as taking place on a different basis than that of the gentiles, through the Law-covenant and not through faith in Christ.[1] But that makes incomprehensible Paul's statement about Christ as Lord of both Greek and Jew (10:12–13) and his anxious prayers on Israel's behalf (10:1–2). Others think that in that famous statement ("All Israel will be saved"), Paul uses "Israel" in a special sense, referring to gentile and Jewish believers.[2] But that hardly fits Paul's careful use of the term "Israel" in these chapters, particularly when he refers to the hardening of some in Israel (11:25) and then the salvation of all (11:26). In fact, most scholars think that Paul's argument in Romans 9–11 is inconsistent: up to the end of chapter 10 (or 11:10), it seems that God's promises are fulfilled in the salvation of a remnant of Israel, but after that point Paul switches track and insists that all Israel must and will be saved.[3] Here I will argue that, for all the changes in focus, Paul pursues a consistent theme that ties his arguments together. From the start, Israel has been constituted by the incongruous mercy of God, which pays no regard to criteria of fittingness or worth (9:6–29). The Christ-event shares this pattern, as role reversals between Jews and gentiles reveal that salvation depends on nothing other than the righteousness and power of God (9:30–10:21). And in the final step of the argument, before the coda of praise (11:33–36), Paul takes the gentile mission as evidence of the "wealth" of God's mercy, whose appli-cation to the *disobedient* gives confidence that God's grace will be powerful enough to reconstitute Israel as a whole (11:1–32). At each step, mercy without condition is the pattern of God's ways.[4]

---

1. This is the so-called *Sonderweg* thesis, that Israel and the gentiles each have their own, "special way" to salvation. One recent advocate is John Gager, *Reinventing Paul* (Oxford: Oxford University Press, 2000).

2. See, e.g., N. T. Wright, *Paul and the Faithfulness of God* (London: SPCK, 2013), 2:1231–52.

3. E.g., Francis Watson, *Paul, Judaism and the Gentiles: Beyond the New Perspective*, 2nd ed. (Grand Rapids: Eerdmans, 2007), 301–43.

4. For a reading of Romans 9–11 parallel to this, see Jonathan A. Linebaugh, "Not the End: The History and Hope of the Unfailing Word," in Todd D. Still, ed., *God and Israel: Providence and Purpose in Romans 9–11* (Waco: Baylor University Press, 2017), 141–63.

THE CREATION OF ISRAEL BY THE MERCY OF GOD
(ROMANS 9:6–29)

"It is certainly not the case that the word of God has fallen" (9:6). The crisis constituted by Israel's unbelief raises the question whether God has gone back on his promises to Israel, but that is an option Paul rules out straightaway. In the first stage of his answer (9:6–29), he gives three examples of divine selection (9:6–18), using antitheses ("not . . . but") to hammer home that God's gracious election does *not* operate by any criteria of worth. In a comparison between God and a potter (9:19–23), the emphasis falls again on the unconditioned nature of the divine decision, while further scriptural texts indicate that God can create a people from "non-people" (including gentiles, 9:24–26) and can select in Israel a remnant, both in judgment and in hope (9:27–29). This passage is thick with scriptural citations, drawn from "the Law and the Prophets" (3:21) and ranging across Israel's history. Together they put the spotlight on God, who *creates* history and forms the people of his choice without regard to their fit or worth.

The whole of Romans 9–11 is designed to show that the word of God has not fallen (9:6) and that "the gifts and the calling of God are irrevocable" (11:29). But to understand how that is so Paul must clarify how that word and those gifts have shaped Israel's history from the very beginning. Many read this first stage in the argument (9:6–29) as showing that God's word never applied to all Israelites: God's promise has not failed because, from the beginning, he selected some and not others, and thus, in the present, he has likewise selected some (who believe in Christ) and not others (who do not).[5] But the issue in 9:6–18 is not *whom* God has chosen and whom he has left out, nor simply *that* he has exercised his choice.[6] The emphasis lies on *how* God has created his people, Israel, as Paul takes care, again and again, to exclude from the reckoning multiple criteria that might have influenced God's choice.

The second half of 9:6 is best translated thus (slightly woodenly): "It is not the case that all who are descended from Israel, these are Israel." As the following verses (9:7–9) make clear, the point is not to designate a subgroup within Israel who are called "Israel" in a special sense but to show that the people of

---

5. See Heikki Räisänen, "Paul, God, and Israel: Romans 9–11 in Recent Research," in *The Social World of Formative Christianity and Judaism,* ed. Jacob Neusner et al. (Philadelphia: Fortress, 1988), 127–208.

6. John Piper puts the emphasis on the sovereignty of God, *The Justification of God: An Exegetical and Theological Study of Romans 9:1–23,* 2nd ed. (Grand Rapids: Baker Academic, 1993).

Israel was never determined by genealogy alone. Abraham had another child (Ishmael), but the Abrahamic family chosen by God was formed via Isaac, not Ishmael. This was according to God's "word of promise" (9:9): the people of Israel was generated (miraculously) by divine promise, not simply through physical descent ("children of the flesh," 9:8). Although Israel is made up of biological descendants of Abraham, not *all* of Abraham's descendants become "Israel." Thus, from the start and at the end of the day, Israel is a creation of God and not of biology. God's choice of one son over another indicates that behind genealogy there is another, more basic criterion for selection—namely, God's selection alone.

The case of Jacob and Esau (9:10–13) tightens the analysis by removing other possible factors. Both were born of the same mother and the same father and were even conceived at the same moment (9:10): there is nothing to distinguish them in their conditions of birth. God's choice took place before they were born and thus before they had done anything—good or bad—to qualify or disqualify them for election. Paul underlines that this choice was "not from works but from the one who calls" (9:12), with "calling" indicating here not invitation but the creative initiative of God (cf. Gal 1:6, 15).[7] All the emphasis lies on God's unconditioned will: there was *no* corresponding condition in the humans concerned. As if to exclude one further criterion, Paul cites the pronouncement that "the greater shall serve the lesser" (Gen 25:23): differentials of status (or age) are so irrelevant as to be turned upside down (9:12).

Paul has thus ruled out all forms of symbolic capital humanly ascribed or achieved: birth, status, and moral behavior are *not* the grounds for God's election. In discussing such scriptural stories, the Jewish philosopher Philo (see chapter 3) was anxious to insist that there *is* a reason for divine selection, perhaps in God's foreknowledge of the character of those unborn: because he knew their name, God foresaw whether they would be good or bad and chose accordingly (*Allegorical Interpretations* 3.65–100). Philo's anxiety is understandable: his aim was not to *dilute* the grace of God but to *explain* it, lest God's choice appear arbitrary or unfair. For Philo (and for others), there must be something about the objects of God's choice that fits them to be chosen. To deny that would bring into question the justice of God—which is exactly the question Paul raises in 9:14: "Surely there is no injustice with God, is there?" Paul knows that he is walking a dangerous path. That he continues is a sign that

---

7. See Beverly R. Gaventa, "On the Calling-into-Being of Israel: Romans 9:6–29," in *Between Gospel and Election: Explorations in the Interpretation of Romans 9–11*, ed. Florian Wilk and J. Ross Wagner (Tübingen: Mohr Siebeck, 2010), 255–69.

his argument rests on the outrageous claim that Israel's election is justified by nothing other and nothing deeper than the will and choice of God.

In the following verses (9:15–18), Paul gives a third example of divine selection and cites God's promise following the crisis of the golden calf: "I will have mercy on whom I have mercy, and I will have compassion on whom I have compassion" (9:15; Exod 33:19). The sentiment in this citation is hopeful: if God will be merciful, as he was at Sinai, there is hope beyond judgment. But it is also disconcerting: the text does not specify to whom God will be merciful (that is God's decision), and it is phrased in the future tense, such that the divine will is unknown and *in principle unknowable*.[8] Another antithesis ("not from (our) willing or running, but from the God who has mercy," 9:16) takes even the human will out of the equation, and divine mercy is contrasted with the "hardening" of Pharaoh, without reference to Pharaoh's actions or character. That silence leads to Paul's scandalous conclusion: "So [God] has mercy on whom he wills, and hardens whom he wills" (9:18).

Why would Paul take us to this cliff-edge, and why in this context? The topic here is the making of Israel, not divine predestination in general or in the abstract. Paul here strips away all natural and reasonable explanations for Israel's election to show that God's mercy never has been, and never will be, dependent on human achievement or status. Israel is suspended from the single (but strong) thread of God's mercy, which is exercised by God alone, irrespective of Israel's attributes. That is disconcerting but also the *only* ground for hope, because in the midst of universal disobedience *everything* depends on the mercy of God (11:28–32).

The double possibility—of mercy or hardening—runs through the potter analogy (9:19–23), which envisages two kinds of pot, "vessels of mercy" and "vessels of wrath prepared for destruction" (9:22–23). That looks like a settled "double predestination," and has often been read that way, but it is important to note two things. These twin possibilities are not based on some pretemporal or natural destiny (as they are in the Qumran *Hodayot*), nor are they quite as final as they seem. The pots "prepared for destruction" are not shown here being destroyed, and that leaves an opening for Paul's hope in Romans 11.[9] But for now the essential point has still to be rammed home: God is in charge of

8. See further, John M. G. Barclay, "'I Will Have Mercy on Whom I Have Mercy': The Golden Calf and Divine Mercy in Romans 9–11 and Second Temple Judaism," *Early Christianity* 1 (2010): 82–106.

9. See the careful discussion of this passage in J. Ross Wagner, *Heralds of the Good News: Isaiah and Paul in Concert in the Letter to the Romans* (Leiden: Brill, 2002), 71–78.

history and his creative power is unlimited. The formation of God's people has always been under God's merciful control, and the (adapted) citations from Hosea in 9:25–26 bear witness to this fact. "I will call those who were not my people, 'My people,' and the one who was not beloved, 'Beloved'" (9:25, citing Hos 2:23). Hosea was speaking about the restoration of disobedient Israel, but Paul applies his words to the calling of God's people as a whole—now constituted not only by Jews but also by gentiles (9:24). If God calls those who are *not loved*, there is hope beyond the present crisis. We may sense here that Paul's gentile mission has given clarity and impetus to his theology of grace: if God can act in mercy *even to gentiles*, one may imagine a future in which even those presently excluded can be integrated again (11:11–32). Sometimes God's purposes operate through choosing a remnant (9:27–29), but even that can be a sign both of God's judgment and of his faithfulness.

Paul has here laid bare the characteristics of Israel's election, as a people created by divine choice, without regard to birth, achievement, disposition, or any other measure of worth. Their existence hangs on God's purpose, which can exclude or include, jettison or preserve, expand or reduce to a remnant, hate or love—and also turn again to love those not loved. Everything is designed to put Israel's past, present, and future into the hands of God, so that when Paul analyzes his present (9:30–10:21) and looks to the future (11:1–32) the primary question is not "What will Israel do now?" but "What is God capable of doing?" It is disconcerting to have the future taken out of human control—but ultimately the only ground of hope.

GOD'S INCONGRUOUS ACT IN CHRIST (ROMANS 9:30–10:21)

The central section of Romans 9–11 focuses on the anomalies created by the Christ-event, whose unconditioned mercy (or "wealth") rearranges the map of history. God's definitive act in Christ constitutes, for Paul, the climax of God's purposes for Israel, but puzzling reversals abound: gentiles succeed without trying, while zealous Israel misses the goal (9:30–10:4); God's "wealth" is given to all, without ethnic conditions (10:5–13); God is found by those who do not seek him, and Israel is provoked by a "foolish nation" (10:19–21).

The section begins with the story of an odd footrace, where the nonrunners (the gentiles) reach the goal, and the runner (Israel), who pursued "the Law of righteousness," has not attained it (9:30–32). These compressed statements indicate Paul's continuing surprise at his mission experience: gentiles respond to the good news, while Jews stumble on the "stone of stumbling and rock of offense" (9:33), a reference to the Messiah.[10] How could one explain such a phenomenon? In the opening verses of chapter 10, Paul commends his fellow Jews for their "zeal for God," but, in ignorance, they "seek to validate their own righteousness" and do not submit to God's (10:2–3). What does he mean by this contrast? Is "their own righteousness" what they seek to achieve by works, trying to gain salvation that only God can give? Or is it their "national" righteousness, where Jews are included and gentiles excluded?[11]

Another reading is possible. As we have seen, "God's righteousness" is identified by Paul with the gift of Christ (3:21–26; cf. Phil 3:4–11), a gift given without regard to Law-observance, from which no true worth can be established. Those who trust in Christ recognize that their worth derives from Christ and in that sense "submit to" the righteousness of God. But many of Paul's Jewish contemporaries have continued to regard Torah-defined righteousness as the criterion for God's gifts, thus opening up a gap between their understanding of "righteousness" and God's. Thus, despite their zeal, they have missed the "goal" (*telos*), which is Christ himself (10:4).[12] The problem with Law-based righteousness is not that it epitomizes human self-reliance, nor that it excludes gentiles, but that it does not and cannot provide a basis of worth before God, which is given wholly and only in Christ.

One might reasonably expect God to distribute his salvific gifts to the fitting or worthy; and in the Jewish tradition, the worthy would be those who are "righteous" in keeping the Law (cf. Phil 3:4–6). But Paul thinks that God has acted in Christ in a way that draws no distinction between "the righteous" and "the unrighteous," the runners and the nonrunners, the Jew and the gentile (9:3–33; 10:12–13). Paul has concluded that the "righteousness from the Law" is not the same as "the righteousness from faith" (cf. Phil 3:9), and he traces this distinction in the difference between what "Moses writes" (in Lev 18:5, cited in Rom 10:5) and what "the righteousness of faith says" (Deut 30:12–14, cited and interpreted in Rom 10:6–8). The latter makes clear that the gift is not something yet to be found (high in the heavens or deep in the abyss) but

---

10. See Wagner, *Heralds of the Good News*, 126–55.

11. For the former reading (characteristic of the Protestant tradition), see Ernst Käsemann, *Commentary on Romans*, trans. Geoffrey W. Bromiley (London: SCM, 1980), 277–82 (he speaks of a "perversion of God's will by pious achievement"). For the latter (characteristic of "the new perspective"), see N. T. Wright, *The Climax of the Covenant* (Edinburgh: T&T Clark, 1991), 241–42 (speaking of "national righteousness" and "racial privilege").

12. The Greek term *telos* can be translated as "end" or "goal" and may here have connotations of both. See Paul W. Meyer, "Romans 10:4 and the 'End' of the Law," in *The Word in This World* (Louisville: Westminster John Knox, 2004), 78–94.

has already been given in the resurrection of Christ.[13] The righteousness that comes from faith/trust is a standing before God that rests on the lordship of Jesus and on the life that has begun to remake the cosmos in the resurrection of Christ (10:9–13).

Thus, the Christ-gift confirms and deepens the pattern of incongruity traced through 9:6–29. As from the beginning, God has belied expectations of appropriateness or fit: his "wealth" is given to all who believe (10:12), regardless of their ethnicity, their righteousness, or their previous quest. If Israel was created and sustained by mercy, not worth, nothing can inhibit that mercy from extending also to the "worthless" gentiles. The strange inversions of the present time confirm the incongruity of this gift, and in these subversions, stumbles, and reversals God brings the paradoxical story of Israel to its climax in Christ. At present, the good news spreads to all the world, but Israel remains a disobedient people (10:14–21). And yet, as Isaiah said, God has "stretched out" his hands (10:21), a symbol of generosity. The story of grace has further to run.

THE MOMENTUM OF MERCY AND THE SALVATION OF ISRAEL (ROMANS 11:1–36)

The image of a "disobedient and contrary people" (10:21) raises the question that opens chapter 11: Has God rejected his people? The answer is a resounding no (11:1), but Paul spells that out in two steps. First, he points to the present remnant (11:1–10) and then to the future for Israel as a whole (11:11–32). That second step has often been considered illogical, an inexplicable twist, as if Paul here suddenly changes the rules of the game. But he has reason to think that the mercy that has flooded the world in Christ will sweep also over the people of Israel, whose existence has depended on mercy right from the start.

As an "Israelite" who has "called on the name of the Lord" (10:13), Paul himself is evidence that God's people have not been abandoned (11:1). Like Elijah, he is accompanied by a "remnant," other Jews who have come to believe in Christ (11:2–5). But it is important to clarify how this has happened. Four times in 11:5–6 Paul uses the term *charis*, including the programmatic statement: "If it is by grace, it is not on the basis of works, otherwise grace would not be grace" (11:6). Why this emphasis? The story of Elijah (concerning the "seven thousand who have not bowed the knee to Baal") might suggest

---

13. See the reading of this passage by Francis Watson, *Paul and the Hermeneutics of Faith* (London: T&T Clark, 2004), 315–41.

that God's choice of a remnant was *in response to* their obedience or "works." That would make God's choice still a gift, but a *congruous one.* In the case of Abraham, Paul insisted that grace worked in the absence of "works" (4:1–5). In Elijah's story there were works (the refusal to commit idolatry), but here too Paul insists on the incongruity of grace: whatever the human activity, it was irrelevant to God's choice and not the reason for his election. We note again the trademark Pauline perfection of grace as an incongruous gift. That is what opens the possibility that God may have mercy even (indeed, especially) on a "disobedient and contrary people" (10:21).

God *may* be merciful on Israel as a whole, but what makes Paul confident that he *will* be? The language of the "remnant" in 11:1–10 is accompanied by references to the "hardening" of others, and one could imagine a permanent split in Israel between the remnant and the rest. But the question and answer of 11:11 indicate that Paul will not stop there: "Have they stumbled so as to fall? No way!" At this point Paul appeals not to Scripture but to the gentile mission (11:11–16). In the success of that mission Paul traces the "wealth" (11:12) of God's mercy, where the least deserving are transformed by grace. If God can do something as anomalous as that, pouring his "riches" into the world, this will surely rebound to the place where his mercy has always been at home. Paul watches Israel's own goods (the favor of God) now spreading around the world, and this, he trusts, will cause Israel to be "jealous" (11:11, 14). "If their (Israel's) transgression means riches for the world, and their lack means wealth for the nations, what will their fullness mean?" (11:12). If God's grace has already had such dramatic effect, how much more will follow?

The olive-tree allegory, deployed in 11:17–24, clarifies Paul's point. Wild olive branches (gentile believers) have been grafted into a rootstock, and natural branches (Jews) cut off, but Paul's first task is to warn gentile believers not to think that they are special or superior. The depiction of Israel as a plant or tree (usually a vine) is common in the Jewish tradition (e.g., Isa 5:1–7; Jer 11:16), but Paul puts unusual emphasis on the *root* as the source of nourishment ("the root of fatness," 11:17) and as the support of the branches ("You do not support the root, but the root supports you," 11:18). What is represented by this root? The people of Israel are not the root, but the natural branches, which may be cut off from the root and later regrafted. The root could refer to the patriarchs, or to Abraham in particular,[14] but as we have seen, both in Romans 4 and in Romans 9, what matters about the patriarchs is not who they were but how

14. See Nils Dahl, "The Future of Israel," in *Studies in Paul* (Minneapolis: Fortress, 1977), 137–58. The commentaries on Romans discuss this question at length.

they came to be chosen. Paul equates staying connected to the root with remaining "in the goodness of God" (11:22), so it seems best to interpret this root as the grace or the mercy of God. Israel, as Paul had pointed out (9:6–18), was constituted by mercy and by promises given without prior condition. It is that same mercy into which gentile believers are now being "grafted," although it is not "natural" to them in the way it is to Israel. But if even wild olive branches can be grafted in, how much more can God restore those for whom this is their original and natural location (11:24).

Branches are cut off for "unbelief" (or "non-trust") or grafted in by "faith" (or "trust", 11:20, 23) because faith, as we have seen, constitutes dependence on a power and a gift outside one's control. To "stand in faith" (11:20) is to live entirely from the gift of God (cf. 4:4–6), and "faith" here, in line with 9:30–10:17, is the faith that confesses Christ as Lord and lives by participation in his resurrection life. This is not an arbitrary addition to the identity of Israel: its existence was always derivative, created and sustained by the calling of God. To draw on the life of Christ, the definitive expression of the goodness of God, is to live by the grace that has maintained Israel from its beginning (cf. 15:8). On Paul's reading, Israel thus draws again—in consummate fashion—on the sustenance of grace and becomes *not less but more like itself*. At the same time, the olive-tree allegory rules out any suggestion that Israel has been superseded by gentiles or that "the church" has taken Israel's place. To the contrary, what Paul envisages is the addition ("grafting in") of gentiles to a mode of existence characteristic of the people of Israel, who are ever dependent on "the gifts and the calling of God" (11:29).[15]

For God to restore Israel to its natural condition is easier to imagine than the current in-grafting of gentile branches: "How much more will those that naturally belong be grafted back into their own olive tree!" (11:24). The future passive (*will be* grafted) points to the agency of God and is notably confident. The miracle of gentile faith, the grafting-in of branches that did not originally belong, points to God's superabundant power, which will surely rehabilitate Israel. This confidence undergirds the "mystery": "A hardening in part has come upon Israel until the fullness of gentiles comes in, and so all Israel will be saved" (11:25–26). The present split within Israel will be resolved in the salvation of the whole. With most scholars, I take "all Israel" to refer to the whole people of Israel.[16] The coming Redeemer (11:26–27) is

15. For theological reflection, see Tommy Givens, *We the People: Israel and the Catholicity of Jesus* (Minneapolis: Fortress, 2014).

16. There is a full discussion of the options in Christopher Zoccali, "And So All Israel

probably Christ (cf. 1 Thess 1:10), who will banish "iniquity" and forgive Jacob's sins—an act of grace that mirrors the justification of Abraham (4:5–8). Israel's Abrahamic identity will thus be restored in Christ, under the impact of the world-enriching mercy of God. The incongruity evident in the formation of Israel (9:6–29) and in the current, paradoxical relation between gentiles and Jews (9:30–10:21) will be the pattern of God's action right to the end. Just as disobedient gentiles have received mercy, so Israel itself will receive mercy from God (11:30–31). If God will have mercy on whom he has mercy (9:15), and if disobedience is precisely where the incongruous mercy of God takes place, Paul trusts that God "has shut up all in disobedience in order that he might have mercy on all" (11:32).

Paul's final acclamation (11:33–36) celebrates the mysteriousness of this counterintuitive phenomenon. From first to last, from the calling of Abraham to the final redemption of Israel, God's mercy operates in the absence of worth. The character of the Christ-gift is the rubric of God's history with Israel and of all God's dealings with the world. The good news is "the power of God for salvation" (1:16). That has always been effective in the story of Israel, and what Paul hopes for in the end is the abundance of grace (5:20–21), the triumph of God's mercy (11:32), and the victory secured by the love of God in Christ (8:39).

Conclusion

This reading of Romans 9–11 has traced a narrative development through these chapters but not inconsistency nor an arbitrary shift at the end. The consistent narrative pattern is the incongruity of divine election, the absence of fit between divine mercy and the worth of its recipients. From start to finish, Israel is constituted by a calling that bears no relation to its worth, and into this Israelite privilege gentiles are drawn by an indiscriminate grace. This gives Paul confidence beyond the current "disobedience" of Israel, since the God who called Israel, without regard to their desert, wills to overcome their "impiety" by his world-embracing mercy, displayed in the extraordinary "wealth" of the gentile mission.

Whence did Paul derive this integrating theme? From his reading of Scrip-

---

Will Be Saved: Competing Interpretations of Romans 11:26 in Pauline Scholarship," *Journal for the Study of the New Testament* 30 (2008): 289–318. It is not clear what exactly is implied by "all," but it certainly means an overcoming of the situation where only a remnant believe.

ture? Certainly, as his citations here show. From his experience of the gentile mission? That seems also to have played a significant part. From the impact of the Christ-event? Clearly so, given the central role of Christ in these chapters (9:30–10:13) and in Romans as a whole. One might have interpreted each of these factors differently, but together they constituted a powerful frame of reference, which thrust into prominence God's unconditioned mercy as the hallmark of God's dealings with Israel and with the world in Christ.

The Christ-event is not just *one* example of this pattern. It is in every respect the definitive act of God's grace: final, complete, decisive, and comprehensive. But it does not come "out of the blue" and is not self-interpreting: it is the completion of the promise to Israel whose existence depends upon the mercy of God. The Messiah is from Israel (9:5), and the Redeemer will come from Zion (11:26): seen in this light, the strange workings of grace in the Christ-event and in the gentile mission are the climax of God's purposes for Israel. At the same time, Paul reads the story of Israel in Romans 9–11 in the light of the Christ-event, such that this history and these Scriptures bear witness to the righteousness of God in Christ. This creates a complex dialectic: Christ is read in the context of Israel, but Israel is also interpreted by reference to Christ. In the subsequent Pauline tradition, a parallel dialectic will be deployed in relation to Christ and creation, where the Christ-event is placed in the framework of all creation, and all creation is, at the same time, Christologically defined (Col 1:15–20; Eph 1:3–10). But here Paul's focus rests on the human story and on the central place of Israel within history. His achievement is to integrate the scriptural witness to Israel's unconditioned call with the good news concerning Christ and the strange success of the gentile mission. A single frame of explanation unites them all: incongruous grace.

CHAPTER 10

The Grammar of Grace and the Gift of Christ

As we have seen, Paul's theology of grace is not confined to his use of a single term, *charis*. It embraces a range of vocabulary and is patterned by a distinctive use of these terms to convey the notion of an *incongruous* gift. We should not confuse the study of a *concept* with the study of a *word*: a concept can be conveyed by a range of different terms, and their meaning is given not in isolation but in their context of use. Because *charis* belongs to the semantic domain of "gift," we have noted the variety of gift-terminology deployed by Paul, but we have also traced some of the deep connections between Paul's language of gift, love (e.g., Rom 5:6–8), mercy (Rom 11:28–32), welcome (Rom 14:3; 15:7), calling (Gal 1:15; Rom 9:25–26), and election (Rom 11:5). Moreover, in observing Paul's use of these terms we have found a consistent pattern, a repeated emphasis on the mismatch between the gracious power of God and the unfitting condition of its recipients. This incongruity, it turns out, is not just one motif in Paul, one idea that crops up here or there. A larger claim can be made: what we have identified in these explorations of Galatians and Romans is the structure or pattern of the leading ideas in Paul, what we might call the "grammar" of his theology.[1]

The grammar of a language concerns the structuring rules by which its words, phrases, and sentences are combined and ordered to make sense. (In your own language you are hardly aware of such a thing, but when you learn a very different language you soon appreciate how languages have their own patterns and structures.) The grammar of Paul's Greek is not especially peculiar, but the grammar of his theology certainly is. For a start, it is noticeable how often he uses paradox and marks his claims with surprising forms of antithesis:

---

1. For this notion (distinct from the old search for the "center" of Paul's theology), see Jonathan A. Linebaugh, "The Grammar of the Gospel: Justification as a Theological Criterion in the Reformation and in Galatians," *Scottish Journal of Theology* 71 (2018): 287–307.

"When I am weak, then I am strong" (2 Cor 12:10); "It is no longer I who live, but Christ who lives in me" (Gal 2:20); "The foolishness of God is wiser than human wisdom, and the weakness of God is stronger than human strength" (1 Cor 1:25). On any reckoning, these are odd expressions, but they indicate more than a love of paradox. They point to the peculiar shape or "grammar" of Paul's theology.

Some theologies work by a principle of extension or supplementation: one can extrapolate from what is true and good about the world or about humanity to what must be true and good about God at a higher level or to a greater degree. Natural beauty points to the greater beauty of God, and human reason gives a reliable clue to the higher reason of the universe. God must be greater, of course, but greater, in this conception of theology, on the same scale. Paul's theology refuses this principle of extension. The wisdom of God is not human wisdom enhanced, and the power of God is not a more powerful version of human power. Grace works not to supplement human capacity but in the absence of human power, not to reward worth but where there is none. Everything functions here by negation and reversal, by loss and gain, by death and new creation. The people of God trust in a God who creates *ex nihilo*, who "raises the dead and calls into existence the things that do not exist" (Rom 4:17).

Paul uses a variety of metaphors for salvation, largely taken from the sphere of social relations: to be saved is to be reconciled, adopted, justified, or freed. All of these are shaped by a pattern of incongruity, of radical alteration or complete reversal. We would expect "sons" to develop into their maturity and hence gain their inheritance, but in Paul's narrative they are relabeled slaves, who will not inherit unless they are both liberated and adopted (Gal 4:1–7). We would expect God to consider in the right ("justify") those who are righteous or worthy by one criterion or another, but he justifies "the ungodly" by a grace that matches no merit (Rom 4:1–8). We would *not* expect that Christ would die for God's enemies, or that the cursed would be blessed, or that the disobedient would receive mercy. At every point salvation works out of its opposite, righteousness from sin, life from death. It is as if Paul bends all his theological grammar into the shape of the death and resurrection of Jesus, so that every facet of God's saving power is first crucifixion then resurrection, first disaster then salvation, first death then life.

This is the pattern of the incongruity of grace, which disregards human canons of possibility, reason, or justice, and creates something out of nothing, where there is no fit or capacity. Even Paul's narratives (regarding Israel, the patriarchs, or himself) are told in a distinctive way, characterized not just by moments of surprise but by a structural pattern of grace in the absence of worth and life in the midst of death.[2] As we have seen, to be baptized is to participate in the death of Christ, to be buried with him, so as to share his "newness of life" (Rom 6:1–6); as Paul puts it regarding himself, "I have died . . . so that I might live" (Gal 2:19).[3]

This grammar of incongruity gives Paul's theology such creativity, enabling him to remap reality in such innovative ways. If God bypasses the traditional systems of order, reason, and justice, it is possible to imagine reality anew. We have already traced that phenomenon in Galatians and Romans, and we will turn here, briefly, to the Corinthian letters, to uncover there also this pattern of grace.

GRACE AND POWER IN THE LETTERS TO CORINTH

The church in Corinth was perhaps the most "successful" of Paul's churches, in terms of its growth and social integration, but in its understanding of the good news it was, in Paul's view, still at the stage of an infant (1 Cor 3:1–3). At the beginning of 1 Corinthians Paul criticizes the Corinthian believers for their factionalism (1 Cor 1:10–17), and he takes their competitive quest for honor to indicate their captivity to the norms of power and wisdom, core values of the urban culture of the Roman world.[4] Since the problem lies so deep, Paul goes to the heart of the good news and puts the spotlight on one thing and one thing only: "Christ crucified" (1 Cor 2:2). Paul's argument has a sharp edge. Elsewhere he reflects on the death of Christ from many angles: it is a form of atonement, effecting forgiveness of sins (Rom 3:21–26; 1 Cor 15:3); it is the moment when Christ absorbed (and "became") the curse that rests on humanity (Gal 3:13; 2 Cor 5:21) and when he overcame the power of Sin (Rom 6:1–10; 8:1–4). But in 1 Corinthians 1–2, Paul brings out something different. Here he depicts the death of Jesus as the epitome of folly and weakness, such

---

2. For an analysis of Paul's autobiographical narratives, see my essay, "Paul's Story: Theology as Testimony," in *Narrative Dynamics in Paul: A Critical Assessment*, ed. Bruce W. Longenecker (Louisville: Westminster John Knox, 2002), 133–56.

3. See Jonathan A. Linebaugh, "'The Speech of the Dead': Identifying the No Longer and Now Living 'I' of Galatians 2.20," *New Testament Studies* 66 (2020): 87–105.

4. "Wisdom" in 1 Corinthians refers to both education and rhetoric, since persuasive public speaking was one of the chief purposes of higher levels of education. See Bruce Winter, *Paul and Philo among the Sophists: Alexandrian and Corinthian Responses to a Julio-Claudian Movement*, 2nd ed. (Grand Rapids: Eerdmans, 2002).

that locating salvation *right there* subverts all that is normally associated with wisdom and power (1:18–25).

Paul here labels the death of Christ repeatedly a *crucifixion*: what he preaches is not just that Christ "died" but that he was *crucified* (1 Cor 1:17, 18, 23; 2:2, 8). In the Roman world, as everyone knew, crucifixion was designed to humiliate its victims; it was a form of elongated public torture that caused extreme pain and maximum shame.[5] The Romans used crucifixion especially for disobedient slaves and provincial rebels, and victims were deliberately elevated high, both for public visibility and to mock their claims to power. In this parody of elevation, the crucified were pinned helpless and naked. Gradually losing bodily control, they were shamed and degraded, rendered subhuman, their corpses normally left as meat for the vultures or crows. One would expect crucifixion to be an aspect of the fate of Jesus that no believer would want to showcase, but Paul insists: "We proclaim Christ crucified" (1 Cor 1:23). God's wisdom and God's power did their deepest work precisely here (1 Cor 1:24–25). There could hardly be a greater challenge to the "civilized" values of the Roman world and its obsession with power: "For God's foolishness is wiser than human wisdom, and God's weakness is stronger than human strength" (1 Cor 1:25).[6]

This counterintuitive message creates some socially surprising results. Who makes up the assembly of believers in Corinth? Not many of you, says Paul, were wise by human standards, not many were powerful, not many of prestigious ancestry (1 Cor 1:26). Education, social influence, and good family background were standard measurements of social worth in the Roman world. One would expect God to pick the "respectable" and the powerful, but in fact he does just the opposite: "God chose what is foolish in the world to shame the wise; God chose what is weak in the world to shame the strong; God chose what is low and despised in the world—things that do not exist—in order to reduce to nothing the things that exist, so that no one might boast before God" (1 Cor 1:27–29). This is an extraordinary claim that matches the extraordinary message of the crucified Christ. God has acted in Christ and in his "calling" of believers (1:26) not to enhance human virtues or to develop human capacities but to subvert these human forms of symbolic capital.[7] God works in the ab-

---

5. The classic work on this topic is Martin Hengel, *Crucifixion* (London: SCM, 1977); cf. John G. Cook, *Crucifixion in the Mediterranean World* (Tübingen: Mohr Siebeck, 2014).

6. For the figure of the fool, the vulgar antithesis to the civilized elite, see Larry L. Welborn, *Paul, the Fool of Christ: A Study of 1 Corinthians 1–4 in the Comic-Philosophic Tradition* (London: T&T Clark, 2005).

7. See John M. G. Barclay, "Crucifixion as Wisdom: Exploring the Ideology of a Dis-

sence of worth, to create something out of nothing. That is exactly the pattern we have seen elsewhere: the incongruity of grace.

Paul's clash with the Corinthians' value system becomes even more pronounced in 2 Corinthians (probably a single letter but perhaps a compilation of letters sent over the course of a few stressful months). From the beginning, it seems, Paul has been an embarrassment to some of the better-off members of this assembly, and other, more "respectable" leaders are beginning to eclipse his influence. He freely admits that his life and ministry are humanly unimpressive, but he traces across his own experience the paradox that God habitually creates from nothing, brings life out of death, in the pattern of the death and resurrection of Jesus. Both Paul and the Corinthians have been wounded, not least by the friction between them, but Paul's response is to call attention to the paradox of grace: just as we share in the sufferings of Christ, so we share in the comfort given by God in the midst of that suffering (2 Cor 1:3–7). Paul himself has come close to death and was reduced to depression or despair—but right there he learned to trust in the God who raises the dead (2 Cor 1:8–11). A little later Paul characterizes his apostolic ministry (and, properly, the life of every believer) as shaped in this peculiar way: we have the treasure of the knowledge of Christ in clay jars, so that the abundance of power might be (and might be seen to be) from God and not from us (2 Cor 4:7). Here again Paul highlights the misfit between divine power and human fragility and in his own buffeted experience finds himself "always carrying in the body the dying of Jesus so that the life of Jesus may also be made visible in our mortal bodies" (2 Cor 4:10–11).[8] Here, as in Romans, the body is the site of God's incongruous power: it is not the body beautiful, nor the body enhanced, but the body of suffering service that bears witness to the risen life of Christ. Once again, Paul draws attention to grace, as it extends to more and more people (2 Cor 4:15), because the pattern he is tracing is another example of the grace that makes human incapacity the site of God's power.

This paradox becomes even more pointed in Paul's emotive pleas in 2 Corinthians 10–13. In comparison with more sophisticated apostles, Paul is being dismissed in Corinth as a blustering fool: "His letters," it is said, "are weighty and strong, but his bodily presence is weak, and his speech is contemptible" (2 Cor 10:10; an ancient form of "body-shaming"). Paul is in a bind: he does not

---

reputable Social Movement," in *The Wisdom and Foolishness of God: First Corinthians 1–2 in Theological Exploration*, ed. Christophe Chalamet and Hans-Christoph Askani (Minneapolis: Fortress, 2017), 15–32.

8. See Timothy Savage, *Power through Weakness: Paul's Understanding of the Christian Ministry in 2 Corinthians* (Cambridge: Cambridge University Press, 1996).

want to play the Corinthians' rhetorical game, but the character of the good news is at stake, not just his personal reputation. So he offers the Corinthians a "boast" of his own, which he is careful to advertise as deeply ironic (2 Cor 11:21). He does not list his honors and achievements but supplies a kind of inverse curriculum vitae, highlighting the weak and shameful aspects of his life (2 Cor 11:21–33). Whatever he might have been given by way of knowledge is matched by a persistent physical deficiency, his "thorn in the flesh" (2 Cor 12:7). He does not spell out what that is, because the point is to spotlight not himself but the grace of God. "Three times I appealed to the Lord about this, that it would leave me. And he said to me, 'My grace is sufficient for you, for my power is perfected in weakness.' So I will boast all the more gladly in my weaknesses, so that the power of Christ might take up residence over me" (2 Cor 12:8–9). Once again, Paul's symbolic capital (his "boast") is ex-centric, derived not from him but from a power that is at work in the absence of human worth.

Here is the grammar of grace, divine power operative in the midst of human weakness. We have traced this grammar in Galatians and Romans in the justification of the ungodly and the reconciliation of enemies, but here it takes shape in the empowerment of the weak. The paradox of strength in weakness reflects the dynamic of the power of God in the powerlessness of crucifixion (1 Cor 1:18–25), or, as Paul puts it here, the weakness of the cross and the power of the resurrection (2 Cor 13:4). Because the issues addressed in the Corinthian letters differ from those in Galatians and Romans, Paul's terminology is different, but the pattern of his theology is recognizably the same. The grace that is given in the absence of worth is the power that is given in the midst of weakness. Grace thereby undermines the human capital in which believers take confidence ("boast") and throws them back, in trust, on the only thing that gives them worth, the gift of God in Christ.

The Gift as Christ

When we use gift-language, we tend to think of *things* given (perhaps even wrapped in gift-paper), and so the question will arise: *What* exactly does God give in grace? For Paul, the Christ-gift is most fundamentally not the giving of a thing but the giving of a person: "The Son of God loved me and *gave himself* for me" (Gal 2:20; cf. Gal 1:4). This gift can be spelled out in various terms: it concerns righteousness, wisdom, holiness, and redemption, but all these, Paul says, are given "in Christ" (1 Cor 1:30). They are not gifts given in addition to Christ, or even by Christ, but the facets of salvation that come through solidarity with Christ and through participation "in" him. Even the Spirit, through which grace is active and experienced in the "hearts" of believers, is "the Spirit of Christ" (Rom 8:9) or "the Spirit of the Son" (Gal 4:6), so that this too is a form of participation in Christ. As we have seen (chapter 8), Paul understands baptism as the reconstitution of the self through identification with Christ: the believer is baptized "into Christ" (Rom 6:3), sharing in his death and burial so as to walk in his "newness of life," as the precursor to sharing in his resurrection (Rom 6:1–5).

We can get another angle on this reality from a passage in Paul's letter to the Philippians. In Philippians 3, Paul uses his own story to demonstrate how the Christ-gift forces a complete reassessment of value or worth, and he sums up what now counts as, simply, "Christ." He first lists (Phil 3:4–6) elements of his life that might cause him to "boast," that is, the things he might count as symbolic capital in human terms ("in the flesh"). His ancestry, his ethnic identity, his Jewish upbringing, his Pharisaic commitment to the Law (Pharisees were famously scrupulous), and his zeal in persecuting the assembly—all these add up to what he calls his "righteousness within the Law" (3:6). But in the next verses (3:7–9) he articulates, in three different ways, a radical cognitive shift. Now the only thing that counts for him, the single and supreme ground of value, is Christ: "Whatever was gain for me, all these I consider loss on account of Christ. . . . I consider all things as loss because of the surpassing value of knowing Christ Jesus my Lord, on whose account I have written off all things as loss, and consider them rubbish, that I might gain Christ and be found in him" (3:7–9).[9] Compared with Christ, *everything else* is "loss," even "rubbish" (*skybala*, 3:8).[10] Paul uses this stark rhetorical contrast to highlight that, in his new value system, there is one thing, and one thing only, that is always of value, in every circumstance, for everyone. Whatever else may be useful or of relative value (in certain contexts and for certain purposes), it cannot be placed in the same category of worth as Christ, or what Paul calls here "being found in him" (3:9).

What does it mean to be "found in Christ"? Paul uses the phrase "in Christ" on many occasions and sometimes uses other spatial language in this connection, like baptism "into Christ" (Gal 3:27; Rom 6:3) or "putting on Christ" (a

---

9. Paul's radical reevaluation of things he previously considered of value has parallels in the Stoic insistence that there is only one thing ("virtue") properly considered "good"; see Troels Engberg-Pedersen, *Paul and the Stoics* (Edinburgh: T&T Clark, 2000).

10. In some contexts, the term can mean "excrement," but its rhetorical force here is not what is dirty but what lacks ultimate value.

clothing metaphor, Gal 3:27; Rom 13:14).[11] In English, we use spatial metaphors for states of being: we might be "in love" or fall "out of love," as if love were a container and we were either in it or out of it. Something similar is possible in Greek, but here the "container" is not a state but a person. When used with a person, the Greek preposition *en* can mean not only "by means of" but also "in identification with," or "in the power of." Sometimes Paul uses the phrase "in Christ" to mean "through Christ," but more often it expresses the fact that something is true for the believer in their identification with Christ and by means of his power. If "the gift of God is eternal life in Christ Jesus our Lord" (Rom 6:23), this is so not just *because of* Christ but inasmuch as believers share in the resurrection life of Christ himself. Thus to be "found in Christ" is to have one's self completely identified with Christ, sharing his story and his status, wrapped up, we might say, in his destiny. Thus, in our passage from Philippians, Paul talks of "sharing in the sufferings of Christ by becoming like him in his death" (3:10), and of "knowing Christ and the power of his resurrection . . . that I may attain the resurrection of the dead" (3:10–11; cf. 3:21). Solidarity with Christ means sharing both in his death and (ultimately) in his resurrection.[12]

Paul's "in Christ" language is thus shorthand for "in identification with Christ" or "in solidarity with Christ." It expresses the way that the self becomes completely associated with, dependent on, and newly aligned to what God has done and will do in Christ. Scholars usually gloss Paul's language with phrases like "union with Christ" or "participation in Christ," although it proves easier to use such phrases than to explain them. In theological traditions influenced by (Greek) philosophical notions of assimilation to God, Paul's language has been interpreted to mean that the believer shares the "nature" or "substance" of Christ, and this has sometimes been described as *theōsis* ("divinization").[13] But it would be better to put this in terms of relationship rather than nature or substance. Paul understands the self as defined by relation: people are constituted by their relationships and derive their selfhood not from some independent or preexisting essence but from their relationships to other people and other powers. Just as in a marriage

---

11. See Michael J. Thate, Kevin J. Vanhoozer, and Constantine R. Campbell, eds., *"In Christ" in Paul: Explorations in Paul's Theology of Union and Participation* (Grand Rapids: Eerdmans, 2014).

12. See Michael J. Gorman, *Inhabiting the Cruciform God: Kenosis, Justification, and Theosis in Paul's Narrative Soteriology* (Grand Rapids: Eerdmans, 2009).

13. For early patristic interpretations, see Ben C. Blackwell, *Christosis: Engaging Paul's Soteriology with His Patristic Interpreters* (Grand Rapids: Eerdmans, 2016). His title gives a Christological twist to the more familiar language of *theōsis*.

one becomes something different through one's relationship to a spouse (Paul uses that analogy in Rom 7:1–6), so the self is, for Paul, reconstituted by its relationship with Christ, and with others in the body of Christ. The "I" that is fully identified with Christ is a different "I," with a new identity, new attitudes and dispositions, new values and goals, new emotions and hopes, a new status before God, and a new destiny in God's purposes.

Thus, what is given by grace is Christ himself, Christ-in-relation-to-the-believer, such that the believer becomes a new person in total self-identification with Christ. That is why Paul speaks of believers being "born" through their conversion (1 Cor 4:15; Phlm 10) and twice uses the striking expression "new creation": "If anyone is in Christ, there is a new creation (or: a new creature): the old things have passed away; look, the new has come to be" (2 Cor 5:17); "Neither circumcision counts for anything, nor the foreskin, but new creation" (Gal 6:15). The language of "new creation" makes clear that this newness is something effected or given by God: no one can recreate themselves. What is given is Christ and, deriving from that, the new self that participates in the gift of Christ.

But how is this participation made possible? In what way is it *given*? Here we may turn to the previous chapter in Philippians, where Paul makes a famous creed-like statement concerning Christ:

> Though [or because] he was in the form of God,
> he did not count it God-like to seize by force,
> but emptied himself, taking the form of a servant, coming to be in
> human likeness.
> And being found in human form, he humbled himself, becoming
> obedient all the way to death, death on a cross.
> Therefore, God has highly exalted him, and given him the name
> above all names,
> that at the name of Jesus every knee should bend, of beings in
> heaven, on earth, and under the earth,
> and every tongue *confess* that Jesus Christ is Lord, to the glory of
> God the Father.
> (Phil 2:6–11)

Complexities aside, the passage's basic pattern is clear. Despite (or better: because) he was in the form of God,[14] Christ did the opposite of what gods

---

14. The Greek could be taken either way; see Gorman, *Inhabiting the Cruciform God*, 9–39.

in mythology were famed for doing: he did not seize or take by force but gave himself into the human condition. Nearly all scholars agree that this passage (alongside Gal 4:4, 2 Cor 8:9, and Rom 8:3) indicates an act of incarnation, whereby Christ takes on the human condition and participates in the limitations and vulnerabilities of human nature. Christ's participation all the way to death, even to crucifixion, indicates that this participation took him to the lowest forms of weakness and folly (cf. 1 Cor 1:18–25); elsewhere, Paul speaks of Christ's participation in flesh, curse, and sin (Rom 8:3; Gal 3:13; 2 Cor 5:21). But this has a purpose and a result: Christ's self is given *into* the human condition but not ultimately given *away*, because in the resurrection and exaltation of Christ a new era is begun and a new life is released, in which others may participate by faith. In other words, Christ participates in the human condition all the way to death, in order that others may participate in *his* condition, all the way to eternal life. By this "interchange" or "mutual assimilation," the self-gift of Christ transforms the human condition, such that those "in Christ" live from the new life, the resurrection life, that derives from their exalted Lord.[15] Their lives are now, as we have seen, ex-centric (see chapter 8), suspended from the life of Christ, such that Paul can even say: "I have been crucified with Christ; it is no longer I who live, but Christ who lives in me, and the life I now live, I live by trust in the Son of God who loved me and gave himself for me" (Gal 2:19–20). This reconstituted self is and always will be the product of a gift.

One common way for Paul to speak of this new life, and to emphasize its origin from outside, is to frame it by reference to the Spirit. Paul can express this in two complementary ways: either as the Spirit of God/Christ taking up residence "in" believers (Rom 8:9, 11) or as believers living "in" or "by" the Spirit (Rom 8:9; Gal 5:25). Each represents the redefinition of the self, whose identity, goals, and values are formed anew by a powerful presence deeper than the normal conditions of human life. The Spirit is "received" as a gift (Gal 3:2, 5, 14), as the existential reality of the Christ-gift, indeed as the Spirit of Christ himself (Rom 8:9). In a passage that encapsulates the mutual participation we have just traced, Paul writes of the sending of the Son, "born of a woman, born under the Law, in order to redeem those under the Law, in order that we might receive adoption as sons" (Gal 4:4–5). The Son participates in the human condition so that redeemed humans may participate in his status, as

---

15. For the language of "interchange," see Morna D. Hooker, *From Adam to Christ* (Cambridge: Cambridge University Press, 1990); for "mutual assimilation," see Susan G. Eastman, *Paul and the Person: Reframing Paul's Anthropology* (Grand Rapids: Eerdmans, 2017).

"sons,"[16] and this is enacted and demonstrated in the presence of the Spirit: "Because you are sons, God sent the Spirit of his Son into our hearts, crying 'Abba, Father'" (Gal 4:6). While some think that Paul understood the "Spirit" (*pneuma*) to be a material phenomenon,[17] what matters is the new relational matrix formed by the Christ-event. Believers are new selves because they are newly repositioned in relation to God, participating in the Son's relation to God (cf. Rom 8:14–16, 29), which transforms both their present condition and their anticipation of the future (as "heirs").

So, what is the gift? One could answer from Galatians 4: adoption, inheritance. But whence do they derive? The text traces those privileges of status back to the "sending" of the Son and links them to the Spirit, or better, the Spirit of the Son. All paths lead back to Christ, whose arrival in "the fullness of time" (Gal 4:4) is the event that constitutes, for Paul, *the Gift*. This is both an "objective" event and a "subjective" reality: this gift happened in the incarnation, death, and resurrection of Christ, but it is received and operative as the total reformulation of the self. It is not a piece of information, nor a possession that one could add to other possessions, but a comprehensive relation that transforms the self at the deepest level and in all its dimensions. And that includes social and ethical practice, as we shall now see.

16. The masculine language links the status of believers to the status of "the Son." But Paul values male and female believers equally, as is clear, for instance, in Romans 16.

17. See Troels Engberg-Pedersen, *Cosmology and Self in the Apostle Paul: The Material Spirit* (Oxford: Oxford University Press, 2010). For discussion of the Spirit in relation to the moral agency of the believer, see Volker Rabens, *The Holy Spirit and Ethics in Paul: Transformation and Empowering for Religious-Ethical Life*, 2nd ed. (Minneapolis: Fortress, 2014).

CHAPTER 11

The Practice of Grace

Across Paul's letters we have found grace to be defined consistently as an *incongruous* gift. It is given "freely" in the sense that it is given without prior conditions and without regard to worth or capacity. But that does not mean that it comes with no expectations of return, no hope for a response, no "strings attached." A gift may be "free" in one sense (given irrespective of worth or desert) but not in another (with no expectation of response). In fact, as we have seen, the Christ-gift carries strong expectations because it is transformative: it remolds the self and recreates the community of believers. The social effects of this divine gift in human gift-practices are, therefore, a *necessary* component of grace. These effects are not instrumental in winning some final or additional gift of grace, but they are the necessary (inevitable and proper) expression of grace in human lives.

Believers, as we have seen, are "under grace" (Rom 6:14; see chapter 8). This condition does not entail the addition of new obligations loaded onto the old, unchanged self but the expression of the new self, founded on a new source of life. As Paul puts it, "If we live by the Spirit, let us also walk in line with the Spirit" (Gal 5:25). Paul expects the grace of God in Christ to cascade through the life of communities, such that the grace received is passed forward by believers and shared among them. In this sense, the return-gift to God is also, at the same time, the forward transfer of grace. "Paying it back" is performed through "paying it forward": believers "give themselves to the Lord" (2 Cor 8:5) by participating in the sharing of gifts (2 Cor 8:7). In this chapter, we will trace this dynamic in three steps: in the practice of gifts within "the body" (1 Corinthians 12); in the reciprocal support that arises from "co-partnership in grace" (Phil 1:7); and in the collection-gift that Paul organized for Jerusalem with a rich theological rationale (2 Corinthians 8–9).

Gifts in the Body

When Paul writes to the Corinthians, he gives thanks for "the grace (*charis*) of God that has been given you in Christ Jesus, for in every way you have been enriched in him . . . so that you are not lacking in any spiritual gift (*charisma*)" (1 Cor 1:4-7). One of the ways grace becomes operative is in the "enrichment" of the community of believers, and one of the ways that wealth is manifest is in the variety of "gifts"—skills, capacities, and services that bind the community together. When Paul picks up this topic in 1 Corinthians 12–14, he gives a list of representative "gifts" (*charismata*), which he also calls "spiritual phenomena" (*ta pneumatika*) since they display the operative presence of grace in the Spirit (1 Cor 12:4-11, 28-30). The list in 1 Corinthians is shaped by the experience of the Corinthian church; elsewhere, Paul offers a rather different catalogue of "gifts" (Rom 12:6-8), which is different again in Ephesians (Eph 4:11). No fixed "menu" appears to exist from which believers are apportioned this or that gift. Rather, what Paul has in mind are skills and services that foster many kinds of communal activity, supporting and developing the community in its internal relations and in its relationship to Christ. More or less anything that fulfills those functions could be considered a *charisma*, and even the capacity to remain single, in undistracted devotion to Christ, could be given this label (1 Cor 7:7).

These gifts are given not for individual enjoyment but for the benefit of all: "To each one is given the manifestation of the Spirit for what is beneficial" (1 Cor 12:7), by which Paul means, what is beneficial for the whole community (cf. 1 Cor 10:23). At this point, famously, he deploys an extended metaphor of the body—a metaphor widely used in antiquity to express the way that a political community (or the universe as a whole) is internally diverse but bound together by the services that each part renders to the others.[1] "In one Spirit," says Paul, "we were all baptized into one body" (1 Cor 12:13), creating a new social unity that is bound tightly to one another just as (and because) it is bound inextricably to Christ (since it is, in fact, "the body of Christ," 1 Cor 12:27). The gifts of the Spirit are distributed around the body, to individual members, so that no member and no gift may be regarded as supreme or self-sufficient, and none can be dispensed with or disparaged as superfluous. "The eye cannot say to the hand, 'I have no need of you,' nor can the head say to the feet, 'I have no need of you'" (1 Cor 12:21). Note the language of "need": it

---

1. See Michelle V. Lee, *Paul, the Stoics, and the Body of Christ* (Cambridge: Cambridge University Press, 2006).

betokens vulnerability, lack, and the necessity to receive. The body (and thus the community in Christ) seems to be specifically designed such that everyone is bound to everyone else, both in gift and in need. The gift relationships may be diffuse: there are more than two parts to the body, and gifts will circulate around it in both direct and indirect forms of reciprocity. What one person gives may be matched by a return from elsewhere in the community. But it is clear that, as gifts circulate, everyone is constantly in the process of both giving and receiving.

In the Corinthian situation, Paul highlights one feature of the body in a specific way, to counter a dangerous tendency in that assembly. Some parts of the body might despise others as dispensable, but, Paul insists, it is the parts of the body that seem to be "weaker" that are all the more necessary, and "those we think less honorable we clothe with greater honor" (1 Cor 12:22-23; he is probably referring to the genitalia). Paul here resists hierarchies of honor or power and directs such comments at the status-divisions that were distorting the Corinthian assembly, where those who were socially and economically stronger were inclined to disparage the "weaker" members of the community, disregarding their opinions and their needs.[2] "Weak" is the term Paul had used to describe those members of the community who could become disastrously compromised in their faith by the cavalier behavior of others. When fellow believers claimed a "knowledge" that emboldened them to eat in pagan temples, Paul feared lest the "weak" follow suit and thereby abandon their exclusive commitment to Christ (1 Cor 8:7-13). Similarly, in his discussion of "the Lord's Supper" (1 Cor 11:17-34), Paul was shocked to hear that at the communal gathering (which probably included a kind of potluck), some members were keeping their own food and drink to themselves, not sharing it with those who, for whatever reason, were unable to bring anything to the meal: "Each of you goes ahead with his/her own meal (*to idion deipnon*), and one is hungry and another is drunk" (1 Cor 11:21).[3] Paul is scandalized: "Do you despise the assembly of God and shame those who have nothing?" (1 Cor 11:22). Paul takes this meal, in which they are ritually bound to Christ, to be the ultimate expression of their belonging, at the same time, most completely to one another. If Christ gave himself "for [each one of] you" (1 Cor 11:24), they had a responsibility to each person "for whom Christ died" (1 Cor 8:11;

2. See Dale B. Martin, *The Corinthian Body* (New Haven: Yale University Press, 1995), 92-96.

3. See Gerd Theissen, *The Social Setting of Pauline Christianity* (Philadelphia: Fortress, 1982), 145-74.

Rom 14:15). The food should not be their own (*idion*) but shared in common (*koinon;* cf. 10:16–17): at this highly symbolic moment of pooling, they should indicate their full commitment to support one another as needs arise.[4]

In the body, individual interests should not be played off against the interests of others. In fact, in a body there can be no division of interests, but "the members should share the same concerns, one for another" (1 Cor 12:25). "If one member suffers, all the members suffer together" (1 Cor 12:26). This is a community where interests have been pooled, where every "I" has been given into a collective "we." The self has not been sacrificed or negated. It has been stripped of its competitive concerns for itself (1 Cor 13:5), but in joining this community it serves a collective interest, where each person will be affirmed and each will flourish. The grace of God has joined people together without regard for their differences in ethnicity, gender, or social and legal status (1 Cor 12:13). It has thereby created a community where each member has the worth accorded by the love of Christ and where new patterns of honor and support are created across old divides. And special attention is to be given to those who are normally invisible or considered of lesser worth.

RECIPROCAL SUPPORT

In modern notions of "charity" or "philanthropy," giving is top-down and (ideally) one-way. The "rich" give to the "poor" and expect, even want, nothing back. Paul's model is different. He does not look for wealthy benefactors to support the rest of the community as self-sufficient patrons. In fact, only in the assembly at Corinth is there evidence for members living at some distance above subsistence-level, and there Paul was acutely aware that economic power distorts social relationships. Neither does he look for one-way relationships in which all the giving is from one side and all the receiving on the other; as we have seen, his model of social relationships (the body) suggests that everyone is, sometimes or in some respects, a receiver as well as a giver. Hence the frequency with which Paul talks of doing things for or to one another (*allēlois* or *eis allēlous*). Such phrases occur no less than thirty-two times in the undisputed letters. Believers are to greet *one another* (with a holy kiss, Rom 16:16; 1 Cor 16:20). They are to welcome *one another* (Rom 15:7), so that the role of the host is accorded not just to one person but to all. They are

4. See David G. Horrell, *The Social Ethos of the Corinthian Correspondence: Interests and Ideology from 1 Corinthians to 1 Clement* (Edinburgh: T&T Clark, 1996).

expected to encourage *one another* (1 Thess 4:18; 5:11) and warn or instruct *one another* (Rom 15:14), since everyone needs the contribution of others. When Paul looks forward to strengthening the believers in Rome with some spiritual gift (*charisma pneumatikon*), he immediately corrects himself: he and the Roman believers will be "*mutually* encouraged by the faith that is in one another, both yours and mine" (Rom 1:11–12). That correction indicates Paul's awareness that the one-way gift can be patronizing, an implicit claim to superior power. He is careful to insist that in the delicate relationships between weak and strong, they are to build up *one another* (14:19); the weak also have something to contribute.[5]

Above all, believers are urged to love *one another* (Gal 5:13; Rom 12:10; 13:8), as the love of God flows within the community not just in one direction but in all. One way that this translates into practice is in "bearing *one another's* burdens" (Gal 6:2). The mutuality in this instruction indicates that there are no self-sufficient individuals able to carry their own load together with that of others: everyone needs the help of other people in carrying his/her own burden. "Burden" (*baros*) can mean many different things, but it can designate a financial need (cf. 1 Thess 2:7, 9). Paul was highly conscious of what it meant to live on the margin economically. Since he often travelled, and it might take time to earn a living on arrival in a new location, he was used to being hungry, thirsty, and inadequately clothed (1 Cor 4:11; Phil 4:12).[6] When writing to the Thessalonians, whom he addresses as craft-workers (1 Thess 4:11) and who suffer from acute social (and probably economic) pressure, Paul urges them to love and support one another (1 Thess 4:9–12), appealing to the ideal of "brotherly love" (*philadelphia*, 4:9), which presumes a comprehensive, unquestionable commitment to support one another. Paul rarely talks about supporting "the poor," perhaps because most of those he addresses are themselves poor and would not use this (distancing) label of themselves.[7] Rather, he expects that everyone within the community is committed to look out for everyone else. What seems to us bland language of "goodness" (Gal 5:22) and "doing good" (Gal 6:9–10) is, in fact, the classic Greek terminology for the giving of benefits, material and social. Paul's assemblies did not, it seems, pool money in a "relief fund," except for the specific purpose of the Jerusalem collection

---

5. On Paul's social ethic, see David G. Horrell, *Solidarity and Difference: A Contemporary Reading of Paul's Ethics* (London: T&T Clark, 2005).

6. Paul speaks of working with his hands (1 Thess 2:9; 1 Cor 4:12) but does not spell out what he does. In Acts 18:3 he is described as a *skēnopoios*, but the term is so rare that it is not certain what it means (builder of temporary dwellings? Tent-maker?).

7. See Justin J. Meggitt, *Paul, Poverty and Survival* (Edinburgh: T&T Clark, 1998).

(see below). Rather, Paul looked for the kind of sharing, swapping, and mutual support that goes on to this day all the time among those who live on the edge of survival.[8] When needs arise ("as you have opportunity," Gal 6:10), believers are expected to help one another out, "sharing the needs of the saints" (Rom 12:13) such that everyone feels responsible for everyone else.[9]

That verb "share" (*koinōneō*, Rom 12:13; cf. Gal 6:6) echoes the language that Paul often uses for the solidarity (*koinōnia*) expected to characterize communities of believers (cf. 2 Cor 13:13; Phil 2:1). The letter to the Philippians is occasioned by the renewal of solidarity between Paul and the Philippians, which extends across a geographical distance and disregards the shame of Paul's current imprisonment. The mutual concern that binds Paul and the Philippians has created a relationship of "give and take" from the beginning (4:15), but this has been revived in the form of a gift sent to Paul in prison, by the hand of Epaphroditus (Phil 2:25–30; 4:10–20). When speaking of this gift, Paul uses the terminology of a business partnership,[10] but the mutual commitment of selves means more to Paul than the money (4:10–14). What matters is that the Philippians are *all* committed to this relationship (the phrase "you all" occurs with notable frequency; Phil 1:4, 7, 8, 25; 2:17, 26) and that they hold him "in their heart" (1:7; cf. 4:10). They have put their selves, and not just their resources, into partnership with Paul: as he says to the Corinthians, "I do not desire what is yours, but you" (2 Cor 12:14). From his side, Paul overrides his personal preferences in order to serve their progress and joy in the faith (Phil 1:25), and gladly spends himself for them (2:17). His aim is that they should rejoice *together* (2:18), he with them and they with him, such that they mutually take pride *in each other* (1:26; 4:1). This pooling of selves entails costs from both sides, but the goal is a shared, conjoint benefit, in which each side will flourish *together with* the other.[11]

Moreover, Paul views all these human relationships as inhabiting an extra dimension. Epaphroditus was committed not just to Paul but also to "the work of Christ" (Phil 2:30); Timothy looked out for the Philippians' interests

8. Ryan S. Schellenberg, "Subsistence, Swapping, and Paul's Rhetoric of Generosity," *Journal of Biblical Literature* 137 (2018): 215–34.

9. Bruce W. Longenecker, *Remember the Poor: Paul, Poverty, and the Greco-Roman World* (Grand Rapids: Eerdmans, 2010).

10. Julian Ogereau, *Paul's Koinōnia with the Philippians: A Socio-Historical Investigation of a Pauline Economic Partnership* (Tübingen: Mohr Siebeck, 2014).

11. See further, John M. G. Barclay, "Paul, Reciprocity, and Giving with the Poor," in *Practicing with Paul: Reflections on Paul and the Practices of Ministry in Honor of Susan G. Eastman*, ed. Presian R. Burroughs (Eugene: Cascade, 2018), 15–29.

but above all for the interests of Jesus Christ (Phil 2:20–21). What Paul and the Philippians have in common is not just a friendship or a financial partnership but a common dependence on the grace of Christ: they are, as Paul puts it, "fellow-sharers in grace" (Phil 1:7).[12] This means that all the gifts that circulate between them are not their own in any strong sense of ownership: they are gifts derived from grace and given onward as a means of participation in the generous self-giving of God. The location of the community within the new reality established by Christ means that every interaction within the community has a double facet: it is both an interaction with one another and, simultaneously, an interaction with Christ (and therefore God). It is important to conceive this aright. Because God is not a third entity *on the same level* or *of the same kind* as humans— that is, not a third agent on the same stage of interaction—it is not a case of interacting with God *or* with human beings. Nor is it the case that believers give to one another while "really" or more "directly" giving to God. Certainly, God is not *identical* with the human agents involved, nor is interaction with God *reducible* to interaction with fellow humans. Nonetheless, the gift-sharing between believers can be viewed *both* as an interhuman interaction *and* as an interaction with God—not either-or but both-and.

This double dimension is evident both in "giving from" and in "giving to." With regard to "giving from," Paul regards the Philippians' gift to him as a form of strengthening and empowerment *from God* (Phil 4:13), just as elsewhere, when he commends the Macedonians' gift, he draws attention first not to their giving but to *God's*: "I want you to know, brothers and sisters, the grace of God given in the assemblies in Macedonia" (2 Cor 8:1). Thus, while Paul acknowledges the gift that he has received from Philippi, he is conscious that in and behind that gift is the "good work" that God has begun and will bring to completion (Phil 1:6). The gift and the giving—and, we might say, the givers themselves—are all to be seen as products of the grace of God. This does not diminish human agency, as if it were a zero-sum calculation where the more there is of God, the less of the human giver. The human giver is neither obscured nor reduced to a puppet, nor is one agency added to another, as if the two were of the same kind. But it is nonetheless true for Paul—and sometimes important to emphasize—that human giving in Christ is sourced and energized by a divine power that is both immanent and transcendent. The gift-sharing that takes place within the community has a second, and deeper, dimension in Christ.

12. See David E. Briones, *Paul's Financial Policy: A Socio-Theological Approach* (London: T&T Clark, 2013).

What about "giving to"? Paul can take the gifts that circulate on the human stage in Christ as also, and at the same time, gifts *to God*. That is how he interprets the Philippians' gift to him: it is truly to him, and part of the *koinōnia* between them, but it is also "a fragrant offering, a sacrifice acceptable and pleasing to God" (Phil 4:18). This Godward-direction of the gift means that it will be returned by God: "My God will fully satisfy every need of yours according to his riches in glory" (Phil 4:19). Paul does not play off against one another the human and the divine destination of the gift, as if the Philippians gave to God *instead of* to Paul, or as if they gave directly to one but indirectly to the other. They give to both, wholly and directly, at the same time, because these are two facets of the same gift. Thus, gift relationships within the community participate in a gift-dynamic that is the source of the giving and is present within it.

The Collection-Gift for Jerusalem

Paul is a practical theologian, and his theology generally revolves around the resolution of issues that concern the practices of believers. This is especially the case with regard to the collection he organized among his assemblies for "the poor among the saints in Jerusalem" (Rom 15:26), which was a financial and social arrangement rooted by Paul in a profound theology of gift. Paul had been part of an earlier collection-project, based in Antioch, in which financial support for believers in Jerusalem ensured that the gentile mission in Antioch stayed connected to its Jerusalem roots (Gal 2:6–10; cf. Acts 11:27–30). Later, after moving west, Paul organized another collection among his assemblies (1 Cor 16:1–4), gathering money that he eventually took to Jerusalem, though with some anxiety over the acceptance of this symbolic financial gesture (Rom 15:25–33).[13] But not all Paul's assemblies were eager to join this project, and when his relationship with the believers in Corinth began to deteriorate, it became uncertain whether they would contribute at all. He thus devised a set of arguments, pleas, and practical arrangements that we can follow in 2 Corinthians 8–9.[14] We are fortunate that this crisis required him to develop his

13. For the history of these projects and their theological underpinning, see David J. Downs, *The Offering of the Gentiles: Paul's Collection for Jerusalem in its Chronological, Cultural, and Cultic Contexts* (Grand Rapids: Eerdmans, 2016). For another reading of the evidence, see Stephan Joubert, *Paul as Benefactor: Reciprocity, Strategy, and Theological Reflection in Paul's Collection* (Tübingen: Mohr Siebeck, 2000).

14. Although some have suggested that chapters 8 and 9 of 2 Corinthians were originally

theology of grace and to draw out in detail the relationship between the Christ-gift and the practice of generosity.

Paul's arguments in 2 Corinthians 8–9 are full of the word *charis*, which sometimes means divine grace (8:1, 9), sometimes favor (8:4), sometimes the collection-gift (8:7), and sometimes thanks (9:15). (This is one of those cases where it helps enormously to read the text in Greek, since English translations necessarily use different words for these different meanings of *charis* and so obscure the connection between them.) Paul displays impressive rhetorical skill in these chapters, but he is not just playing on words. The different uses of *charis* suggest that divine grace *flows through* believers and is expressed in their giving to others, and that the momentum of this flow generates thanks to God in recognition of the source of the gift. Here, if you like, is the circle of *charis*: from God in Christ, through and among believers, and back to God in *charis* or *eucharistia* (thanksgiving).

The argument begins (2 Cor 8:1–6) by recounting the generosity of the Macedonian believers, whose example Paul uses to goad the Corinthians into action (cf. 9:1–5). But instead of saying, as we might expect, "We want you to know about the generosity of the assemblies of Macedonia," Paul says, "We want you to know about the *grace of God given to* the assemblies of Macedonia" (2 Cor 8:1). The Macedonians' generosity (out of extreme poverty) was entirely of their own volition (2 Cor 8:3), but it was ultimately attributable not to themselves but to God. Thus, right from the start, Paul figures human gift-giving as the product of divine gift-giving, a flow of divine *charis* into human *charis*, as if the human agents were conduits or channels. Later, in order to counter the Corinthians' anxiety lest generosity might deplete their resources, Paul assures them that "God is able to provide you with every blessing in abundance, so that by always having enough of everything, you may share abundantly in every good work" (2 Cor 9:8). That again figures God as the source of the gift, while it encourages the Corinthians to think of the world as a rich source of open-ended possibility in which God is able to multiply resources, provided they are not hoarded but given (2 Cor 9:10–12).

If God's grace is the origin of the gift that flows *through* the Macedonians and Corinthians to Jerusalem, this collection-project is to be seen, first and foremost, in its relation to God. When Paul describes the reception of the gift in Jerusalem, he says that "the worship expressed in this ministry not only

---

separate letters, their internal structure and rhetorical links indicate a carefully crafted unity; see Kieran J. O'Mahony, *Pauline Persuasion: A Sounding in 2 Corinthians 8–9* (Sheffield: Sheffield Academic, 2000).

supplies the needs of the saints but also overflows with many thanksgivings to God" (2 Cor 9:12). The recipients in Jerusalem will no doubt be grateful, but their thanks will go primarily to the God who enabled and sourced this giving. The collection-gift will tie Paul's assemblies to Jerusalem in long-distance love and mutual concern, but only because they recognize in each other the gift or grace of God: the "saints" in Jerusalem, Paul says, will "long for you and pray for you, because of the overwhelming grace of God that rests on you" (2 Cor 9:14).[15] The giving of this gift is an act of worship to God, and the receipt of the gift issues in thanksgiving to God. In other words, the gift that binds the givers with the receivers also, and at the same time, binds them both to God.

We may focus this point by looking closely at 2 Corinthians 8:9, which is the first and most important warrant for the gift (2 Cor 8:7) and establishes its theological basis. The verse is normally translated: "For you know the generous act of our Lord Jesus Christ, that though he was rich, yet for your sakes he became poor, so that by his poverty you might become rich." This is a perfectly possible translation, but it creates some difficulties. It suggests a model of giving in which the giver gives up wealth, or gives it away, and becomes materially poor for the sake of others, whereas Paul seems at pains to assure the Corinthians that he is not asking them to endure hardship in contributing to this collection (2 Cor 8:13; cf. 9:8–11). It also leaves unclear in what sense the Corinthians are to think of themselves as being made "rich," or how this relates to Paul's request. The Greek clause *plousios ōn*, which is normally translated "although he was rich," can also be translated "*because* he was rich" (i.e., in a causal, not a concessive sense), and this makes better sense of the whole verse.[16] It allows for an understanding of "wealth" not in terms of what you have (and then give up) but in terms of how you give. It was *because of* his wealth (in generosity) that Christ gave, and it is in this sense also that believers become "rich."[17]

15. Even in this case, Paul envisages a long-term relationship of mutuality: he uses the manna story (Exodus 16) to indicate that the surplus of one is designed to meet the need of the other, *and vice versa* (8:13–15). See John M. G. Barclay, "Manna and the Circulation of Grace: A Study of 2 Corinthians 8:1–15," in *The Word Leaps the Gap: Essays on Scripture and Theology in Honor of Richard B. Hays*, ed. J. Ross Wagner, C. Kavin Rowe, and A. Katherine Grieb (Grand Rapids: Eerdmans, 2008), 409–26.

16. Note the parallel with Phil 2:6 (if translated "because he was in the form of God"), discussed in chapter 10.

17. For further detail, see John M. G. Barclay, "'Because He Was Rich He Became Poor': Translation, Exegesis, and Hermeneutics in the Reading of 2 Cor 8.9," in *Theologizing in the Corinthian Conflict: Studies in the Exegesis and Theology of 2 Corinthians*, ed. Reimund Bieringer et al. (Leuven: Peeters, 2013), 331–44.

Let's see what happens when we translate the verse this way: "For you know the grace of our Lord Jesus Christ that, *because* he was rich, for your sake he became poor, so that by his poverty you might become rich." What does it mean for Christ to be "rich" and for believers to be made "rich"? The best clue is in the immediately preceding verses, where Paul talks of the generosity of the Macedonian churches, how "during a severe ordeal of affliction, their abundant joy and their extreme poverty have overflowed in a wealth of whole-hearted commitment (*ploutos tēs haplotētos*)" (2 Cor 8:2). Paul uses the same terminology at the end of chapter 9, when he speaks about the Corinthians being "enriched for all *haplotēs*" (2 Cor 9:11). (*Haplotēs* is often translated "generosity," but it means the spirit of the gift rather than the quantity, a wholehearted, unstinting commitment to giving.) Both these texts signal that what Paul means by "wealth" is not so much what one has (the wealth of possessions) but how one gives, wealth in the spirit of giving. Thus, if Christ was rich, it was not because he possessed much but because he was full of the self-giving love of God. Similarly, if believers "become rich" or are "enriched," it is not so that they may possess much (in either material or spiritual terms), but so that they may *give* in an equally sincere, unstinting fashion. Thus we may take the verse like this: "For you know the grace of our Lord Jesus Christ that, because he was rich (that is, rich in divine self-giving), for your sake he became poor (in the incarnation, strategically limited in his capacities), so that by his poverty (his participation in the human condition) you might become rich (participating in his wholehearted self-giving)."

On this reading, Paul presents the Christ-gift in 2 Cor 8:9 not so much as an *example* to be imitated but as an event in which to participate. An example remains a story or model external to the self, something to admire and emulate, but not internal to the self and its motivations. But for Paul, believers are not just inspired by the example of Christ but reconfigured by solidarity with Christ or participation "in" him. In fact, this verse seems to summarize the pattern of mutual participation that we traced at the end of chapter 10: Christ participates in the human condition in order to enable human participation in Christ. Here, believers do not become rich materially (this is not a version of a prosperity gospel), nor do they become rich in the enjoyment of spiritual blessings. They become rich precisely as Christ was and is rich, that is, in the self-diffusing love that is the core of the life of God. Grace, as we have seen, is not a *thing* passed over and passed on; it is a relationship that remakes the self, an encapsulation within the gift-giving dynamic of God. Thus, human gift-giving is a form of participation in grace, as believers are drawn into something both utterly beyond them and wholly integral to what they do.

If human giving is placed within such a frame, this affects the understanding of possessions. If believers view what they have as what they have been given, and if this has been given not for them alone but to be shared with others, their instinct is not to accumulate wealth but to share it. In fact, possessions themselves become ambiguous things. On the one hand, they must belong to their possessors to a sufficient degree that they may be *given* (one cannot give what one does not possess). On the other hand, they are not *owned* in the sense that those who possess them have the right to dispose of them exactly how they wish. Interestingly, Paul traces the principle of divine gift also within creation: "He who supplies seed for the sower and bread for food will supply and magnify your seed and increase the fruits of your righteousness" (2 Cor 9:10). That suggests that the created world is more than just an analogy for "spiritual" blessings: it is the terrain in which God's generosity is already witnessed in its multiplying power. And as it is God's, its fruitfulness is to be enjoyed but not exploited, deployed for the benefit of all, not only of some, honored as a gift, with accountability to its Giver. The ingredients for an ecological ethic and for a radical Christian perspective on property "rights" may be found at this point. If all of creation is divine gift, it is not ours to exploit how we will nor to be used without a deep sense of accountability. The modern instrumental view of nature as "resource" has brought us to the brink of disaster, since our only concern has been its economic utility. Paul's answer would not be to give nature a semideified persona but to direct our accountability to God, the Giver, to whom we return our gratitude in honoring the gifts of creation and in sharing them with others, both in our own generation and for generations to come. And then we do not have the "right" to dispose of our money or possessions in whatever way we want. The modern assumption that no one can question my "right" to use "my" resources in my own, autonomous way runs directly against the theology we have witnessed in Paul's letters. Perhaps it is only when creation is seen as gift to be received with gratitude, and to be nurtured, maintained, and shared, that we can begin to reverse our exploitative relationship to our environment and can find a sustainable way to live in, with, and for the gifts that indicate God's enriching presence in the world.

CHAPTER 12

Grace and Other Perspectives on Paul

Our reading of Paul from the perspective of grace has encompassed not just a single term (*charis*), nor only a single motif, but the shape or "grammar" of the whole of Paul's theology (see chapter 10). From this perspective, we have examined entire letters (Galatians and Romans) but also significant features of the theological landscape in other Pauline texts. The connection between theology and ethics; the meaning of the cross, of the incarnation, and of participation in Christ; the social and economic practices of gift; the community-oriented gifts of the Spirit; the reconstitution of the self in Christ—all these we have found to be shaped by Paul's theology of grace and integrated by it. In that sense, this book sketches the outlines of a whole "perspective" on Pauline theology, though there are many features that could be further developed. In recent years, there has been much talk among Pauline scholars about "perspectives" on Paul, old and new.[1] So how does the approach outlined in this book compare with other perspectives on Paul, traditional and contemporary?

Paul's theology of grace has been central to disputes that have divided churches and separated whole streams of theological interpretation. The relationship between grace and free will, grace and works, justification and judgment, faith and love—these have been the storm center of centuries-long controversies within the Western theological tradition, dividing heirs of Augustine, separating Protestants from Catholics, and creating bitter disputes among Protestants themselves. But grace has also been a topic central to the relationship between Christianity and Judaism, which has often been expressed

---

1. For an overview, see Stephen Westerholm, *Perspectives Old and New on Paul: The "Lutheran" Paul and His Critics* (Grand Rapids: Eerdmans, 2004). For a reading of current controversies, see N. T. Wright, *Paul and His Recent Interpreters: Some Contemporary Debates* (London: SPCK, 2015). For a longer view of key trajectories in the history of interpretation, see my *Paul and the Gift* (Grand Rapids: Eerdmans, 2015), 79–182.

in a false antithesis between Christian "grace" and Jewish "works." As we have seen (chapter 3), the work of E. P. Sanders led to a thorough reconfiguration of this topic, and the resulting ferment in Pauline studies has spawned many new ways of configuring Paul's relationship to his Jewish heritage. In this book we have reexamined the subject of grace and disaggregated its different meanings and perfections, and on that basis we have charted a path that leads beyond entrenched positions and current controversies. How so? In this chapter, I will summarize some of the ways in which this reading of Paul moves beyond influential paradigms, under four headings: Protestant perspectives;[2] Catholic perspectives; "the new perspective on Paul"; and the approach to Paul labelled "Paul within Judaism."[3] In each case, I will trace how the readings of Paul offered in this book can repair weaknesses in other lines of interpretation.

PROTESTANT PERSPECTIVES

Grace has been central to Augustinian-Protestant readings of Paul, and several features of the theology of grace explored in this book overlap with that tradition.[4] Shared features include: the identification of grace with the Christ-event; the understanding of "faith" as receptive trust; and the emphasis on grace as intrinsically undeserved or unconditioned (in my terms, "incongruous"). Recent "apocalyptic" readings of Paul (inspired by Karl Barth) represent a radicalization of this tradition, emphasizing the "newness" of the Christ-gift, the revelatory character of the good news, and the powerful agency of God

---

2. These have been dubbed the "old" perspective on Paul (in contrast to the "new"). But the label may be misleading: some of the oldest readings of Paul contain features of the "new" perspective! See Matthew J. Thomas, *Paul's 'Works of the Law' in the Perspective of Second-Century Reception* (Tübingen: Mohr Siebeck, 2018). Moreover, many of the Protestant Reformers' readings of Paul were dependent on Augustine, who is hardly a "Protestant"! But my focus here is on the ways in which the Augustinian tradition has been refracted and supplemented in the Protestant tradition.

3. The "gift perspective" outlined in this book is placed in conversation with these other four in Scot McKnight and B. J. Oropeza, eds., *Perspectives on Paul: Five Views* (Grand Rapids: Baker Academic, 2020).

4. Many New Testament scholars display a less than adequate understanding of the Lutheran and Calvinist traditions. For a recent authoritative treatment, see Stephen J. Chester, *Reading Paul with the Reformers: Reconciling Old and New Perspectives* (Grand Rapids: Eerdmans, 2017). Cf. Michael Allen and Jonathan A. Linebaugh, eds., *Reformation Readings of Paul: Explorations in History and Exegesis* (Downers Grove, IL: InterVarsity Press, 2015).

in liberating a captive humanity.[5] However, there are three interrelated ways in which the "gift-perspective" developed in this book departs from classic Protestant interpretations of Paul:

1. I have emphasized that for Paul the *unconditioned* gift—given in the absence of worth and without regard to worth—is not also *unconditional* in the sense of expecting no return. We noted an important distinction among the perfections of grace, between incongruity (without regard to worth) and noncircularity (with no expectation of return). This indicated that a gift that is "free" in one respect (irrespective of merit or desert) is not necessarily free in the other (requiring or expecting no form of response). The confusion between these two senses of "free" has been a major cause of difficulty within the Protestant tradition, making it hard to explain the place of Christian practice ("works") within the scheme of salvation or to give due weight to Paul's depictions of judgment according to works. In the Lutheran tradition, the law-gospel antithesis has given rise to anxiety around the language of "obligation," which has made it difficult to account for Paul's sense that believers are "under grace" (Rom 6:14).[6] Our own reading of Paul has attempted to repair this problem by insisting that divine grace given without regard to preexisting worth (indeed, where there is none at all) is designed to be transformative, reconstituting human agents whose "newness of life" has a necessarily different set of orientations, allegiances, and obligations. These are not new burdens placed onto the old, incapable self but the proper expression of the new life realigned to Christ and newly energized by the Spirit.[7] Clearly Paul does not advocate a "cheap grace": although grace works in the midst of sin, it causes such a fundamental reconfiguration of the self and of the community of grace that new values and new patterns of life are its inevitable and necessary expression.

5. The seminal work on this front was by J. Louis Martyn; see, especially, his *Galatians: A New Translation with Introduction and Commentary*, Anchor Yale Bible Commentary 33A (New York: Doubleday, 1997). Douglas Campbell has developed this reading in ways that clash with traditional Protestant readings of Paul; see *The Deliverance of God: An Apocalyptic Reading of Justification in Paul* (Grand Rapids: Eerdmans, 2009). For analysis of both, see my *Paul and the Gift*, 147–50, 171–73.

6. This has been less problematic in the Reformed (Calvinist) tradition, which has maintained, nonetheless, a clear distinction between justification and sanctification. For nuanced analysis of the difference between these two Protestant traditions, see Jonathan A. Linebaugh, ed., *God's Two Words: Law and Gospel in Lutheran and Reformed Traditions* (Grand Rapids: Eerdmans, 2018).

7. My reading has at this point some affinities with Matthew W. Bates, *Salvation by Allegiance Alone* (Grand Rapids: Baker Academic, 2017), though I consider the primary meaning of *pistis* in Paul to be trust, not faithfulness or allegiance.

2. We have found that Paul, when discussing what is *not* the basis of justification, sometimes speaks of "works of the Law" (e.g., Gal 2:16) and sometimes of "works" in general (e.g., Rom 11:6). Where the Protestant tradition has tended to treat these as equivalent, and has taken both as symbols of a self-reliant attitude or self-made salvation, we have seen reason to maintain the specificity of "works of the Law" (as the observance of the Jewish Torah) and to take this phrase as a reference to the Jewish symbolic capital assumed to make the one who observes the Law a fitting recipient of divine grace (see chapters 3 and 4). Because Paul radicalizes grace as an incongruous gift, he discounts this and all other forms of human worth, so that "works" (specific or general) represent a form of worth now considered inconsequential in comparison with the sole value of "being found in Christ" (Phil 3:6–9). As we have seen, there are other forms of worth that Paul also discounts, such as ethnicity, ancestry, social status, and gender, which explains why he advances his theology of grace in the course of his gentile mission. This reading challenges the tendency in Protestantism to place works and faith into an overarching or comprehensive antithesis. Although faith (or trust) is the core of the new life that is dependent on the unconditioned gift of God in Christ, the term "works" is not, in itself, a signal of human self-reliance; within the frame of the new life, "working" and "good works" are exactly how this trust is expected to be active (Gal 5:6; cf. Eph 2:9–10). Nor does Paul play off divine against human agency, as if the effect of grace is to *replace* the human actor with the action of the Spirit. To be sure, the believer's agency is now energized by, and enveloped within, the agency of the Spirit/Christ, but it would be misleading to deploy here a generalized contrast between passive and active, grace and work.[8]

3. The Protestant tradition has typically construed Judaism as a religion of "works," a form (even the quintessential form) of "works-righteousness," in which legalistic achievement takes the place of divine grace. The grace-perspective advanced in this book strengthens resistance to this caricature of Judaism and helps us place Paul better *within* the spectrum of views among his Jewish contemporaries concerning the operation of God's mercy/grace. Christianity is not uniquely a "religion of grace." In fact, Paul was not the only Jew of his day who took God's grace to operate incongruously in the absence of worth. What makes his profile distinct is not that he, and he alone, "believed

---

8. The theological tradition has spoken of "synergism" (two agencies in collaboration) and "monergism" (the one agency of God/the Spirit). Paul's theology (and his Greek in Phil 2:13) might encourage us to deploy the term "energism," with its noncontrastive model of the relationship between divine and human agency. See chapter 6.

in grace," but that he took the Christ-event to be the definitive expression of God's unconditioned grace and understood this incongruity to relativize the distinction between Jews and non-Jews, and thus to legitimize the gentile mission. Paul does not reject "Judaism" as a "legalistic" religion. In fact, he considers Israel's very being as founded on the unconditioned mercy of God. He is therefore hopeful for the future of the Jewish people, despite the fact that many had so far failed to recognize the gift of the Messiah (see chapter 9).

CATHOLIC PERSPECTIVES

Paul's letters were, of course, closely read and carefully interpreted well before the Protestant Reformation, and they continue to play a significant role in Christian theologies outside of the Protestant tradition.[9] Although the Catholic tradition is diverse, there are certain features in the traditions that run from patristic interpreters through Aquinas to modern-day Catholic reception of Paul that one might bundle together as "Catholic perspectives on Paul," and that are worth comparing with the perspective developed in this book.[10]

Grace is, of course, a central theme within all Christian theology, and it plays a pivotal role in the Catholic tradition. Commonly, in the Catholic tradition, the concept of grace is paired with nature: as a "supernatural" gift, grace perfects but does not abolish nature.[11] Grace, on this reading, takes nature to a level that is beyond its "natural" capacity but is, at the same time, paradoxically, what nature is fitted for and designed toward. The category "nature" does not, in my view, play a significant role in Paul's theology, but the thesis of this book contains an important element of agreement with Catholic tradition: the grace of God in Christ is *transformative.* Believers are not left as they were, altered

---

9. For reasons of space, I omit here discussion of the interpretation of Paul within the Orthodox traditions, which continue to draw inspiration from John Chrysostom's close engagement with the letters of Paul. See Athanasios Despotis, ed., *Participation, Justification, and Conversion: Eastern Orthodox Interpretation of Paul and the Debate Between Old and New Perspectives on Paul* (Tübingen: Mohr Siebeck, 2017).

10. For a recent Catholic reading of Paul, see Brant Pitre, Michael P. Barber, and John A. Kincaid, *Paul, a New Covenant Jew: Rethinking Pauline Theology* (Grand Rapids: Eerdmans, 2019).

11. Edward T. Oakes, *A Theology of Grace in Six Controversies* (Grand Rapids: Eerdmans, 2016), 1–46. The Protestant instinct is to contrast grace with sin, rather than to explore its complex relation to "nature." See the reflections on this significant difference by Karen Kilby, "Paradox and Paul: Catholic and Protestant Theologies of Grace," *International Journal of Systematic Theology* 22 (2020): 77–82.

only in their legal status before God. They are reconstituted and reoriented by their receipt of grace, such that the practice of love and generosity, in the power of the Spirit, is integral to the expression of salvation. In our reading of Paul, we have stressed how the *incongruous gift* is designed to *create congruity* between the believer and the righteousness or holiness of God. That helps to make sense of Paul's language of judgment by works (see chapter 7). On this point, readers in the Catholic tradition are apt to agree.[12]

Two things, however, should be said by way of clarification:

1) Paul does not distinguish between two acts, or stages, of grace, that is, between an initial grace in justification and a final grace in eschatological judgment/justification. Believers live, from start to finish, out of the single gift of life in Christ, and their life "under grace" does not "merit" eternal life in the sense that it is instrumental toward a salvific gift yet to be given. To be sure, it is possible for believers to "fall from grace" (Gal 5:4), and Paul warns that if they "sow to their flesh" they will reap destruction (Gal 6:8). But if they stay in step with the Spirit (Gal 5:25), that is because they remain within the kindness or grace of God (Rom 11:22), continuing in the gift that grounds their new existence, not earning the right to acquire it. The future judgment of which Paul speaks does not, then, determine salvation on the basis of human "collaboration" with grace.[13] It scrutinizes whether the single gift, already given through participation in the life of Christ, has been expressed and active in the works of the believer.

2) Paul does not reify grace as a thing transferred to the believer, such that it could be said to inhere within them as a "habitual grace." Such language suggests an ontology of substance in which the human being is constituted by its substances, now supplemented by, or infused with a divine substance, grace.[14] While we have seen value in deploying Bourdieu's notion of *habitus* (see chapter 8), this is not the same as the theology of a "habitual grace," if grace is thereby seen as a substance enhancing the natural powers of the human. I have

12. See, e.g., the response to *Paul and the Gift* by Brant Pitre in McKnight and Oropeza, *Perspectives on Paul*, and by Nathan Eubank, "Configurations of Grace and Merit in Paul and His Interpreters," in *International Journal of Systematic Theology* 22 (2020): 7–17.

13. For the language of "collaboration," see *Catechism of the Catholic Church* (London: Burns and Oates, 2010), §§2001, 2003, 2008, 2025. For the larger point, see §2027: "No one can merit the initial grace which is at the origin of conversion. Moved by the Holy Spirit, we can merit for ourselves and for others all the graces needed to attain eternal life, as well as necessary temporal goods."

14. This is sometimes connected to an interpretation of justification as "making righteous." See Oakes, *Theology of Grace*, 47–91.

argued that Paul's language of grace is better understood in relational terms: grace reconstitutes the self at the deepest level by reordering its identity-in-relation. Believers are remade by being brought into a new relational matrix with God and with others. This new relationship is transformational at every level, as believers now participate in the new dynamic of grace, inaugurated in the death and resurrection of Jesus. As I argued in chapter 10, what is given in grace is not a "thing" but Christ himself, together with the new self that arises out of this transformative gift. That requires philosophical and theological unpacking, but it is doubtful whether Aristotelian notions of substance will be our best resource for that task.[15]

THE NEW PERSPECTIVE ON PAUL

"The new perspective on Paul" arose in the wake of E. P. Sanders's redescription of Second Temple Judaism (see above, chapter 3).[16] It encompasses a range of views, but they are united in their emphasis that Paul's theology was centrally concerned with the gentile mission and with the formation of new communities (not just refashioned individuals) in which gentiles were not required to become Jews by adopting "works of the Law." Where the theological tradition has mined Paul's letters for their theological concepts (such as faith and grace), and has sometimes treated them in abstraction, in "the new perspective" emphasis is placed on the historical context of Paul's work and the social dimensions of his theology.[17] For James Dunn and N. T. Wright, Paul disagreed with his fellow Jews, but not over the structure of salvation: what he reacted against was "ethnocentrism" or "nationalism" since the Christ-event had thrown salvation open to all.[18] In Wright's narrative scheme, God's

15. For a contemporary exploration using psychological (second-person perspective) and neuroscientific modes of analysis, see Susan G. Eastman, *Paul and the Person: Reframing Paul's Anthropology* (Grand Rapids: Eerdmans, 2017).

16. I have discussed "the new perspective" at greater length in *Paul and the Gift*, 151–65. See also Francis Watson, *Paul, Judaism and the Gentiles: Beyond the New Perspective*, 2nd ed. (Grand Rapids: Eerdmans, 2007).

17. This matched new interest in the socio-historical and sociological analysis of the Pauline communities, as inspired by Wayne Meeks, *The First Urban Christians: The Social World of the Apostle Paul* (New Haven: Yale University Press, 1983).

18. See, e.g., James D. G. Dunn, *The Epistle to the Galatians* (London: Black, 1993), and his two-volume commentary on Romans (*Romans 1–8* and *Romans 9–16*, Word Biblical Commentary 38A and 38B [Grand Rapids: Zondervan, 1988]). Wright's reading of Paul is most accessible in *Paul: Fresh Perspectives* (London: SPCK, 2005).

promises to Abraham (for his offspring and for "all nations") set the course of covenant history, which has stalled in the condition of "exile"; Jesus as Messiah took on Israel's (unfulfilled) task to bring blessing to the nations and redefined the people of God around himself.[19]

Several features of "the new perspective" are taken up in this book, which also follows in the wake of Sanders's revolution. In common with this perspective, I reject the caricature of Judaism as a religion of works-righteousness and consider the scope and terms of the gentile mission to be integral to Paul's theology of faith, justification, and grace. The historical context and the historical specificity of Paul's theology must be taken seriously, together with its primary concern with the formation of communities.

However, "the new perspective" often fails to connect these social phenomena to their proper Pauline base, his theology of grace. What legitimates Paul's new communities is not just that they are the fulfillment of the Abrahamic promises: as we have seen, Paul's opponents thought that too and insisted on male circumcision (see chapter 4). These communities transcend ethnic distinctions between Jews and non-Jews, but not because of some principled opposition to "nationalism," nor because Paul was an advocate of "inclusion" or "equal rights."[20] The radical terms of Paul's mission were founded, rather, on the incongruous grace of God in Christ, given without regard to ethnic (or any other) worth. The fact that Paul did not require his gentile converts to adopt the symbolic capital of the Jewish tradition ("the works of the Law") can be explained best by the subversive power of an unconditioned grace that calls into question all previously constituted criteria of worth. Paul was not driven by some general antipathy to "ethnocentrism," nor by some corresponding drive toward the "universal." What reshapes his theology is the unconditioned Christ-gift that relativizes (but does not erase) "natural" and socially constructed differentials and that impels him to take the "good news" to all, precisely because it belongs to none.[21]

Wright is correct that Paul's theology operates within the large frame of the

---

19. For the full-scale version, see N. T. Wright, *Paul and the Faithfulness of God*, 2 vols. (London: SPCK, 2013). I have offered a critical review in *Scottish Journal of Theology* 68 (2015): 235–43.

20. For this way of framing Paul's theology, see Krister Stendahl, *Paul among Jews and Gentiles* (London: SCM, 1977), 2, 28–29, 130–31.

21. There are tendencies in "the new perspective" to read Paul as an advocate of the "universal" over the "particular," an antithesis derived from Enlightenment politics and pushed to an extreme in Daniel Boyarin, *A Radical Jew: Paul and the Politics of Identity* (Berkeley: University of California Press, 1994).

scriptural story and the history of Israel. But to appreciate the deep structures of Paul's theology one needs not only a wide-screen but also a 3D perspective. Whenever Paul tells narratives, of humanity (Rom 5:12–21), of Israel (Rom 9:6–29), of his converts' lives (Gal 4:8–10), or of his own (Gal 1:11–16), he tells them according to a distinctive pattern, shaped by the grammar of grace (see chapter 10). He does not merely plot the present on the timeline of the "covenant story." Rather, he is concerned, time and again, to demonstrate how God's grace creates the impossible, turns disaster into salvation, and operates by mercy alone. That is why Abraham, for Paul, is not just the father of a mul-tiethnic people but the programmatic origin of a people constituted by the power of grace, a power that operates where human worth is zero and human capacity nil (see chapter 7). And that is why, *pace* Wright, Paul still has hopes for the future of the nation of Israel (Rom 11:11–32). Because this is a people constituted by mercy, and because the wealth of this grace has spread in Christ to all the nations, Paul is confident that the grace of God will prove salvific for Israel, within and beyond its current "disobedience" (see chapter 9).

"PAUL WITHIN JUDAISM"

In recent years, a number of scholars have identified themselves as a coalition concerned to affirm that Paul stood unambiguously "within Judaism."[22] In reaction against the use of Paul's theology to denigrate Judaism and to justify the split between "Christianity" and Judaism, it is insisted that Paul consid-ered himself a Jew (not a "Christian"—a term created only later) and that he remained always faithful to his people and to the Jewish Law (the Torah). Statements about "freedom" from the Jewish Law relate only to Paul's mission to the gentiles, supporting his insistence that the Law was not to be imposed on them. Paul wanted to bring gentiles into relation to Israel's God and to Abra-ham but in their own Christ-dependent way, distinct from Israel's relationship to God.[23] Since his letters address gentiles, not Jews, it is a categorical mistake

22. There is considerable diversity within this group, but, in general, they continue the post-Holocaust pattern of interpretation pioneered by Lloyd Gaston, Krister Stendahl, and John Gager. For representative essays, see Mark D. Nanos and Magnus Zetterholm, eds., *Paul within Judaism: Restoring the First-Century Context to the Apostle* (Minneapolis: Fortress, 2015).

23. See Caroline Johnson-Hodge, *If Sons, Then Heirs: A Study of Kinship and Ethnicity in the Letters of Paul* (Oxford: Oxford University Press, 2007); Paula Fredriksen, *Paul: The Pagans' Apostle* (New Haven: Yale University Press, 2017). For some scholars within this

to read his letters (at least, his letter to the Galatians) as speaking about Jews and Judaism.[24]

The reading of Paul's theology offered in this book also affirms that Paul stands self-consciously within the Jewish tradition. He self-identifies as a "Jew" (Gal 2:15) or "Israelite" (Rom 11:1), and his engagement with Scripture, Israel, and the mercy of God is best understood *within* the discussions and debates of Second Temple Judaism (see chapter 3).[25] Paul also regards the Jewish people as, in an important sense, special to God, recipients of an irrevocable "call" (Rom 11:28; see chapter 9). But it is crucial to recognize the basis of this calling in the unconditioned mercy of God. For Paul, this mercy constitutes the "root" of Israel's identity and hope (Rom 11:17–24), and it has been exercised in a definitive fashion in Israel's Messiah, Jesus (Rom 9:4–5; 15:8). As is clear in Romans 9–11, it was impossible for Paul to think about Israel's identity except in relation to the gift of God in Christ, and it was impossible to think about the gentile mission except in relation to the destiny of Israel. Paul takes the good news concerning Christ to be for all, "both for the Jew—first—and also for the Greek" (Rom 1:16; 2:9–10; 3:22–23): "For there is no distinction between Jew and Greek: the same Lord is Lord of all, and is rich toward all who call upon him" (Rom 10:12; cf. 1 Cor 1:22–24).

This means that when Paul speaks *to* gentiles (as the primary, implied audience in Galatians and Romans), he must also speak *about* Jews, because the salvation of the whole world is founded on God's mercy to Israel.[26] Where Paul discusses Israel's disobedience (like the prophets and like other Second Temple Jews), that is not to suggest that Israel's sin is worse than others' but to highlight the power of Sin, which conquers even the best human intentions and frustrates even the best possible Law (Rom 2:17–29; 7:7–25). Such passages have been misused by Christians to suggest that Jews have a supersized sin of

---

group, Israel's salvation is regarded as distinct from Christ and secured already through the Mosaic covenant; for others, it is crucial that Paul understands Jesus as Messiah ("Christ"), and thus the Messiah for Israel.

24. See on this last point Matthew Thiessen, *Paul and the Gentile Problem* (Oxford: Oxford University Press, 2016).

25. We should note, however: the more variegated one recognizes Second Temple Judaism to have been, the more difficult it is to maintain that Paul, because he was a Jew, *must* have thought or lived in a certain way. And while Paul was a Jew, he might still have been anomalous; see John M. G. Barclay, *Jews in the Mediterranean Diaspora from Alexander to Trajan (323 BCE–117 CE)* (Edinburgh: T&T Clark, 1996), 381–95.

26. Note the distinction here between the audience (to whom Paul is speaking) and the subject-matter (what he is speaking about).

arrogance, exclusivity, or self-reliant boasting, but Paul's purpose is to indicate that even the Torah, the greatest defense against Sin, has failed and that only grace given to the *unrighteous* can match the depth of the human problem. Paul is confident about Israel's future (according to the "mystery" of Rom 11:25–26), not because Israel is unaffected by Sin, but because God has created and sustained Israel by grace and can graft back in those branches that are presently cut off (11:24, 28–32).

As we have seen, Israel is in Paul's view most truly itself when it trusts in its Messiah, Jesus, and this definitive gift means that Paul places his whole Jewish heritage at the service of, and subordinate to, the ultimate value of "knowing Christ" (Phil 3:4–11; see chapter 10). If the Torah can be observed in serving the Lord, Christ, that is good (Rom 14:1–11; see chapter 8). But if Torah-observance would destroy the unity among believers or would form a barrier to gentile access to Christ, it would be better for Jews like Peter and Paul to live "in a gentile fashion" (Gal 2:11–14; see chapter 4). Speaking as a Jew in Christ (Gal 2:15–17), Paul says he has "died to the Law" in order to live to God (Gal 2:19) because the Law is no longer the supreme norm for those whose identity and allegiance have been reconfigured by the gift of Christ (Gal 2:19–21). Paul's stance here is subtler than a simple binary choice between comprehensive obedience to the Law or utter repudiation of it. Subject to the authority of Christ, Paul can certainly live like a Jew where that serves the purposes of the good news (1 Cor 9:19–23). But because that good news announces a gift given without regard to previous criteria of worth, every cultural tradition (Jewish and non-Jewish) is subject to its supreme criterion of value, and every practice made relative to the purposes of Christ.[27]

Paul stands, indeed, "within Judaism" in the sense that he participates in its internal debates regarding God, grace, and the interpretation of Scripture. But because he interprets that grace as an incongruous gift, definitively given in Christ, his Jewish conceptuality is reconfigured in radical and often paradoxical ways. We must not return to Christian caricatures of Judaism or to reading Paul as if he lambasted an inherently defective "Judaism." But the Christ-gift has recalibrated *everything* once regarded as symbolic capital (Phil 3:8; Gal 6:14), and that includes Paul's Jewish allegiances, now fulfilled in Christ and subordinated to him.

---

27. See further, in dialogue with Caroline Johnson-Hodge, John M. G. Barclay, "An Identity Received from God: The Theological Configuration of Paul's Kinship Discourse," *Early Christianity* 8 (2017): 354–72.

The reading of Paul offered in this book thus intersects with both long-established and more recent lines of interpretation. It has the capacity to resolve some of the old confessional disputes around grace but also to put more recent lines of interpretation on a stronger exegetical base and to repair some of their weaknesses. Every reading is, of course, answerable to the text and can be established only by patient and painstaking exegesis.

But I have made here at least a prima facie case that a fresh consideration of the familiar topic of grace does not take us back to old disputes but forward to new ways of configuring the total shape of Paul's thought. It is now time to suggest what resources this might supply for the contemporary task of "thinking with Paul."

CHAPTER 13

Paul and the Dynamics of Grace Today

Many people in the modern West think of God in something like the way they think of Santa Claus: that is, as a genial figure whom you address only when you want something, and then you hope he will be kind if he considers you sufficiently good. I have argued in this book that the pattern of Paul's good news is very different, in fact, the *inverse* of this Santa Claus image. According to the well-known Christmas song, "Santa Claus Is Coming to Town," it is Santa's task to keep a list of those who do right and wrong, and he will distribute his gifts accordingly. In other words, Santa's gifts are conditioned: he gives to those who have been good. Like most responsible givers, he wishes to give only to worthy recipients, and he finds out who they are. However, once his gifts have been given, there is no resulting relationship, no expression of gratitude, and no expectation of a gift in return. (Children write requests to Santa, but does anyone ever write him a thank-you letter or ask him how he's doing after Christmas?) In other words, Santa's gifts are congruous but noncircular. They are given to worthy recipients but have "no strings attached." They fit the moral ideals of modern, Western individualism.

Paul's message of grace was the opposite: incongruous and circular. The Christ-gift was given to the "ungodly"—in the absence of worth—and it was given to all, without regard to any preconstituted worth of gender, ethnicity, status, or success. There was no "list" and no selection determined by "who's naughty or nice." But it was given in order to transform the human recipients and to establish a permanent relationship: the receipt of this gift is necessarily expressed in gratitude, obedience, and transformed behavior. This grace is free (unconditioned) but not cheap (without expectations or obligations). Those who have received it are to remain within it, their lives altered by new habits, new dispositions, and new practices of grace.

We have focused in this book on the (undisputed) letters of Paul. If we were to range more widely across the New Testament, the pattern of grace would be largely the same. In the gospels, Jesus associates with the stigmatized, the lost, and the worthless: with prostitutes, tax-collectors, illiterate fishermen, children, and women marginalized by illness or ethnicity. His association represents the welcome of God. Jesus proclaims "the year of the Lord's favor" (Luke 4:18–19) without regard to the standard criteria of worth, indeed often provocatively against them. He tells stories of a mercy that crosses ethnic distinctions (the parable of the good Samaritan, Luke 10:29–37), of forgiveness to the hopelessly indebted (Matt 18:23–35), and of a divine love that awaits the return of the prodigal son (Luke 15:11–32). This is an unmerited, incongruous mercy like that announced by Paul, though expressed in a different idiom. At the same time, this grace is anything but cheap: Jesus is excoriating in his criticisms of those who disobey God and makes heavy demands of his disciples. This is not a grace where "anything goes." Time after time, Jesus makes clear that strong expectations are laid on those who are welcomed into the kingdom: the forgiven are expected to forgive (Matt 6:12), the fig tree is expected to bear fruit (Luke 13:6–9), the disciples are called to serve (Mark 10:41–45), the wealthy are expected to give (Luke 19:1–10), and the loved are commanded to love (John 13:34–35). These are not means to earn a second gift but the proper result when "salvation has come to this house" (Luke 19:9).

The letters written (probably) after Paul within the Pauline tradition display the same pattern of a free but demanding gift. The extraordinary welcome of non-Jews is a matter of continuing celebration: those who were estranged from God and "dead" in their sins are now included in God's people by an unconditioned gift (Eph 2:1–21). The point can be generalized: "The saying is sure and worthy of full acceptance, that Christ Jesus came into the world to save sinners" (1 Tim 1:15). This salvation is given "not according to our works, but according to God's own purpose and grace" (2 Tim 1:9). But this grace does not leave its recipients as they were: Jesus Christ "gave himself for us, that he might redeem us from all iniquity and purify for himself a people of his own, zealous for good deeds" (Titus 2:14). This is not, as has sometimes been claimed, a descent from the gospel of grace into "moralism." These "good deeds" are the works of compassion and mutual support that circulate within the community of believers and spill out from them to others—in other words, the practice of grace in community-building generosity that we traced above (see chapter 11). Here, too, the grace of God is transformative—given without boundaries or conditions in order to remake its recipients.

Bu what are the implications for us today? How can Paul's theology of grace be recontextualized in our own time and place? It is important to be aware of what this question entails. We cannot simply transfer texts and concepts across the distance of time and culture that separates us from Paul. Our own cultural contexts are very different from his, and we need a range of creative skills in interpretation to identify the right points of resonance. Theological interpretation looks to learn from the ways in which Paul's theology has been received and reapplied down the centuries. While it takes inspiration from understanding his letters in their original historical context, it also claims a necessary freedom to rethink his theology for new contexts, in different language, and with the aid of additional theological resources. By way of illustration, I will outline here three ways in which Paul's theology of grace could have resonance today: in equipping communities to challenge inherited systems of worth; in addressing contemporary crises in personal self-esteem; and in fostering the practice of reciprocal generosity, forms of giving not *to* but *with* the poor.

Challenging Communities

Paul's theology of grace was developed in and for the creation of innovative communities that crossed previous boundaries and challenged preestablished hierarchies of worth. It required expression in social terms and could be real only if it had effect in the creation of countercultural practices. Since God's calling in grace did not take account of the standard taxonomies of ethnicity, status, or gender, the communities it founded needed to demonstrate its presence in meals, meetings, and patterns of mutual care that were not bound by conventional practice.

To what extent, and in what ways, do churches today demonstrate this grace-shaped ethos and its capacity to challenge culturally dominant evaluations of worth? It is frighteningly easy for churches to be shaped, at a deep and subconscious level, by their societal norms, and to assume that the standard cultural assumptions regarding ethnicity, race, class, status, and gender are endorsed by the good news of Christ. Implicitly (and sometimes explicitly) barriers are erected between "people like us" and "others," whether the attitude toward those others is dismissive or patronizing.[1] Churches easily settle into a homogeneous subculture, where certain sorts of people attend one church,

---

1. See J. Louis Martyn, "From Paul to Flannery O'Connor with the Power of Grace," in his *Theological Issues in the Letters of Paul* (Edinburgh: T&T Clark, 1997), 279–96. He comments here on a powerful short-story ("Revelation") by Flannery O'Connor, regarding deep prejudices against people of lower social status.

and certain sorts another, such that ingrained assumptions become reinforced because one's community is unmixed.[2] Even within the one church, different services for different "types" of people may reinforce the social cultures of each. As Paul realized, it is difficult to break out of inherited social norms, which run deep in the *habitus* of a culture. But he insisted on a theology of the cross that subverted those assumptions and on a theology of grace that recalibrated all standards of worth. That theology of grace has been best articulated by those who have broken through class barriers (e.g., early Methodism), have challenged racial injustice (e.g., Martin Luther King), and have articulated the worth of all, abled and disabled (e.g., the L'Arche communities). All these have demonstrated the subversive power of grace, which takes no account of "elite" ancestry, "superior" education, the color of our skin, or the capacities of our bodies. Paul's theology of grace is, in fact, a rich resource for Christians in challenging racism, gender prejudice, and all forms of negative stereotype.

Creating and sustaining communities that cross the cultural assumptions of our society is no easy task, and there is no simple formula for how to do so in the name of grace. Paul founded and supported communities where "there is neither Jew nor Greek, neither slave nor free, no male and female" (Gal 3:28). This did not mean the abolition of these categories, but it did require that the hierarchies of worth conveyed by them were undermined and that every identity was reoriented to the "superior worth" of knowing Christ (Phil 3:8). This meant, first and foremost, that every believer was honored and loved as a brother or sister in Christ, whether they were slave, freedman, or free (Phlm 16; 1 Cor 7:21–24). Slaves were not of lesser value than the free because legal status was not what gave anyone worth before God. Paul did not, and perhaps could not, envisage an economic structure in which slavery was abolished, and he leaves ambiguous what it means for believers to own slaves whom they regard as siblings. In our different economic and social conditions, and equipped with a theological ethic that repudiates the ownership of humans, we would develop Pauline resources into a more comprehensive ethic of social justice.[3] In relation to gender, Paul could rethink gender identities to such an extent that he could overturn assumptions about sexuality and marriage and

---

2. For comments in this connection on the Christian role in apartheid, see Richard Burridge, *Imitating Jesus: An Inclusive Approach to New Testament Ethics* (Grand Rapids: Eerdmans, 2007), 347–409.

3. For reflections on the partial, but only partial, overlap between Paul's notions of freedom and equality and those we have inherited from the Enlightenment, see John M. G. Barclay, "What Makes Paul Challenging Today?" in *The New Cambridge Companion to St. Paul*, ed. Bruce W. Longenecker (Cambridge: Cambridge University Press, 2020), 299–318.

promote the benefits of singleness (1 Corinthians 7). He also opened possibilities for women's leadership that did not match the traditional norms of gender and status (e.g., Phoebe and Prisca in Rom 16:1–5; Junia in Rom 16:7).[4] In our different historical context, and with additional theological tools, we can and should develop this Pauline resource further than he could imagine, but the essential point is authentically his: grace is not given differentially with regard to gender, or with regard to age, wealth, status, or race. On this basis, any discrimination, any inequality in treatment, any attribution of secondary status is an affront to the good news of the grace of God in Christ.

Paul insists on the practice of grace in the context of communal meals at Antioch (Gal 2:11–14), at Corinth (1 Cor 11:17–34), and at Rome (Rom 14:1–15:6). In its meals, and especially at "the Lord's Supper" (1 Cor 11:20), the community is constituted by its mutual welcome and by the welcome it has received from Christ. At this meal (now variously named "Communion," "Eucharist," "Lord's Supper," or "Mass"), the church is recalled most clearly to its status as a community created by an undiscriminating grace. Where Christ's body is given "for you," the community hears the value of each member, for whom Christ died (1 Cor 8:11; Rom 14:15), and believers are reminded, physically and mentally, that they are children of God by grace alone. At that moment, cultural prejudices concerning ethnic origin, educational attainment, age, and class should fall away, as believers become recipients of grace and thus most truly themselves.

For Paul, the value of each person resides in the worth that they are given by the love of God in Christ. Believers are required to care about others "for whom Christ died" (1 Cor 8:11), and since, as Paul says, Christ died for all (2 Cor 5:14–15), we may regard everyone as accorded the same worth in that single act of unconditioned grace. That would constitute a starting point for a distinctively Christian contribution to the current discussion about the basis of human rights and the individual's worth. The American Declaration of Independence states, "We hold these truths to be self-evident, that all men are created equal, that they are endowed by their Creator with certain unalienable Rights, that among these are Life, Liberty and the pursuit of Happiness." Nowadays we are not at all sure how these claims can be regarded as "self-evident," and it is clear that no one can take them for granted. In the United Nations' *Universal Declaration of Human Rights*, reference to the "Creator" disappears, and we have only the assertion, "All human beings are born free and equal

---

4. Amidst the vast literature on Paul and gender, see the well-informed reconstruction of the life of Phoebe in Paula Gooder, *Phoebe: A Story* (London: Hodder & Stoughton, 2018).

in dignity and in rights. They are endowed with reason and conscience and should act towards one another in a spirit of brotherhood." Ever since this was drafted, there has been no consensus regarding the basis of this equality "in dignity and rights." In practice, the influence of power, wealth, and national self-interest ensure that some lives matter more than others and that some people's dignity is denied. Traditionally, Christian theology has affirmed the dignity of each individual on the basis of their creation in "the image of God" (*imago Dei*), but it is not wholly clear what that motif entails or whether it can bear such weight. Pauline theology would point in a different direction, locating the value of each person not (only) in nature but in grace.[5] On that basis, racial, gender, and social discrimination are affronts to "the truth of the good news," which announces the indiscriminate grace of God in Christ.

Because You're Worth It

We live in an age when self-esteem, or self-worth, is under intense pressure, especially among young people. Indeed, research in Western societies shows that crises of self-worth have reached epidemic proportions. Schools, colleges, counselors, churches, and health workers report a sharp and shocking rise in the number of people suffering anxiety, self-doubt, depression, and loss of self-esteem. These ailments manifest in numerous ways: self-harm, panic attacks, eating disorders, sleep disorders, obsessive behavior, suicidal thoughts, and, tragically, suicide. The problem has multiple roots, but it seems to be exacerbated by social media, with its requirement to project an attractive self-image in popularity, appearance, body-shape, and success. The combination of impossibly high expectations and fragile egos is a recipe for distress. In an age when people fear the judgment of their peers more than the judgment of God, we have become increasingly petulant, critical, even cruel, and it is proving hard to take.

In Paul's good news, human worth is founded on the grace of God, which is not dependent on any form of symbolic capital, ascribed or achieved. No one can, and no one needs to, make themselves "worth it" in the most important arena of all. One might speak here of a "psychology of grace."[6] In response to

5. In Col 1:15–20, Christ is hailed as "the image of God" and as the integrating power of all creation. In that frame, the value of all that exists is given a Christological foundation, such that creation and grace cohere. Thus, the worth of each individual would reside both in their creation and in their reconciliation, and both of these would hold true "in Christ."

6. See the work of the psychotherapist and theologian Dorothy W. Martyn, *Beyond*

the contemporary crises in self-esteem, many have urged that people should "let go of who you think you are supposed to be and embrace who you are."[7] But that does not help if "who you are" crumbles under your own embrace, as happens for many people today. If that embrace does not come from outside of ourselves, and if it is not completely authoritative and utterly secure, we are left wishing ourselves into worth, rather than knowing we have it.

In his Heidelberg Disputation of 1518, Martin Luther articulated his final thesis (28) as follows: "The love of God does not find, but creates what is pleasing to it. Human love comes into being through what is pleasing to it" (my translation). The point of the contrast is simple but profound. Human love is by attraction: we are drawn to something good, beautiful, or useful, to something that is already present in the object. We cannot love something that we cannot see or imagine, and we turn away from evil and ugliness because they are unattractive to us. What attracts or repels us depends, of course, on our own standards of value; we love what we count as worthy of our love. By contrast, on the basis of the good news, but against the dominant philosophical tradition, Luther insisted that the love of God does not *find* something pleasing to it, which draws God's love toward it. Rather, it *creates* what is pleasing and good, confers it, and fashions it out of nothing. As Luther commented on this thesis: "Therefore sinners are attractive [to God] because they are loved; they are not loved because they are attractive. . . . This is the love of the cross, born of the cross, which turns in the direction where it does not find good which it may enjoy, but where it may confer good on the bad and needy person."[8] Grace, in other words, is unconditioned. It does not depend on human accounts of worth but gives worth, the only worth that counts, the worth of being loved by God.

That is, of course, easier to affirm than to feel. Against our individualistic desire to know and feel this from ourselves, Paul offers a social vision of a community in which each person honors and affirms the other: "Take the lead in showing honor to one another" (Rom 12:10). That is a powerful injunction: it gives each person the responsibility to ensure that others hear what they might not be able to tell themselves. And, of course, the speech has to be accompanied by practice. As we have seen, Paul was furious when believers were shamed or humiliated (1 Cor 11:22); he expected practice, at meals and

Deserving: Children, Parents, and Responsibility Revisited (Grand Rapids: Eerdmans, 2007).

7. This is the subtitle of Brené Brown's well-known book, *Gifts of Imperfection* (Center City, MN: Hazelden, 2010).

8. Martin Luther, *Heidelberg Disputation*, in *Luther's Works* (St. Louis: Concordia; Philadelphia: Fortress, 1955–1986), 31:39–70, Thesis 28.

elsewhere, to express the worth of each one "for whom Christ died" (Rom 14:15). That is why patient, resilient, and long-term relationships are, in the end, the only way to express the truth of the worth of one another. If close relationships are fragile and few, they may prove insufficient, and a diverse community like a church, for all its difficulties, might prove in the long term more resilient than a single, or limited, support-base. Moreover, the church can articulate that the worth of each person is dependent on a reality greater than its own fallible resources—that, when all else fails, the love of God does not.[9] What we need are better, fuller, and more down-to-earth ways of making this message clear and practical, and in the present psychological state of many young people, few things seem more existentially urgent.

GIFT, RECIPROCITY, AND "CHARITY"

As we saw in chapter 11, Paul's theology of grace presses toward the practice of generosity since grace draws believers into participation in the generous self-giving of God. But if all that we have is what we have been given, and if it is given that it may be shared, that alters the frame in which we think about ownership and property and challenges the assumption that we have the "right" to use what we own in whatever way we wish. In the history of modernity, assertions of the right of private property arose in defense of individuals and families against the predatory tendencies of landowners and states. But such rights have become an end in themselves, divorced from wider social responsibilities, such that the state is now understood to exist to defend the rights of private property rather than to provide a framework for mutual care. As we cherish the right to utilize "our" resources however we wish, we have become a critical threat to our planet and to its future sustainability. Here Paul's theology of divine gifts, which we hold in trust for others, has the capacity to generate alternative notions of ownership, foregrounding our accountability to the Giver and thus to others, including future generations.[10] Central Western values, like autonomy and choice, are beginning to show their limitations if they do not serve a larger social purpose, and Paul's theology of gift-sharing,

---

9. See Philip Yancey, *What's So Amazing about Grace?* (Grand Rapids: Zondervan, 1997).

10. For theological reflections on this matter, see Kathryn Tanner, *Economy of Grace* (Minneapolis: Fortress, 2005) and her penetrating analysis of the perils of finance capitalism, *Christianity and the New Spirit of Capitalism* (New Haven: Yale University Press, 2019).

community, and reciprocity could offer resources for a more balanced and sustainable political economy.

We noted, in chapter 11, the significance of reciprocity in the Pauline ethic of gift: Paul does not idealize the one-way gift but figures the body as a dynamic community of gift and receipt. Although the Christian concept of love has often been associated with self-sacrifice and self-negation, Paul's theology offers resources for a more nuanced picture.[11] Paul does not figure the interests of the self as necessarily in competition with the interests of others, as if in a zero-sum calculation where benefit for one must mean loss for the other. When the self is given *into* a collective "we," its interests are not lost but pooled, and the benefits are shared. This raises a significant question against modern notions of "altruism," a concept that typically operates with a binary opposition between "my" interests (egoism) and the interests of the other (altruism). Although some Christians have been keen to adopt this model of altruism, we have found in Paul many indications that point in a different direction. Although the self must shed whatever serves its own good *at the expense of others*, it can and should flourish within a shared good where its interests are fulfilled *in conjunction with* the interests of others.

Paul's model of reciprocity therefore contributes to notions of giving that are neither top-down nor one-way. As many analysts now recognize, forms of "charity," "service," or "philanthropy" that operate in the mode of one-way giving often turn out to be toxic.[12] Both at the international level (in international "aid") and in more local, charitable enterprises, the one-way gift frequently proves to be patronizing, demeaning, and disempowering. Well-intentioned giving on this model can backfire, creating resentment or continuing dependency rather than partnership, growth, and mutual respect. A Pauline ethic of reciprocity and interdependency provides resources for the development of alternative models of gift, which, on theological grounds, can apply outside the church as well as within it. Indeed, there is a strong resonance here with the social vision of the "common good," and, at the local level, with forms of community development known as "asset-based community development." The philosophical and pragmatic roots of this perspective lie in sources as diverse as Paulo Freire's liberation insights and Saul Alinsky's rules of com-

---

11. For theological treatments of Christian love, see Gene Outka, *Agape: An Ethical Analysis* (New Haven: Yale University Press, 1972).

12. For recent discussion, see Steve Corbett and Brian Fikkert, *When Helping Hurts* (Chicago: Moody, 2009); Robert D. Lupton, *Toxic Charity: How Churches and Charities Hurt Those They Help (And How to Reverse It)* (New York: HarperCollins, 2011).

munity organizing,[13] but its primary principles include: the expectation that the community itself will already contain multiple gifts, ready to be discovered and developed; the determination to bring in outside resources, financial or personal, *only* in such a way as to develop and enhance the gifts within the community; and the desire to create partnerships, cooperation, and solidarity both within local communities, and, where appropriate, with other agencies. Paul's theology of community aligns closely with this vision in many respects, especially in the formation of communities of mutual dependence, where every member of the body has something to contribute and no one can say of another, "I have no need of you" (1 Cor 12:21).[14] In this respect, it is unhelpful (even harmful) to speak of "the poor" or "deprivation," if one thereby implies the presence of nothing but lack. On a Pauline model of the body, everyone has something to give to others, and one should expect to give not *to* the poor but *with* them.[15]

These are just some of the ways in which the theology we have explored in this book could provide resources of relevance to our contemporary world. Although the theme of grace has traditionally been heard to apply primarily to the individual ("I once was lost, but now am found"), I have tried to highlight here its social dimensions, in line with the fact that Paul developed this theology in the context of his gentile mission and in relation to the formation of communities, not just the conversion of individuals. To be sure, the implications are individual as well as communal, psychological as well as social, but for Paul individuals will hear and experience the good news primarily in relationships with others. As we have found, "theology" for Paul cannot be divorced from "ethics," and if the good news is not expressed in transformed behavior, it is received in vain. Approaching Paul afresh from the perspective of gift or grace helps us to see his whole theology in a new light; it solves some of the long-standing conundrums in Pauline studies and has contemporary resonance in multiple dimensions. Careful exegesis and a well-founded historical understanding of Paul's letters turn out, in this respect, not to distance

13. Paulo Freire, *Pedagogy of the Oppressed* (Harmondsworth: Penguin Books, 1972); Saul Alinsky, *Rules for Radicals: A Pragmatic Primer for Realistic Radicals* (New York: Vintage Books, 1989).

14. For further discussion, see John M. G. Barclay, "Paul, Reciprocity, and Giving with the Poor," in *Practicing with Paul: Reflections on Paul and the Practices of Ministry in Honor of Susan G. Eastman*, ed. Presian R. Burroughs (Eugene, OR: Cascade), 15–29.

15. For the significance of the preposition "with," see Samuel Wells, *A Nazareth Manifesto: Being with God* (Chichester: Wiley-Blackwell, 2015).

Paul from ourselves but to throw out new challenges and fresh possibilities. In our current intellectual and political conditions, that is highly welcome, and it is notable that several philosophers, including some from outside the Christian tradition, have recently rediscovered Paul and have hailed the present as Paul's "new moment."[16] If it is so, one of Paul's greatest contributions to our contemporary world must be his theology of grace.

16. John Milbank, Slavoj Žižek, and Creston Davis, *Paul's New Moment: Continental Philosophy and the Future of Christian Theology* (Grand Rapids: Brazos, 2010).

Bibliography

Translations of Ancient Texts

Hesiod, *Works and Days*. Translated by Dorothea Wender. London: Penguin, 1973.

John Chrysostom, *Homilies on Romans*. Translated in *A Select Library of the Nicene and Post-Nicene Fathers of the Church*. Edited by Philip Schaff. Vol. 11. Edinburgh: T&T Clark, 1996.

Pelagius, *Commentary on St Paul's Epistle to the Romans*. Edited and translated by Theodore de Bruyn. Oxford: Clarendon, 1993.

Seneca, *On Benefits*. Translated by Miriam Griffin and Brad Inwood. Chicago: University of Chicago Press, 2011.

Tertullian, *Against Marcion*. Edited and translated by Ernest Evans. 2 vols. Oxford: Clarendon, 1972.

Other Works Cited

Alinsky, Saul. *Rules for Radicals: A Pragmatic Primer for Realistic Radicals*. New York: Vintage Books, 1989.

Allen, Michael and Jonathan A. Linebaugh eds. *Reformation Readings of Paul: Explorations in History and Exegesis*. Downers Grove, IL: InterVarsity Press, 2015.

Anderson, Gary A. *Charity: The Place of the Poor in the Biblical Tradition*. New Haven: Yale University Press, 2013.

Atkins, Margaret, and Robin Osborne, eds. *Poverty in the Roman World*. Cambridge: Cambridge University Press, 2006.

Badiou, Alain. *Saint Paul: The Foundation of Universalism*. Translated by Ray Brassier. Stanford: Stanford University Press, 2003.

Barclay, John M. G. "'Because He Was Rich He Became Poor': Translation, Exegesis, and Hermeneutics in the Reading of 2 Cor 8.9." Pages 331–44 in *Theologizing in the Corinthian Conflict: Studies in the Exegesis and Theology of 2 Corin-thians.* Edited by Reimund Bieringer, Ma. Marilou S. Ibita, Dominika A. Kurek-Chomycz, and Thomas A. Vollmer. Leuven: Peeters, 2013.

———. "Crucifixion as Wisdom: Exploring the Ideology of a Disreputable Social Movement." Pages 15–32 in *The Wisdom and Foolishness of God: First Cor-inthians 1–2 in Theological Exploration.* Edited by Christophe Chalamet and Hans-Christoph Askani. Minneapolis: Fortress, 2017.

———. "Faith and Self-Detachment from Cultural Norms: A Study of Romans 14–15." *Zeitschrift für neutestamentliche Wissenschaft* 104 (2013): 192–208.

———. "'I Will Have Mercy on Whom I Have Mercy': The Golden Calf and Divine Mercy in Romans 9–11 and Second Temple Judaism." *Early Christianity* 1 (2010): 82–106.

———. "An Identity Received from God: The Theological Configuration of Paul's Kinship Discourse." *Early Christianity* 8 (2017): 354–72.

———. *Jews in the Mediterranean Diaspora from Alexander to Trajan (323 BCE–117 CE).* Edinburgh: T&T Clark, 1996.

———. "Manna and the Circulation of Grace: A Study of 2 Corinthians 8:1–15." Pages 409–26 in *The Word Leaps the Gap: Essays on Scripture and Theology in Honor of Richard B. Hays.* Edited by J. Ross Wagner, C. Kavin Rowe, and A. Katherine Grieb. Grand Rapids: Eerdmans, 2008.

———. *Obeying the Truth: A Study of Paul's Ethics in Galatians.* Edinburgh: T&T Clark, 1988.

———. *Paul and the Gift.* Grand Rapids: Eerdmans, 2015.

———. "Paul, Reciprocity, and Giving with the Poor." Pages 15–29 in *Practicing with Paul: Reflections on Paul and the Practices of Ministry in Honor of Susan G. Eastman.* Edited by Presian R. Burroughs. Eugene: Cascade, 2018.

———. *Pauline Churches and Diaspora Jews.* Grand Rapids: Eerdmans, 2016.

———. "Paul's Story: Theology as Testimony." Pages 133–56 in *Narrative Dynamics in Paul: A Critical Assessment.* Edited by Bruce W. Longenecker. Louisville: Westminster John Knox, 2002.

———. "What Makes Paul Challenging Today?" Pages 299–318 in *The New Cam-bridge Companion to St. Paul.* Edited by Bruce W. Longenecker. Cambridge: Cambridge University Press, 2020.

Barclay, John M. G., and Simon J. Gathercole, eds. *Divine and Human Agency in Paul and His Cultural Environment.* London: T&T Clark, 2006.

Barton, Carlin A. *Roman Honor: The Fire in the Bones.* Berkeley: University of California Press, 2001.

Bates, Matthew W. *Salvation by Allegiance Alone.* Grand Rapids: Baker Academic, 2017.

Bird, Michael, and Preston M. Sprinkle, eds. *The Faith of Jesus Christ: Exegetical, Biblical, and Theological Studies*. Milton Keynes: Paternoster, 2009.

Blackwell, Ben C. *Christosis: Engaging Paul's Soteriology with His Patristic Interpreters*. Grand Rapids: Eerdmans, 2016.

Bonhoeffer, Dietrich. *The Cost of Discipleship*. London: SCM, 1948.

Bonner, Gerald. *St. Augustine of Hippo: Life and Controversies*. Norwich: Canterbury, 1963.

Bourdieu, Pierre. *Outline of a Theory of Practice*. Translated by Richard Nice. Cambridge: Cambridge University Press, 1977.

Boyarin, Daniel. *A Radical Jew: Paul and the Politics of Identity*. Berkeley: University of California Press, 1994.

Breytenbach, Cilliers. *Grace, Reconciliation, Concord: The Death of Christ in Graeco-Roman Metaphors*. Leiden: Brill, 2010.

Briones, David E. *Paul's Financial Policy: A Socio-Theological Approach*. London: T&T Clark, 2013.

Brown, Brené. *Gifts of Imperfection*. Center City, MN: Hazelden, 2010.

Brown, Michael L. *Hyper-Grace*. Lake Mary, FL: Charisma House, 2014.

Brown, Peter. *Augustine of Hippo*. New York: Dorset, 1967.

Burke, Kenneth. *Language as Symbolic Action: Essays on Life, Literature, and Method*. Berkeley: University of California Press, 1966.

———. *Permanence and Change: An Anatomy of Purpose*. Berkeley: University of California Press, 1954.

Burridge, Richard. *Imitating Jesus: An Inclusive Approach to New Testament Ethics*. Grand Rapids: Eerdmans, 2007.

Campbell, Douglas. *The Deliverance of God: An Apocalyptic Reading of Justification in Paul*. Grand Rapids: Eerdmans, 2009.

———. *The Rhetoric of Righteousness in Romans 3:21–26*. Sheffield: JSOT Press, 1992.

Carson, D. A., Peter T. O'Brien, and Mark A. Seifrid, eds. *The Complexities of Second Temple Judaism*. Vol. 1 of *Justification and Variegated Nomism*. Tübingen: Mohr Siebeck, 2001.

Catechism of the Catholic Church. London: Burns and Oates, 2010.

Chester, Stephen J. *Conversion at Corinth: Perspectives on Conversion in Paul's Theology and the Corinthian Church*. Edinburgh: T&T Clark, 2003.

———. *Reading Paul with the Reformers: Reconciling Old and New Perspectives*. Grand Rapids: Eerdmans, 2017.

Cook, John G. *Crucifixion in the Mediterranean World*. Tübingen: Mohr Siebeck, 2014.

Corbett, Steve, and Brian Fikkert. *When Helping Hurts*. Chicago: Moody, 2009.

Croasmun, Matthew. *The Emergence of Sin: The Cosmic Tyrant in Romans*. Oxford: Oxford University Press, 2017.

Dahl, Nils. "The Future of Israel." Pages 137–58 in *Studies in Paul*. Minneapolis: Fortress, 1977.

Das, Andrew A. *Solving the Romans Debate*. Minneapolis: Fortress, 2007.

Dawson, J. David. *Christian Figural Reading and the Fashioning of Identity*. Berkeley: University of California Press, 2002.

de Boer, Martinus C. *The Defeat of Death: Apocalyptic Eschatology in 1 Corinthians 15 and Romans 5*. Sheffield: Sheffield Academic, 1988.

———. *Galatians: A Commentary*. New Testament Library. Louisville: Westminster John Knox, 2011.

———. "Paul's Quotation of Isa 54.1 in Gal 4.27." *New Testament Studies* 50 (2004): 370–89.

Derrida, Jacques. *Counterfeit Money*. Vol. 1 of *Given Time*. Translated by Peggy Kamuf. Chicago: University of Chicago Press, 1992.

deSilva, David A. *Honor, Patronage, Kinship, and Purity: Unlocking New Testament Culture*. Downers Grove, IL: InterVarsity Press, 2000.

Despotis, Athanasios, ed. *Participation, Justification, and Conversion: Eastern Orthodox Interpretation of Paul and the Debate Between Old and New Perspectives on Paul*. Tübingen: Mohr Siebeck, 2017.

Donfried, Karl P., ed. *The Romans Debate: Revised and Expanded Edition*. Grand Rapids: Baker Academic, 2011.

Downs, David J. *The Offering of the Gentiles: Paul's Collection for Jerusalem in its Chronological, Cultural, and Cultic Contexts*. Grand Rapids: Eerdmans, 2016.

Dunn, James D. G. *Romans 1–8*. Word Biblical Commentary 38A. Grand Rapids: Zondervan, 1988.

———. *Romans 9–16*. Word Biblical Commentary 38B. Grand Rapids: Zondervan, 1988.

———. *Jesus, Paul, and the Law*. London: SPCK, 1990.

———. *The Epistle to the Galatians*. London: Black, 1993.

———. *The New Perspective on Paul: Collected Essays*. Tübingen: Mohr Siebeck, 2005.

Eastman, Susan. "Israel and the Mercy of God: A Re-Reading of Galatians 6.16 and Romans 9–11." *New Testament Studies* 56 (2010): 367–95.

———. *Paul and the Person: Reframing Paul's Anthropology*. Grand Rapids: Eerdmans, 2017.

———. *Recovering Paul's Mother Tongue: Language and Theology in Galatians*. Grand Rapids: Eerdmans, 2007.

Ellis, Paul. *The Hyper-Grace Gospel*. Birkenhead, New Zealand: KingsPress, 2014.

Engberg-Pedersen, Troels. *Cosmology and Self in the Apostle Paul: The Material Spirit*. Oxford: Oxford University Press, 2010.

———. *Paul and the Stoics*. Edinburgh: T&T Clark, 2000.

Esler, Philip F. *Galatians*. London: Routledge, 1998.

Eubank, Nathan. "Configurations of Grace and Merit in Paul and His Interpreters." *International Journal of Systematic Theology* 22 (2020): 7–17.

Fee, Gordon D. *God's Empowering Spirit: The Holy Spirit in the Letters of Paul*. Grand Rapids: Baker Academic, 2011.

Fredriksen, Paula. *Paul, the Pagans' Apostle*. New Haven: Yale University Press, 2017.

Freire, Paulo. *Pedagogy of the Oppressed*. Harmondsworth: Penguin Books, 1972.

Gager, John. *Reinventing Paul*. Oxford: Oxford University Press, 2000.

Gathercole, Simon J. "A Law unto Themselves: The Gentiles in Romans 2:14–15 Revisited." *Journal for the Study of the New Testament* 85 (2002): 27–49.

———. *Where is Boasting? Early Jewish Soteriology and Paul's Response in Romans 1–5*. Grand Rapids: Eerdmans, 2002.

Gaventa, Beverly R. ed., *Apocalyptic Paul: Cosmos and Anthropos in Romans 5–8*. Waco: Baylor University Press, 2013.

———. "Galatians 1 and 2: Autobiography as Paradigm." *New Testament Studies* 28 (1986): 309–26.

———. "On the Calling-into-Being of Israel: Romans 9:6–29." Pages 255–69 in *Between Gospel and Election: Explorations in the Interpretation of Romans 9–11*. Edited by Florian Wilk and J. Ross Wagner. Tübingen: Mohr Siebeck, 2010.

———. *Our Mother Saint Paul*. Louisville: Westminster John Knox, 2007.

———. *When in Romans: An Invitation to Linger with the Gospel According to Paul*. Grand Rapids: Baker Academic, 2016.

Gill, Christopher, Norman Postlethwaite, and Richard Seaford, eds. *Reciprocity in Ancient Greece*. Oxford: Oxford University Press, 1998.

Givens, Tommy. *We the People: Israel and the Catholicity of Jesus*. Minneapolis: Fortress, 2014.

Godelier, Maurice. *The Enigma of the Gift*. Translated by Nora Scott. Chicago: University of Chicago Press, 1999.

Gooder, Paula. *Phoebe: A Story*. London: Hodder & Stoughton, 2018.

Gorman, Michael J. *Cruciformity: Paul's Narrative Spirituality of the Cross*. Grand Rapids: Eerdmans, 2001.

———. *Inhabiting the Cruciform God: Kenosis, Justification, and Theosis in Paul's Narrative Soteriology*. Grand Rapids: Eerdmans, 2009.

Gruen, Erich. *Diaspora*. Berkeley: University of California Press, 2002.

Hampson, Daphne. *Christian Contradictions: The Structures of Lutheran and Catholic Thought*. Cambridge: Cambridge University Press, 2001.

Harrison, Carol. *Rethinking Augustine's Early Theology: An Argument for Continuity*. Oxford: Oxford University Press, 2006.

Harrison, James R. *Paul's Language of Grace in its Graeco-Roman Context*. Tübingen: Mohr Siebeck, 2003.

Hayes, Christine. *What's Divine about Divine Law? Early Perspectives*. Princeton: Princeton University Press, 2015.

Hays, Richard B. "Christology and Ethics in Galatians: The Law of Christ." *Catholic Biblical Quarterly* 49 (1987): 268–90.

———. *Echoes of Scripture in the Letters of Paul*. New Haven: Yale University Press, 1989.

———. *The Faith of Jesus Christ: The Narrative Substructure of Galatians 3:1–4:11*. 2nd ed. Grand Rapids: Eerdmans, 2002.

Heilig, Christoph. *Hidden Criticism? The Methodology and Plausibility of the Search for a Counter-Imperial Subtext in Paul*. Minneapolis: Fortress, 2017.

Hengel, Martin. *Crucifixion*. London: SCM, 1977.

Hooker, Morna D. *From Adam to Christ*. Cambridge: Cambridge University Press, 1990.

Horrell, David G. *The Social Ethos of the Corinthian Correspondence: Interests and Ideology from 1 Corinthians to 1 Clement*. Edinburgh: T&T Clark, 1996.

———. *Solidarity and Difference: A Contemporary Reading of Paul's Ethics*. London: T&T Clark, 2005.

Hubbard, Moyer V. *New Creation in Paul's Letters and Thought*. Cambridge: Cambridge University Press, 2002.

Jackson, T. Ryan. *New Creation in Paul's Letters: A Study of the Historical and Social Setting of a Pauline Concept*. Tübingen: Mohr Siebeck, 2010.

Johnson-Hodge, Caroline. *If Sons, Then Heirs: A Study of Kinship and Ethnicity in the Letters of Paul*. Oxford: Oxford University Press, 2007.

Joubert, Stephan. *Paul as Benefactor: Reciprocity, Strategy, and Theological Reflection in Paul's Collection*. Tübingen: Mohr Siebeck, 2000.

Käsemann, Ernst. *Commentary on Romans*. Translated by Geoffrey W. Bromiley. London: SCM Press, 1980.

———. "'The Righteousness of God' in Paul." Pages 168–82 in *New Testament Questions of Today*. Translated by W. J. Montague. Philadelphia: Fortress, 1969.

———. "On Paul's Anthropology." Pages 1–31 in *Perspectives on Paul*. Translated by Margaret Kohl. London: SCM, 1971.

Kilby, Karen. "Paradox and Paul: Catholic and Protestant Theologies of Grace." *International Journal of Systematic Theology* 22 (2020): 77–82.

Kirk, J. R. Daniel. *Unlocking Romans: Resurrection and the Justification of God.* Grand Rapids: Eerdmans, 2008.

Lee, Michelle V. *Paul, the Stoics, and the Body of Christ.* Cambridge: Cambridge University Press, 2006.

Levenson, Jon D. *The Love of God: Divine Gift, Human Gratitude, and Mutual Faithfulness in Judaism.* Princeton: Princeton University Press, 2016.

Lieu, Judith M. *Marcion and the Making of a Heretic: God and Scripture in the Second Century.* Cambridge: Cambridge University Press, 2014.

Linebaugh, Jonathan A. *God, Grace, and Righteousness in Wisdom of Solomon and Paul's Letter to the Romans: Texts in Conversation.* Leiden: Brill, 2013.

———, ed. *God's Two Words: Law and Gospel in Lutheran and Reformed Traditions.* Grand Rapids: Eerdmans, 2018.

———. "The Grammar of the Gospel: Justification as a Theological Criterion in the Reformation and in Galatians." *Scottish Journal of Theology* 71 (2018): 287–307.

———. "Not the End: The History and Hope of the Unfailing Word." Pages 141–63 in *God and Israel: Providence and Purpose in Romans 9–11.* Edited by Todd D. Still. Waco: Baylor University Press, 2017.

———. "'The Speech of the Dead': Identifying the No Longer and Now Living 'I' of Galatians 2.20." *New Testament Studies* 66 (2020): 87–105.

Longenecker, Bruce W. *Remember the Poor: Paul, Poverty, and the Greco-Roman World.* Grand Rapids: Eerdmans, 2010.

Lupton, Robert D. *Toxic Charity: How Churches and Charities Hurt Those They Help (And How to Reverse It).* New York: HarperCollins, 2011.

Macaskill, Grant. *Living in Union with Christ: Paul's Gospel and Christian Moral Identity.* Grand Rapids: Baker Academic, 2019.

Mannermaa, Tuomo. *Christ Present in Faith: Luther's View of Justification.* Edited and translated by Kirsi Irmeli Stjerna. Minneapolis: Augsburg Fortress, 2005.

Martin, Dale B. *The Corinthian Body.* New Haven: Yale University Press, 1995.

Martyn, Dorothy W. *Beyond Deserving: Children, Parents, and Responsibility Revisited.* Grand Rapids: Eerdmans, 2007.

Martyn, J. Louis. "Apocalyptic Antinomies in Paul's Letter to the Galatians." *New Testament Studies* 31 (1985): 410–24.

———. *Galatians: A New Translation with Introduction and Commentary.* Anchor Yale Bible Commentary 33A. New York: Doubleday, 1997.

———. *Theological Issues in the Letters of Paul*. Edinburgh: T&T Clark, 1997.

Maston, Jason. *Divine and Human Agency in Second Temple Judaism and Paul*. Tübingen: Mohr Siebeck, 2010.

Matlock, R. Barry. "The Rhetoric of πίστις in Paul: Galatians 2.16, 3.22, Romans 3.22 and Philippians 3.9." *Journal for the Study of the New Testament* 30 (2007): 173–203.

Mauss, Marcel. *The Gift*. Translated by W. D. Halls. London: Routledge, 1990.

McCosker, Philip. "Grace." Pages 206–21 in *The Cambridge Companion to the Summa Theologiae*. Edited by Philip McCosker and Denys Turner. Cambridge: Cambridge University Press, 2016.

McFarland, Orrey. *God and Grace in Philo and Paul*. Leiden: Brill, 2015.

McKnight, Scot and B. J. Oropeza, eds. *Perspectives on Paul: Five Views*. Grand Rapids: Baker Academic, 2020.

Meeks, Wayne. *The First Urban Christians: The Social World of the Apostle Paul*. New Haven: Yale University Press, 1983.

Meggitt, Justin J. *Paul, Poverty and Survival*. Edinburgh: T&T Clark, 1998.

Meyer, Paul W. "Romans 10:4 and the 'End' of the Law." Pages 78–94 in *The Word in this World*. Louisville: Westminster John Knox, 2004.

Milbank, John, Slavoj Žižek, and Creston Davis. *Paul's New Moment: Continental Philosophy and the Future of Christian Theology*. Grand Rapids: Brazos, 2010.

Moll, Sebastian P. *The Arch-Heretic Marcion*. Tübingen: Mohr Siebeck, 2010.

Morales, Rodrigo J. *The Spirit and the Restoration of Israel*. Tübingen: Mohr Siebeck, 2010.

Morgan, Teresa. *Popular Morality in the Early Roman Empire*. Cambridge: Cambridge University Press, 2007.

———. *Roman Faith and Christian Faith: Pistis and Fides in the Early Roman Empire and Early Churches*. Oxford: Oxford University Press, 2017.

Nanos, Mark D., and Magnus Zetterholm, eds. *Paul within Judaism: Restoring the First-Century Context to the Apostle*. Minneapolis: Fortress, 2015.

Newsom, Carol. *The Self as Symbolic Space: Constructing Identity and Community at Qumran*. Leiden: Brill, 2004.

Nussbaum, Martha. *The Fragility of Goodness: Luck and Ethics in Greek Tragedy and Philosophy*. Second edition. Cambridge: Cambridge University Press, 2001.

Oakes, Edward T. *A Theology of Grace in Six Controversies*. Grand Rapids: Eerdmans, 2016.

Ogereau, Julian. *Paul's Koinōnia with the Philippians: A Socio-Historical Investigation of a Pauline Economic Partnership*. Tübingen: Mohr Siebeck, 2014.

O'Mahony, Kieran J. *Pauline Persuasion: A Sounding in 2 Corinthians 8–9*. Sheffield: Sheffield Academic, 2000.

Outka, Gene. *Agape: An Ethical Analysis*. New Haven: Yale University Press, 1972.

Parker, Robert T. "Pleasing Thighs: Reciprocity in Greek Religion," Pages 105–22 in *Reciprocity in Ancient Greece*. Edited by Christopher Gill, Norman Postlethwaite, and Richard Seaford. Oxford: Oxford University Press, 1998.

Parry, Jonathan. "*The Gift*, the Indian Gift, and the 'Indian Gift.'" *Man* 21 (1986): 453–73.

Patout Burns, J. *The Development of Augustine's Doctrine of Operative Grace*. Paris: Études Augustiniennes, 1980.

Peterman, Gerald W. *Paul's Gift from Philippi: Conventions of Gift Exchange and Christian Giving*. Cambridge: Cambridge University Press, 1997.

Piper, John. *The Justification of God: An Exegetical and Theological Study of Romans 9:1–23*. 2nd ed. Grand Rapids: Baker Academic, 1993.

Pitre, Brant, Michael P. Barber, and John A. Kincaid. *Paul, a New Covenant Jew: Rethinking Pauline Theology*. Grand Rapids: Eerdmans, 2019.

Prothro, James B. *Both Judge and Justifier: Biblical Legal Language and the Act of Justifying in Paul*. Tübingen: Mohr Siebeck, 2018.

Rabens, Volker. *The Holy Spirit and Ethics in Paul: Transformation and Empowering for Religious-Ethical Life*. 2nd ed. Minneapolis: Fortress, 2014.

Räisänen, Heikki. "Paul, God, and Israel: Romans 9–11 in Recent Research." Pages 127–208 in *The Social World of Formative Christianity and Judaism*. Edited by Jacob Neusner et al. Philadelphia: Fortress, 1988.

Riches, John K. *Galatians through the Centuries*. Oxford: Blackwell, 2008.

Sahlins, Marshall. *Stone Age Economics*. 2nd ed. London: Routledge, 2004.

Saller, Richard P. *Personal Patronage under the Early Empire*. Cambridge: Cambridge University Press, 1982.

Sanders, E. P. *Judaism: Practice and Belief, 63 BCE–66 CE*. London: SCM, 1992.

———. *Paul and Palestinian Judaism*. London: SCM, 1977.

———. *Paul: The Apostle's Life, Letters, and Thought*. London: SCM, 2016.

———. *Paul, the Law, and the Jewish People*. Philadelphia: Fortress, 1983.

Savage, Timothy. *Power through Weakness: Paul's Understanding of the Christian Ministry in 2 Corinthians*. Cambridge: Cambridge University Press, 1996.

Schellenberg, Ryan S. "Subsistence, Swapping, and Paul's Rhetoric of Generosity." *Journal of Biblical Literature* 137 (2018): 215–34.

Schliesser, Benjamin. *Abraham's Faith in Romans 4*. Tübingen: Mohr Siebeck, 2007.

Schrift, Alan D., ed. *The Logic of the Gift*. London: Routledge, 1997.

Schüssler Fiorenza, Elisabeth. *In Memory of Her: A Feminist Theological Reconstruction of Christian Origins*. New York: Crossroad, 1992.

Schütz, John H. *Paul and the Anatomy of Apostolic Authority*. Cambridge: Cambridge University Press, 1975.

Schwartz, Seth. *Were the Jews a Mediterranean Society?* Princeton: Princeton University Press, 2010.

Stegemann, Hartmut, with Eileen Schuller (with translation of texts by Carol Newsom). *1QHodayot^a with incorporation of 1QHodayot^b and 4QHodayot^{a-f}* DJD XL. Oxford: Clarendon, 2009.

Stendahl, Krister. *Paul among Jews and Gentiles*. London: SCM, 1977.

Stone, Michael E. *Fourth Ezra*. Hermeneia. Philadelphia: Fortress, 1990.

Stowers, Stanley. *A Rereading of Romans: Justice, Jews, and Gentiles*. New Haven: Yale University Press, 1994.

Tanner, Kathryn. *Christianity and the New Spirit of Capitalism*. New Haven: Yale University Press, 2019.

———. *Economy of Grace*. Minneapolis: Fortress, 2005.

Thate, Michael J., Kevin J. Vanhoozer, and Constantine R. Campbell, eds. *"In Christ" in Paul: Explorations in Paul's Theology of Union and Participation*. Grand Rapids: Eerdmans, 2014.

Theissen, Gerd. *The Social Setting of Pauline Christianity*. Philadelphia: Fortress, 1982.

Thiessen, Matthew. *Paul and the Gentile Problem*. Oxford: Oxford University Press, 2016.

Thomas, Matthew J. *Paul's 'Works of the Law' in the Perspective of Second-Century Reception*. Tübingen: Mohr Siebeck, 2018.

Timmins, Will. *Romans 7 and Christian Identity: A Study of the "I" in Its Literary Context*. Cambridge: Cambridge University Press, 2017.

Veyne, Paul. *Bread and Circuses*. Abbreviated and translated by Brian Pearce. London: Penguin Books, 1990.

von Reden, Sitta. *Exchange in Ancient Greece*. London: Routledge, 1995.

Wagner, J. Ross. *Heralds of the Good News: Isaiah and Paul in Concert in the Letter to the Romans*. Leiden: Brill, 2002.

Wallace-Hadrill, Andrew, ed. *Patronage in Ancient Society*. London: Routledge, 1989.

Watson, Francis. *Paul and the Hermeneutics of Faith*. Grand Rapids: Eerdmans, 2004.

———. *Paul, Judaism and the Gentiles: Beyond the New Perspective*. 2nd ed. Grand Rapids: Eerdmans, 2007.

Wawrykow, Joseph P. *God's Grace and Human Action: "Merit" in the Theology of Thomas Aquinas*. Notre Dame: University of Notre Dame Press, 1995.

Webster, John. *Barth's Ethics of Reconciliation*. Cambridge: Cambridge University Press, 1995.

Wedderburn, Alexander J. M. *The Reasons for Romans*. Edinburgh: T&T Clark, 1988.

Welborn, Larry L. *Paul, the Fool of Christ: A Study of 1 Corinthians 1–4 in the Comic-Philosophic Tradition*. London: T&T Clark, 2005.

Wells, Samuel. *A Nazareth Manifesto: Being with God*. Chichester: Wiley-Blackwell, 2015.

Westerholm, Stephen. *Perspectives Old and New on Paul: The "Lutheran" Paul and His Critics*. Grand Rapids: Eerdmans, 2004.

Winter, Bruce. *Paul and Philo among the Sophists: Alexandrian and Corinthian Responses to a Julio-Claudian Movement*. 2nd ed. Grand Rapids: Eerdmans, 2002.

Wright, N. T. *The Climax of the Covenant*. Edinburgh: T&T Clark, 1991.

———. *Justification*. London: SPCK, 2009.

———. *Paul: Fresh Perspectives*. London: SPCK, 2005.

———. *Paul and His Recent Interpreters: Some Contemporary Debates*. London: SPCK, 2015.

———. *Paul and the Faithfulness of God*. 2 vols. London: SPCK, 2013.

———. "Paul and the Patriarch." Pages 554–92 in *Pauline Perspectives: Essays on Paul 1978–2013*. London: SPCK, 2013.

Yancey, Philip. *What's So Amazing about Grace?* Grand Rapids: Zondervan, 1997.

Yinger, Kent L. *Paul, Judaism, and Judgment According to Deeds*. Cambridge: Cambridge University Press, 1999.

Zahl, Paul. *Gift in Practice: A Theology of Everyday Life*. Grand Rapids: Eerdmans, 2007.

Zetterholm, Magnus. *The Formation of Christianity at Antioch*. London: Routledge, 2003.

Zoccali, Christopher. "And So All Israel Will Be Saved: Competing Interpretations of Romans 11:26 in Pauline Scholarship." *Journal for the Study of the New Testament* 30 (2008): 289–318.

Index of Authors

Index of Scripture and Other Ancient Sources